D1092792

IN THE SHADOW OF
ARNHEM

IN THE SHADOW OF
ARNHEM

THE BATTLE FOR THE LOWER MAAS,
SEPTEMBER–NOVEMBER 1944

KEN TOUT

SUTTON PUBLISHING

First published in the United Kingdom in 2003 by
Sutton Publishing Limited · Phoenix Mill
Thrupp · Stroud · Gloucestershire · GL5 2BU

British Library Cataloguing in Publication Data
A catalogue record for this book is available from the British Library.

ISBN 0-7509-2821-2

Typeset in 12/15.5pt Garamond 3.
Typesetting and origination by
Sutton Publishing Limited.
Printed and bound in England by
J.H. Haynes & Co. Ltd, Sparkford.

To those who were killed or deprived of a normal life in costly but unsung battles back down the Arnhem road. The wider story of their sacrifices and heroism has been neglected because of popular concentration on the equally heroic but unfortunate epic of the 'bridge too far' at Arnhem.

Contents

List of Illustrations

Acknowledgements

In preparing this book I have been fortunate in the number of participants in these same battles who have since produced works of historical or literary importance, particularly Denis Whitaker, George Blackburn, Bill Close, Ian Hammerton and W.R. Bennett. I therefore make no excuse for drawing on their reminiscences as they have kindly encouraged me to do. Sadly Denis died during the period of my research but his widow and co-writer, Shelagh, has continued his encouragement.

A younger writer of a monumental piece of research on Walcheren, Paul Crucq, has also generously opened his files and contacts to me. Professor Terry Copp and his *Canadian Military History* journal are fundamental sources on Canadian operations.

Several people in Holland and Belgium have gone out of their way to help, including Luc van Gent, Karel Govaerts, Louis Kleijne, Freddy Pille, Dr Ger Schinck and Jan Wigard.

In the UK a number of people pointed me on to, or helped me make, further contacts. Among these were John Brown, Bill James, Don Scott and others mentioned in the notes. Tess Carpenter, who was also 'there', was at hand for translations. As always, archivists were ever ready to support, including those at the IWM, Mrs Beech at Keele University Air Photo Library, David Fletcher at Bovington Tank Museum, and the staff of the York and Lancaster, Leicesters, Shropshire and Welsh Museums, as well as the Polish Institute. Now fully on stream is the relatively new Second World War Experience Centre, founded by First World War expert Dr Peter Liddle in Horsforth, whose staff and volunteers were at my service, and to which I am consigning my research papers from previous books.

Among my own 1NY comrades, sadly Bill Moseley died during the writing of this book, but his widow, Jean, was happy to extend his permission to quote. Kenny Jack has also left us, cheerful to the end. Rex Jackson, MM, continues to find unusual books for his old tank mate. A special mention for Reg Spittles: not only is he a continuing fount of reminiscences, he now visits Northampton schools to speak about the realities of war, reflecting the work done by Louis Kleijne and others around the battlefields. My wish would be that more UK schools would open their doors to veterans like Reg at a time when, perhaps more than any moment since 1945, the new generations need to know about the realities of oppression, aggression and liberation.

Finally, but first in the queue of the helpful and encouraging, my wife, Jai, still struggling to find 'dustable' areas amid the chaos of my office, but, more often, dispelling the dust of years from my brain. And the staff of Sutton Publishing: Jonathan Falconer, Nick Reynolds and a number of others at Sutton who have always been at hand to help with sensitive and professional advice. Thank you to them all and apologies to any I may have omitted, either above or in the complicated search for personal permission to quote.

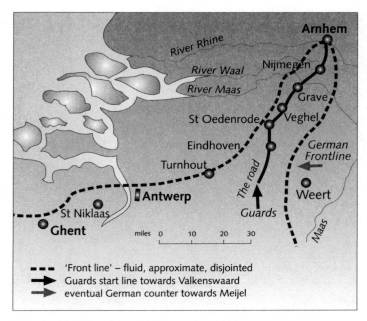

Map 1   The 'Thumb' – 19/20 September 1944.

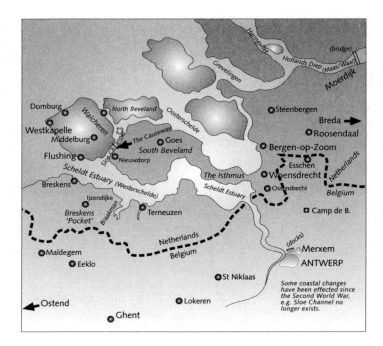

Map 2   German retreat to Moerdijk, 1944.

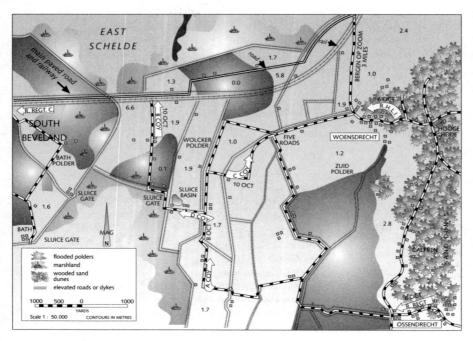

Map 3   South Beveland Isthmus *(adapted from W.R. Bennett).*

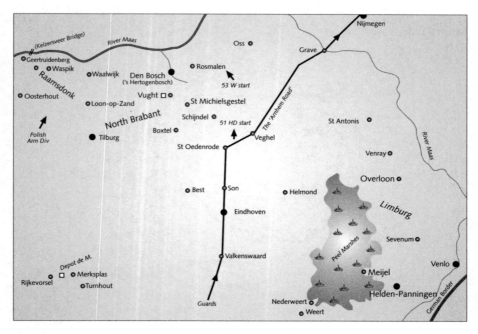

Map 4   Limburg and North Brabant, 1944. The two month-long task of extending the flanks of the Arnhem road up to the barrier of the Maas.

CHAPTER ONE

Beggary and Bravery

The people branded as 'lunatics' stood and watched the sane men shooting each other and wondered. Was this some strange form of entertainment put on for their benefit by the establishment? Some perverse ballet? Some horrific cabaret?

The inmates were not to know, nor could they have appreciated, that they were about to be present at an act of bravery as incredible as any that might be found in the annals of the British Army. A new name was to be added to the elite roll of the bravest of the brave: names like that of John Frost at the Arnhem bridge, Leonard Cheshire, Lord Lovat, Wg Cdr Guy Gibson, Lt Col 'H' Jones, John William Harper.

John William *who?*

Like a ready-made fortress *le Depôt de Mendicité* straddled the Allied line of advance on 29 September 1944. The rank and file of the British Army were notorious for their ability to mispronounce foreign names like 'Wipers' (Ypres) in 1914 or 'Bugger's Bus' (Bourguebus) in Normandy 1944. Now *Mendicité*, with its accented final 'tay', was a tough one, and instantly became the 'Monday City' for many. Few front-line soldiers in 1944 spoke French and therefore might not know that *Mendicité* meant 'Beggary': *Depôt de Mendicité* – the 'Beggary Deposit'.

Both John William Harper, 'Jack' to family and friends, and John R. Dean, 'Dixie' to his mates, were worried about the Monday City. It was just a blob on the map between Rijkevorsel (pronounced 'rake-for-sell') and Merxplas in north Belgium. They had been told that it was a lunatic asylum and that the loonies were still inside. So there would be no devastating air raid or huge artillery barrage to mash the buildings into ruins before the infantry attack. Nothing larger than hand-thrown grenades or small mortar bombs, delivered with pin-point accuracy by the company mortar sections, would be used.

The attackers, from the Hallamshires and Leicestershires, had at first envisaged a vast, solid, single building like a British asylum. When Harper's company were told that they had to find a back way in, they anticipated charging straight up to the edifice and smashing through doors and windows while under direct fire from defenders who would be using patients as protection. In fact the *Depôt de Mendicité* was a totally different proposition. It was more of the style of a huge military camp. The confusion was not confined to front line troops, for 1 Corps HQ itself reported the Hallams and Leicesters 'attacking a factory' that day.

The original name of the institution, founded in 1822, would have confounded even the most capable linguists in the attacking 49th 'Polar Bear' Division: *Maatschappij van Weldadigheid voor de Zuidelijke Nederlanden.*

King Willem I of the Netherlands (Belgium was then part of the Netherlands) had instituted a colony for tramps. In 1870 the hospitality was extended to include paupers, beggars and drunkards, and gained its 1940s name. Gradually parts of the compound were turned over for use as a civil prison.[1]

It was the occupying German authorities of the First World War who set up a lunatic asylum there, providing secure accommodation for mentally ill people from Belgium and northern France, many of whom could, at that time, be treated only by restraint methods. Just before the Second World War, Jewish refugees were also offered shelter. Then with the 1940 German occupation Belgian and Dutch hostages were interned in the prison section.

Some idea of the size of the establishment may be gained from the fact that up to 6,000 persons could be accommodated there, of whom at the time of the battle 1,740 were prisoners. Only a relatively small percentage of the 1940s residents were classed as lunatics, the majority being vagabonds. But it is reasonable to estimate that several hundred occupants were mentally ill, and the prison also housed many who were criminally insane. This vast establishment, originally set up as 125 small farms for indigent families, lay as a physical obstacle across the Allied route and posed a unique humanitarian problem for the commanders planning their attack.

After the collapse of the German armies in Normandy, the Allies had rushed across France and most of Belgium in a drive towards the heartland of Germany. But in the north of Belgium the German resistance began to stiffen behind the many wide waterways and deep ditches of the low lands. Already men of the 49th 'Polar Bear' Division had been forced to fight bitter skirmishes around Rijkevorsel.[2] Accompanying tanks of the Polish Armoured Division were held up by a bridge across a wide moat. The moat was part of the *Mendicité* complex, a twenty-foot-wide water obstacle designed to prevent inmates from exiting but equally effective in preventing invaders from entering.

So both Cpl Jack Harper and Sgt Dixie Dean had good cause to be worried. Jack Harper's platoon of the Hallamshires was to lead the way across 300 yards of open ground without shelter against undamaged, well-prepared defences. Dixie Dean with the 1st Leicesters was responsible for getting the vital mortars supplied for their daunting task as substitutes for Lancaster bombers and siege guns. Each company had two of the light 3-inch mortars. Each mortar section was commanded by a sergeant with a no. 18 radio set in touch with the company (coy) commander, so that speed and accuracy could be assured as the infantry advanced.

Dixie Dean, later RSM (Regimental Sergeant Major), remembers the battle vividly:

At dawn on Friday 29th September, the Bn attacked the *Depôt de Mendicité* which was a lunatic asylum and this was without doubt the most deadly action we had fought to date [they had fought through Normandy!]. The plan for this attack was given out by the Adjutant, Captain North. 'A' Coy to go south of the main road, 'B' Coy north, 'C' pass through 'B', then 'B' in reserve. . . . 'A' Coy moving through the woods were the first to run into the enemy and Lt Guy was killed. . . . They lost direction in the confusion and were pinned down for hours by the enemy.[3]

To the left of the Leicesters' position, men of C, the lead coy of the Hallamshires, looked out from the thick woods and studied their task. Capt Mike Lonsdale-Cooper with Lt Judge and Cpl Harper had no illusions about that pleasant green level sward stretching from the trees to a far embankment. Yorkshire 'Tykes', from the champion cricket county of the 1930s, they would have seen the area as an ideal place for a cricket match with long boundaries each end. Now their bowlers would have to demonstrate their skills at lobbing hand grenades. The bomb, which fitted in the palm of the hand, was normally lobbed rather than thrown direct, firstly in order to drop vertically beyond obstacles and secondly to allow three seconds for the fuse to activate, so that the enemy had no time to pick up the grenade and throw it back.

Dug deep into the far embankment and as yet invisible, the enemy had available, in addition to their own long-handled grenades, the awesome Spandau machine-gun (m-g). The defenders of the asylum had been reinforced by a fresh battalion and were lined up in considerable numbers around the perimeter. Facing Lonsdale-Cooper's coy may have been four or more of the rapid-firing m-gs, each of which could spit out over a thousand rounds a minute, or nearly twenty bullets a second, and every bullet potentially fatal. The rapid fire meant that the m-gs were not very accurate in comparison to a sniper's accuracy. Yet they produced a whirling cone of bullets, widening as they sped spinning from the muzzles, and forming a dense horizontal hail of death over a wide area of ground.

It might appear hopeless for men to attempt a 300-yard walk, or weaving trot, in the face of such fire, remembering that the weight of weapons and equipment made it difficult for even the fittest infantryman to sprint such a distance. But Lonsdale-Cooper and Judge knew there were also a few factors in their favour. As soon as the m-gs started to fire, their positions would be revealed and they would be prime targets for the Hallams' mortar bombs, which could be on target with less than a minute's notice. In addition the elite German units were congregated around Arnhem so that those defending the *Depôt de Mendicité* would be less skilled and resolute than the superhuman, infallible German soldiers of more recent Allied myths.

Rapid though it was, the Spandau could not fire incessantly without pauses to reload or to make changes of target, which could affect accuracy. Because of the great expenditure of ammunition those m-gs had to fire relatively short bursts. German hand grenades, too, were known to be fallible. Normal German Army units, as distinct from the SS, were being reinforced with poor quality 'dug out' men, some very old or very young for front-line duty. Ordinary enemy soldiers would be as fearful and ready to hide from hostile fire as were the attackers themselves.

Having said that, there was a real possibility that the entire Hallamshire coy could be wiped out or forced to go to ground, seeking shelter in the sparse contours of the rough field. There was no advantage in argument or delay. Judge and Harper and their comrades set off across that horribly open space the size of a test match cricket field. Immediately they were greeted by crashing, blazing torrents of fire, heralding high velocity bullets and jagged shards of iron as well as solid clods and stones wrenched from the ground by explosions. It was like walking through a cloud of smoke in which every particle was a shrieking, tearing sliver of sharp death.

As the wary, sweating infantrymen chose their own way forward, some hastening to gain the embankment, others diving, leaping up, swerving in fruitless attempts to become invisible, men began to fall. Roy Simon had been wounded in Normandy in June, had spent time in British hospitals, and now was back with his comrades for his first battle in Belgium. He was shot almost immediately. Another young recruit, nervously waiting to hear his first shots fired in anger, probably never heard the bullet that killed him. Lt Judge was hit in the neck and fell, incapable of thought or action. Harper walked on.

In his brief return to war Roy Simon had been a hero, modest though he was about it:

We were in a ditch on the edge of this wood and what happened next was Errol Flynn stuff. We were lined up and they were shelling us and Lonsdale-Cooper was at the side of me and he said, 'Right. Get ready', and he were looking at his watch. Then all of a sudden he blows his whistle and I gets half out of the ditch and nowt happens.

Nobody moved! And he says to me, 'Come on, Simon,' he says, 'You're one of the old lads, show them how it's done.' So I gets up and I shouts, 'Come on the Hallams, let's go' and I sets off running. . . . We got half way across and I was running like the clappers with nothing to fire at, and everything seemed to be coming at us.[4]

As men fell, some mates ran faster while others took more urgent evasive action. It mattered not which action the individual took. Death and wounding ranged everywhere, horizontally, vertically, diagonally. And as the advance shortened the distance remaining, it brought the attackers within range of the defenders' stick grenades. Then the infamous *Nebelwerfers*, groups of six mortar bombs with their 'Moaning Minnie' sirens, found the range and added to the inferno. In the lead, Harper, briefly noticing that Judge was down and that he was now in charge of the point attackers, walked on.

The 'running', as Simon described it, of a fully accoutred infantryman tends eventually to become more of a shambling, stumbling progress across uneven ground. The more active leaders could not move too far in advance of their less agile supporters. Five minutes could have elapsed during the erratic movement as the advancing ranks staggered, thinned, disintegrated, disappeared.

On the defenders' side there may have been some damping down of fire. Weapons became overheated. Ammunition needed to be replenished. Wounds had to be dressed. Dead bodies dragged out of the way. Pits, demolished by enemy fire, cleared of debris or new refuge found.

Above all the defender would be impressed by the success of his own fire as the vast majority of the attacking force sought refuge in depressions in the earth or lay about as dead or badly wounded bodies in full view. The vigorous attacking force, a clear, tempting target, had faded into a vague chimera with one or two indistinct figures still moving in the landscape. Just one slight man wearing a corporal's stripes still trudged on, near at hand and easy for someone else to shoot somewhere else along the unbroken line of the embankment defences.

There are moments of minor climax in battle when the defender thinks 'We've won that round!' And relaxes for a moment. Pauses before the next round. Takes a deep breath. Lights a fag. Has a puff. Passes it to a mate. Checks the gun. Urinates.

And then the vague figure with the corporal's stripes becomes a yelling monster leaping at the gun pits, throwing bomb after bomb which explode in all directions, spreading lethal splinters at cowering foes. Lobbing more bombs over the embankment where skulking defenders are bewildered by the sudden assault. Leaping up high and alone on to the embankment where he has no right to be, and which is supposed to be the domain of the defenders, and where he now dominates the slit trenches that had seemed so safe.

In battle there can be a kind of hysteria which inspires a wave of attackers to forget the odds and accomplish miracles. There is a similar hysteria which affects surprised defenders, causing sometimes instant surrender, sometimes confused flight, sometimes berserk response. The ordinary German soldiers, confronted by this apparition in their midst, wilted and suffered themselves to be overawed and scattered, dead, wounded, fleeing or surrendering. Harper, undaunted, climbed back over the earthen bulwark, shepherding four prisoners and still firing at those who were retreating.

With Lt Judge disabled, the coy commander had gathered men together in the shelter of the 'home' side of the embankment. Their orders were clear. Find a back way into the depot and exploit. Harper offered to cross the obstacle again to find out whether the moat beyond could be waded. As he descended at the far side on to the banks of the moat, the entire area was still being deluged by fire from several directions. Carefully he crouched down by the moat, or may even have stepped down into it, to test its depth. Nobody else was there to see, in any case. Clearly it was too deep to ford. He returned to Lonsdale-Cooper with his report. The major ordered him to get the survivors of his platoon on to the banks of the moat.

Harper, in the lead, crossing the embankment for the third time, found the German gun pits on that side still empty. Ordering covering fire at the buildings beyond the water, he encouraged his men over the obstruction and down into the pits, only one man being hit in the process. He then went walking along the bank, alone, totally exposed, looking for a possible crossing place of the twenty-foot-wide water obstacle.

On that side of the embankment the close-range crossfire from within the depot was, if anything, worse than it had been in the open field. There were more Spandaus located beyond hand-grenade range in or between the buildings. By some miracle Harper managed to move a considerable distance along the bank, still looking for a ford.

His quest took him beyond the battalion's boundary where he found an outpost of the Leicesters. They had located a ford and were able to point it out to him. Once more the corporal made his way back through the inescapable turbulence of air displaced by myriad hurtling projectiles and almost visibly ablaze with tracer fire and explosions. Enemy gunners, angry and baffled, continued to aim at the lone figure, and to miss, possibly due to the undisciplined frenzy of firing. Up to that point, because of the exigencies of battle and the finality of the outcome, there is no clear indication as to whether Harper, at some time or in some way, might have been wounded. It would have been typical of him to carry on anyway.

Capt (later Maj) Mike Lonsdale-Cooper had also risked his life, climbing over the embankment and venturing out on to the banks of the dyke. Jack Harper, mission accomplished, was able to direct the major to the vital ford. The back door to the 'Monday City' was open. At that precise moment, a chance bullet, or one fired with more precision by a more careful sniper, found him at last, and he fell grievously wounded. Mike Lonsdale-Cooper quickly realized that nothing could be done. There on the bank of the moat John William Harper, a reluctant soldier, had died.[5]

Other soldiers of the Sheffield Battalion, the Hallamshires, fought and suffered as the unit probed into the asylum. Arnold Whiteley was accompanying Maj Cooper across the moat:

We made our crossing and as we ran across you could hear the bullets whizzing. We were well spaced out and it were only Maj Cooper who got hit. Of course, when we got under cover of banking on the other side, I said, 'Thank God nobody got hit', and he said, 'You speak for your bloody self!' He was shot straight through his left arm. Another six inches in and he would have been finished.

Roy Simon in his brief cameo battle found that shots were hitting his mates from an angle high up, perhaps from a roof in the complex:

I looked around and our lads were going down and stretchers were being called for. . . . Where I was laid down I raised my rifle to my shoulder. I was just going to pull trigger when all of a sudden I heard this terrific bang at the side of my ear. I stood straight up and spun round and fell back, but this L/Cpl caught me. Then I felt this warmth down me back and I said to this Lance Jack, 'What's me back like?' He said there was blood coming out and the same bullet had passed through me and hit him in the wrist.

One of the young lads came running over with both hands up in the air and he had been shot through both wrists while taking aim. Then Gerry started mortaring us. Shells were falling in a pattern and bodies were going up all round.

Meanwhile Arnold Whiteley with others had arrived inside the barriers to the asylum and observed just how close the fighting was:

The lads who were in close proximity were eye-ball to eye-ball over this banking and they must have seen each other and killed simultaneously. There was only a few yards between our dead and theirs. We got into the compound and they starting giving themselves up and I was with Maj Cooper when the lads started to tell him about Cpl Harper and his deeds.

After his wounding Roy Simon had either fainted or dozed off, sitting with his back against the side of a trench. Suddenly he came to his senses to see with horror that several German soldiers were approaching him. Were they going to shoot him? Or take him prisoner? What a fate, to spend the rest of the war in a prisoner-of-war camp. He could do nothing about it:

They were coming closer to me. They looked at two or three of our lads and then came to me. I tried to raise my rifle. Then somebody said it was all right and that they'd do me no harm as they were stretcher bearers. One of them looked at me and he were nearly old enough to be me Granddad.

It gradually sank into Roy's befuddled mind that the German stretcher-bearers were themselves prisoners and that the battle was over and won. So the Germans attended to him:

They picked me up and, using my rifle as a chair, carried me along this earthen bank and then turned over a little bridge. We went into this kind of a barn and they sat me down. A German came over and treated my wound with my own field dressing and covered it with some of theirs. He took his own coat off and put it round me to keep me warm.

Roy also saw Mike Lonsdale-Cooper come in with his arm in a sling. But the German medic's kindness almost caused Roy problems. On his way back down the line he was thought to be a German prisoner of war because he was wearing the German greatcoat. His Yorkshire accent soon dispelled that impression. Nearly sixty years later Roy was taken back to the battle site by regimental historian Don Scott. He was amazed to find the little barn still there. He was able to sit again on the same seat built into the wall where he sat while his wound was dressed.

To the right of the Hallams' attack, the Leicesters were going in through the front door, as it were. Their experience was very similar. Their regimental aid post, established in a nearby house, was soon very busy. Sgt Dixie Dean saw several of his friends being rushed into the post, 'Major Blackstock and Sgt Goodlad of "A" and Sgts Goodacre and Payne, and Ptes Lewitt and Bradshaw of "C" among others'.[6]

References to a 'back door' and 'front door' are figurative and could be misleading, as this was not a single simple building. A more complete description of what the Leicesters saw in front of them would be informative as they would have had a clear view from the bridge, which formed the main entrance across the moat. The waterway itself, with its high embankment, was 7 km long and between 10 and 12 metres wide throughout its length. It enclosed a domain of 600 hectares (nearly 1,500 acres). There were 27 km of streets and lanes running through the compound and dividing up the various sections of the complex.[7]

The 'dormitories' for the paupers were solid four-storey buildings, a wide avenue of them leading up to a large chapel. The prison buildings surrounded an inner square of 4 hectares. There was a Great Farm and a Small Farm. The population required its own hospital, workshops, stores, offices and so on. In addition to other areas providing casual work for the unskilled 'vagabonds', there was also a large brickworks, its tall stacks of bricks forming yet more narrow alleys to be explored.

As he supervised the ammunition for the mortars of the various companies now advancing into this unfamiliar maze, Dixie Dean had a good general view of the battalion's progress. He saw B Coy wading across the moat at the place which they had pointed out to Jack Harper. He observed C Coy passing through B in an enthusiastic charge, then being caught in ruthless m-g crossfire until they were counter-attacked and temporarily surrounded by a fresh German battalion, from 719th Infantry Division, whose presence was unknown to the British commanders.

In any other battle the word would have gone out for rocket Typhoons or medium artillery to strafe the defenders. But with the harmless civilians, many of them seriously mentally ill, still in the complex it could only be urgent calls to Dixie Dean's 'pop-gun' mortars to assist the infantrymen. One Leicester attacker recorded that, at this point, 'The Germans let out the inmates who were just standing around looking at us as if we were the mad ones. They were being killed left, right and centre but there was nothing we could do to save them.'

The next hazard to which the mortars were directed was the area of brickworks within the prison area. Maj Denaro led the attack into this section which was a maze of alleyways formed out of the stacks of bricks.

To the Leicesters this was unknown ground but the defenders knew its layout and used the brick stacks for shelter. Denaro and his men had to rush each alleyway, one by one, losing men at every turning. Here again, a normal artillery bombardment would have flattened the loose brick stacks and saved many casualties among the soldiers, but would also have wrought massive slaughter of incapable patients, paupers and civil prisoners.

Dixie Dean's recollections of the fight are tragic, with the constant refrain of good comrades being cut down in a ruthless fight where the man at the sharp end paid the price of laudable humanitarian considerations:

> The enemy was in an ideal position in a kind of brickworks, with its alleyways and mounds affording good cover. Maj Denaro had gone forward and was killed here. Cpls Hodges and Beck and L/Cpls Smith, Kiddier and Mitchell were all killed here. Making good use of the dykes and ditches the enemy continued to play havoc with 'C' coy and Sgt Skelton, L/Cpl Clements and Ptes Palmer, Elliott, Preston and Hart were all killed. As the enemy withdrew the occupants of the asylum were released, thus providing cover for the retreating troops.

What distressed many of the Leicesters after the battle, where they had witnessed Denaro's inspiring leadership and sad death, was that, because he died, he was denied the Distinguished Service Order award which his men thought should have been his. Under the awards system an officer killed in action could only receive the rare VC or a Mention In Despatches, but not the more appropriate DSO or MC. The men could not understand why this should be so. Surely bravery to the death should be quite as good an eligibility as bravery with survival?

This strange quirk of the awards system did not diminish the admiration of the men for those who did receive awards. One who received the Military Cross, all the more significant because it was an immediate award, was Lt V.F.W. Bidgood. His platoon had been in a similar advance to that of Lt Judge and Cpl Harper. Their target was the small bridge over the moat near the main entrance.

Like Judge's platoon, they had open ground to cross from their sheltering wood, about 250 yards. Again the advance had to be made against defences which had escaped the ravages of air or heavy artillery bombardment. Again the Spandaus ripped out their deadly challenge with a noise faster than any side drummer could play. Again men fell as they braved the open spaces. By the fortune which favours some and not others, a number of Bidgood's platoon survived and, joined by Sgt Poole's platoon, they subdued the defenders of the bridge, ran across it and established a small 'bridgehead' within the compound.

Men of all ranks exhibited similar valour. At the bottom of the military hierarchy and without a rifle, Pte C.H. Woods won the Military Medal. Woods was a stretcher-bearer and went forward with the lead platoons. Once the bridge had been secured, the infantrymen found or dug cover on either side of it. The enemy poured m-g and mortar on the bridge to try to prevent Leicester reinforcements from moving up. Woods, forward of the bridge and finding several wounded men in need of urgent treatment, crossed the bridge time and time again assisted by volunteer bearers. A number of lives were saved by the prompt surgical treatment enabled by the extremely high-risk rescue work of Woods.

Sgt Dean noted that the Leicesters' C Coy had been reduced to forty-three men surviving out of nearly a hundred. A Coy 'had taken a pretty good hammering but the Bn had good reason to be proud of its first really BIG show' of the autumn campaign. Dixie and his weary mortar men were delighted next day on advancing again to hear 'our heavy guns keeping up a seemingly never-ending barrage and accompanied by heavy bombers and Typhoons'. They were also thinking 'If only . . . !'

The taste of victory was not as sweet as might have been the case if it had been a real fort or a factory which had been cleared of the enemy. Soldiers expected to find other soldiers dead and dying on a battlefield. They found it more difficult to deal with the sight of numbers of helpless civilians similarly slaughtered. Outside the buildings lay those civilians who had been caught in the crossfire – paupers, prisoners, 'lunatics' and, perhaps most sadly, detained Belgian and Dutch heroes and hostages who had been betrayed by fate at the moment of release. And the atmosphere within some of the buildings was depressing, even frightening.

Walter Shea was with the 62nd Anti-Tank Regt, Royal Artillery. His unit was moving up in close support for the infantry against possible counter-attack. As they moved into the buildings Shea was not feeling particularly bellicose. He recorded years later:

They'd got there a big civil prison. What they done they let them out
. . . they'd opened the cages and these were criminally insane people.
The German troops were falling back. And the prison guards they
weren't anywhere to be seen. There were the two of us. We had a pistol
and a Sten gun, but walking in there, and several of these insane
people wandering around loose, even with our guns we were feeling
quite a bit wary of them. We weren't happy anyway because we lost
our C.O. killed there – a wonderful guy.[8]

The British Army does not 'send up medals with the rations', and the
number of awards for gallantry that day illustrates the fierceness of the
fighting. Apart from Harper, who won the VC, and Denaro, who died
denied a medal, the DSO went to Capt P. Upcher; the MC to Lt Bidgood
and Lt F.A. Gaunt, who was with Denaro in the brickworks; and Military
Medals to Sgts W. Irwin and T. Johnson, L/Cpl W.A. Saunders, and Ptes
C.H. Woods and H.T. Gill, the latter also a stretcher-bearer. Their
efforts, and those of their comrades, had cleared the main road for the
waiting Polish armoured division to dash on its way towards Tilburg.
The dead were buried eventually in Leopoldsburg war cemetery.

Some of the local people had suffered badly during the battle, even
without counting the damage to property. Sixty-three-year-old Frans
Mertens was serving a sentence in the prison wing. For him, liberation
was good news and bad news. Suddenly he was afforded the chance of an
unexpected early release. Then equally suddenly he received an
undeserved death sentence. He was killed by a rifle bullet, perhaps fired
by the Germans, perhaps by the British. Nobody could tell in the
confusion.

Prison warden August Meeusen, aged fifty-nine and looking forward
to retirement from the service, was killed, as were a further nine
detainees. Seventeen of the inmates were badly wounded. The confusion
looked to be a good thing for some German soldiers who hastily doffed
more visible elements of weaponry and uniform and mixed with the
crowd of inmates, hoping thus to escape prisoner-of-war captivity.

The official citation for Cpl Harper's Victoria Cross clearly details the
enormity of the mission undertaken by Harper and his colleagues:

In Northwest Europe, on September 29th, 1944, the Hallamshire Battalion of the York and Lancaster Regiment attacked the *Depôt de Mendicité*, a natural defensive position surrounded by an earthen wall, and then a dyke strongly held by the enemy.

Corporal Harper was commanding the leading section in the assault. The enemy were well dug in and had a perfect field of fire across 300 yards of perfectly flat and exposed country. With superb disregard for the hail of mortar bombs and small arms fire which the enemy brought to bear upon this open ground, Corporal Harper led his section straight up to the wall [earthen embankment] and killed or captured the enemy holding the near side. During this operation the platoon commander was seriously wounded and Corporal Harper took over control of the platoon.

The citation then describes Harper's three sallies over the 'wall' and his lone walk to find a crossing place over or through the moat. It ends: 'the success of the Battalion in driving the enemy from the wall and back across the dyke must be largely ascribed to the superb self sacrifice and inspiring gallantry of Corporal Harper. His magnificent courage, fearlessness, and devotion to duty throughout the battle set a splendid example to his men and had a decisive effect on the course of the operations.'

The citation was written by a staff officer, but those who 'were there' might demur at the use of the word 'fearlessness'. Certainly Harper was courageous and devoted to duty and sacrificial, but whether he was without fear is a moot question. The vast majority of front-line soldiers knew fear and many had to fight it as vigorously as they fought the physical enemy.

What is known about Harper's personality would suggest that, like other quiet men, he had won a prolonged battle against fear without totally eliminating it.

Who, then, was this John William Harper? Whence came he? And what sort of man was he?

Mike Lonsdale-Cooper, by then a major, wrote to Harper's wife while recovering from his own wound. He said, after briefly describing the battle, and stating that Harper's death came from a sniper's bullet and that he died 'instantly':

> He was a very brave man and the best type of N.C.O. and it was an honour to have him with me in battle and out. He was always quietly efficient, always cheerful, and somehow gave everybody a feeling of confidence . . . we are mourning the loss of a brave soldier and a very fine man.

Surprisingly, although a memorial plaque was placed in nearby Doncaster, Harper's own village of Hatfield Woodhouse in Yorkshire had no memorial to him until fifty-eight years after the battle. Then ex-mayor and present Rotarian treasurer, John Brown, proposed a public appeal for remembrance of the VC in that tiny country hamlet where he was born. In 2002, outside the chapel of the churchyard at Hatfield Woodhouse, an impressive black granite stone was unveiled to recall Harper's bravery.[9]

A visitor to the cemetery might well encounter a local villager visiting a family grave. If questioned the villager is likely to claim relationship with Jack Harper, perhaps at the second, third or fourth remove, or as an in-law, and of child, grandchild or great-grandchild generation. One local remarked that the village might well be called Harper Woodhouse. Of his much closer surviving relatives, including a sister and a brother, sister Joan Willis, nearing eighty, was delighted to talk to John Brown about her memories of Jack.

It was a large rural family, brothers Jack, George, Frank, Stan and Pete and just the one little sister, Joan. The boys were a boisterous lot and sometimes became too rough for their little sister. It was always Jack who stepped in and brought the other boys to order. Was he then a fierce, aggressive boy?

'Nay,' says Joan, 'he were the quietest man you could ever hope to know.'

In the 1920s and 1930s men came home to eat their food and the women worked in the kitchen. With her mother going out to work on the farm, Joan often found herself alone in the kitchen with a huge pile of dirty dishes and pans, to be scoured and washed by hand. It was always Jack who, against the conventions of the time, sneaked into the kitchen to give little sister a hand with the washing up and even more menial tasks.

Quiet, reserved and gentle, Jack rarely went out except to play football, his one delight, or to go to a film. He was of medium height, with black hair and, in civilian life, no 'tache'. It may be that as a soldier he developed a moustache to make himself look fiercer than he really was. He met a girl called Lilian who lived in Drax, then only a few huddled houses, but later a notorious centre of modern power production. They were married at Drax and, as Hatfield Woodhouse offered little employment, they moved to the nearby market town of Thorne, so pretty amid its canals, and settled in a modest villa at 25 Southend. Jack got a job as a peat cutter.

In the Middle Ages Thorne had been a port set among almost impassable marshes. By a coincidence it was engineers from the continent, those who conquered the water problems of the Low Countries, establishing canals and dykes like those at *Depôt de Mendicité*, who drained the Thorne marshes, beginning with Cornelius Vermuyden in the days of James I. The draining of the marshes bequeathed to Thorne the largest expanse of lowland peat in the country, intersected by continental-style canals and dykes.

Peat was then cut by hand, in long rolls similar to the rolls of turf used for laying lawns. Its main use had been as fuel, but its suitability as garden compost was becoming more important. Jack Harper and his mates were paid by the chain, the old imperial measure of 22 yards. The rate per chain was low and a hard week's work was needed to maintain a household, although there were no children of the marriage.

When Jack Harper saw the surroundings of the *Depôt de Mendicité* there must have been some sense of familiarity about the flat, open spaces, and the canals, and the dykes dug deep and built high to discipline the vagaries of the waters. It seems that he walked towards the *Depôt*, holding his rifle as calmly and deliberately as though he was carrying a peat-cutting spade across the levels. There may well have been some kind of catharsis about his last conscious moments on the banks of a waterway so similar to the dykes around Thorne.

The well-authenticated character of Cpl Harper, VC, once again underlines the fact, known to most soldiers, that when the going gets tough it is rarely the boastful 'tough guy' who performs the feat of ultimate bravery and self-sacrifice. It is the quiet man who, when the deadly crisis threatens, steps forward. Too many film producers and novel writers have followed the line of a plot which has criminals being recruited to carry out a dangerous mission which no-one else will undertake. Few criminals make first-class soldiers. It is unlikely that any German penal battalion was as efficient a military formation as the rigorously puritan *Hitlerjugend* Division.

Proponents of the 'scoundrel makes the best soldier' theory, looking to invent a potential VC in the 1940s, would have been unlikely to place him in the kitchen, helping little sister with the washing up.

CHAPTER TWO

Mad Tuesday and Black Friday

Mad Tuesday, 5 September 1944, witnessed the farce of a war which ended too soon. Black Friday, 13 October, made it clear that the end was not yet – not soon. And not easily to be achieved. For many it was the betrayal and destruction of burgeoning hope.

There were elements of visible stage farce about Mad Tuesday: lusty German soldiers robbing nursemaids of prams in which to pack their kit; brutal *Sicherheitsdienst* extermination guards throwing down their helmets and running away from jeering children; drunken soldiers singing '*wir fahren gegen Engeland*' – 'we're off to [conquer] England' – and mounting captured cart-horses to clatter away east towards the Fatherland; radios, totally banned and invisible for four years, pouring forth London news broadcasts on every street corner.

Mad Tuesday fell five years and four days after Hitler's initial invasion of Poland, which led on to the invasion of the Netherlands, Belgium, France, which necessitated the liberation landings of Allied troops on 6 June 1944 in far away Normandy. Throughout June, July and August, clandestine radio sets in those countries told of the dogged and costly battles still only just off the Normandy beaches. Then the German resistance cracked. Allied armies raced across the length and breadth of France. Suddenly Brussels was free and the guns could be heard in Antwerp. There seemed no way that the German high command could halt the stampede of retreat. Generals were captured in their pyjamas as the shock troops drove on.

Armoured divisions from five countries fought alongside armoured and infantry brigades from another three, and overwhelming air forces;

and local resistance groups emerged to fight in the open. There was no way that the fragile line of disciplined elite German troops could stem a flood which was like the old stories of the sea rushing through broken dykes into the same Low Countries.

And in Antwerp, Woensdrecht, Bergen-op-Zoom, Breda and all stations between, everyone could see the enemy headquarters troops packing what loot they could, but leaving most of it, to join the panic escape from the vengeance of the occupied countries.

One woman from Woensdrecht watched in amazement which turned to relief, which then turned to joy, though all too soon:

> Wandering soldiers, far from home, looking like vagabonds, trying to find their way to the *Heimat*. . . . The game was finished. No food, no drinks. The very strict leaders from before were also gone. The fanatical discipline was gone like snow before the sun. The urgency of food and peace plagued those soldiers day and night. The rumour was spreading that Breda was already in the hands of the British. Chaos was total. . . . Tomorrow the Tommies will be here.[1]

Now some local people felt emboldened to shout insults at the retreating hordes. Dutch flags were hung out of windows. But angry soldiers, maddened by panic, shame and disbelief, fired remaining ammunition at the flags and the houses and the jeering civilians. It was still dangerous until the Allied tanks actually rumbled down the streets. *Dolle Dinsdag* the locals called it – Mad, Crazy, Delirious Tuesday.

But where were the Allied tanks? Rumble of distant guns. But no booming of tank engines or squeaking of tank tracks or spattering of infantry small arms fire. Many British soldiers savoured the warmth of welcome from civilians enjoying their earliest breath of freedom, and the welcome was a reflection of the subjugation, slavery and hopelessness which for so long had precluded use of that magic Dutch word, '*Bevrijding*!' – liberation.

Maj Bill Close, MC, a typical British tank squadron leader with 3rd Royal Tank Regiment (3RTR), had frequently been at the forefront of Normandy battles where an advance of 500 yards was thought to be most laudable. He had therefore enjoyed the unique armoured race across France, 386 miles in eight days, and was now thrilled to be driving into the target city of Antwerp, the desired port which would solve all the supply problems of the Allies. On the wireless he heard Maj John Dunlop's C Squadron ordered to hasten to the docks. His own squadron was to head for the railway station. But he found the mission difficult for reasons much different from those horrific days of Operation Goodwood in Normandy:

> The Belgian population surged on to the streets and it became impossible to advance. Every tank was greeted by cheering crowds who clambered up on to the turrets. Crews were overwhelmed with flowers, bottles and kisses. I had a company of the 1st Herefords with me; at least I thought I had, but conversing with their company commander, he informed me he could only muster about thirty riflemen, as most of the others had disappeared among the ecstatic civilians.[2]

Another tank man, Tpr 'Spud' Taylor, was astonished to see, leading his tank, 'youngsters, boys and girls on cycles, riding in front of us as we bowled along, although Fritz wasn't far away. On reaching the village we were mobbed by the population, until, as if by magic, they all disappeared as we were showered with mortar bombs.'[3]

Typical of the civilian reactions was the experience of tank gunner Cpl Bill Moseley, advancing into Gierle, being adopted by the Geerts family and, in spite of the shortage of food, being served an omelette made from twenty-five eggs for the crew of five:

> We swopped our tinned food for their fresh. The children soon divested us of our chocolate and sweet rations. The omelette was served with fried tomatoes and great bowls of succulent chips. It must have been 10 o'clock by the time we had finished and prepared to leave, but they would not hear of it; the whole family, including the children, took us over to the estaminet where we spent the rest of the night drinking Belgian 'Tipsy' beer, playing pool and being regaled with tales of the Belgian Resistance. The estaminet finally closed at about 4.30 a.m. when the beer ran out![4]

So in the towns and villages within the sound of the guns but beyond the reach of the tanks, they waited for *Bevrijding* while the occupying enemy and their collaborators ran for their lives. In the wild rout there were also the 'quislings', the members of the Dutch Nazi party. There were ordinary *Wehrmacht* soldiers who had been enjoying convalescence from the Russian front. There were German civilians, Gestapo men and administrators, generally more hated than the men in army uniform. All were looking for any kind of transport which moved faster than tired legs could run.

As crowds of Dutch and Belgian people gleefully shouted, 'Come and see the Germans running!', some were more cautious. Teresia Carpenter was born and brought up in Breda and would one day marry her British tank driver hero. But Mad Tuesday found her parents undecided about the delirious celebrations:

> When we emerged from our cellar to see the soldiers walking through our street we were told not yet to hang out our flags in case the Germans might return. Our home had been severely hit by shells, the roof partly blown off and some walls ripped asunder. We were able to move into a house just round the corner which had been left by German collaborators at the approach of the Allied forces.[5]

The liberated people had good cause to rejoice. It was not a simple cultural preference for British or Canadians instead of Germans. There was a history of intense hatred. One present-day Dutch burgomaster who, as a baby, was subjected to dire sufferings during the liberation battles, sketched out the reasons for the widespread delight. The unreasoning, almost hysterical relaxation of Mad Tuesday was entirely understandable, he thought. There were four main reasons which brought *Bevrijding* delirium to such a peak at that particular time.[6]

Firstly, there had been an increasing pursuit of Jews by Nazi police ordered to ship people of Jewish blood away to extermination camps. Earlier in the war Dutch Jews had simply been 'asked' to report to a 'Jewish Council' in order to be sent on 'voluntary work' in labour camps mainly in Germany. News of the real purpose of such camps sent many Jews into hiding. During 1943 the *razzias* (searches) began in earnest. By the autumn of 1944, more than 25,000 Dutch families were hiding Jews, at the peril of the lives of all of them, fugitives and hosts alike. The hiding places were mainly in Brabant and Limburg, areas now close to liberation and seized with the hopes of Mad Tuesday.

Secondly, the German need to reinforce their fleeing armies, mobilising all males from fifteen to sixty, meant that there was a serious shortage of labour in that country. Allied bombing meant more and more repair and construction work for which hands were few. Dutch and Belgian males were therefore being rounded up in large numbers to supply the required labour.

Many Dutch and Belgian men of ages fifteen to sixty had formerly been allowed to remain at home, in reserved occupations such as doctors, farmers and bakers, and essential personnel in the transport and power industries, as well as the physically handicapped. They were now mobilised to dig trenches along the River Maas, together with Russian prisoners of war and German civilians outside of military age.

Thirdly, with the advance of the Allies and encouragement from the Dutch government in exile in London, the Resistance was becoming more active, in country notably difficult for Resistance activities. Reprisals were aimed at all members of the community, both relatives of Resistance workers and also random hostages.

Fourthly, Germany had now ordered the arrest of all former Dutch Army soldiers. These men had been released after the capitulation in 1940 but were now viewed as potential Resistance fighters. This order provoked strikes of workers throughout the Netherlands. Repressed strikes developed into riots. In a brief period 80 strike leaders were executed, 95 civilians were killed in the streets and 400 were seriously wounded.

Add to those current issues the long-term problems of food and material shortages exacerbated by Nazi greed and arrogance, and the overwhelming desire to be liberated is understandable. An interminable dream seemed to be wakening into reality.

Another version of events describes how:

in the beginning they heard the guns, forty, thirty, twenty km away. The roar of exploding shells which, in 1940, had heralded the dreaded German invasion now brought the promise of impending Allied rescue. Telephones were silent, service disrupted, rumours filled the vacuum. The most convincing evidence . . . the German occupation force was in full flight. The people awoke, that Mad Tuesday, to an incredible sight: barracks lay empty, with food still on tables, clothes on pegs. . . . German stragglers who had not yet left got a boot in the behind from the now-emboldened citizens: 'Go home, German. Get out of my house!' they cried.

And then it all went wrong. The clockwork of the hectic advance had run down. Literally it had 'run out of gas'. Miles covered and expectations raised had failed to take into account what any forecourt petrol pump assistant could have advised. Supplies will only enable so many vehicles to travel so many miles. And supplies still had to be brought those 400 miles from temporary docks off the open Normandy beaches. The great port of Antwerp had been captured, more or less. But Allied generals seemed to have forgotten that the port lies miles up a relatively narrow river, on both banks of which resolute German troops still sat tight, barring the way to Allied shipping. The great mad bubble of *Bevrijding* exhilaration burst overnight.

In Bergen-op-Zoom, its inhabitants feverishly waiting, it was the sight of Canadian prisoners of war being marched through the city which dispelled the jollity. These were 'grim evidence of battles being waged to the south'.[7] Allied attacks were now meeting ferocious resistance from small but well-placed German units. Dutch labour was being forced to construct tank and infantry defences as well as obstacles to prevent air landing attacks.

Yet it all happened again, twelve days later. Mad Tuesday now became Mad Sunday, *Dolle Zondag*. Little wonder! The citizens of those same regions looked up and saw a vast, unparalleled armada of planes thundering invincibly overhead, troop carriers, gliders, fighters, bombers. Then out of the troop carriers blossomed thousands of parachutes, all the way from Son to Arnhem, flowers of promise of real freedom. White emblems of peace.

The public telephone system stayed open, from Arnhem back through Nijmegen, Grave and Eindhoven to the waiting towns and villages, Breda, Antwerp, Middelburg, Flushing, Bergen-op-Zoom, Tilburg, Vught. Sons, uncles, grandmothers, neighbours, police, tradesmen phoned back the news. An entire airborne army had landed behind an already stricken and fragmented enemy. This time one could go mad with no fear of future recriminations.

Dutch rail workers went on strike throughout the country. Public funeral processions were held in Brabant for Allied airmen shot down during the battles. Hidden Resistance leaders came out into the open. Young baker's assistant Will Lagarde stood and watched the endless procession of planes and the circus entertainment of floating, swinging, landing parachutists. His town, Oss, would be liberated and stay liberated. But the guns would roar and the shells would fall into the streets for more than a month before the silence of true peace became permanent.[8]

As a Canadian historian has put it graphically:

> For the people of Bergen-op-Zoom and the surrounding countryside, the months of September and October 1944 were marked by elation, despair, tragedy, courage and finally triumph through liberation. But the liberation seemed so long in coming, for despite being only some 25 kilometres north of Antwerp, which fell on 4 September, the city's Canadian liberators did not occupy its *centrum* until 27 October 1944.[9]

A tank soldier, waiting to advance on 22 October 1944, found himself on night guard duty walking the same Arnhem road near St Oedenrode which had been traversed by the lead tanks of the Guards and 'liberated' five weeks earlier. The previous night enemy patrols had penetrated from their positions just left of the road and killed several infantrymen as they slept. The tank men on prowler guard around their '*laager*' were instructed to patrol in twos, without noisy boots and walking back to back.[10] This was dangerous for the patrols but both dangerous and disheartening for the local people of St Oedenrode, isolated in what appeared to be an immovable front-line situation.

The failure of the Allies to capture Arnhem and the determination of the Germans to defend the Scheldt estuary had two main repercussions from Mad Sunday onwards. The first was a bitter wait, with reinforced enemy control and a starvation diet for the Dutch, for those in Brabant another month or six weeks, for those north of the Maas another seven months in atrocious winter conditions, far worse than the normal freeze.

The second factor involved Allied troops, many tired from Normandy battles and the conquest of the Channel ports. They had been encouraged by some leaders, including FM Montgomery, to expect victory and release from the threat of death by Christmas. Now every unit and every fighting man, at some point or other, had to endure bloody battles against hopeless odds in towns and villages whose saga would never be proclaimed in the way in which the epic of Arnhem has been celebrated, through that winter of sub-zero temperatures and on into the next spring.

The experience of just one war-scarred battalion in one unsung battle underlines the fallacies of Mad Tuesday and Mad Sunday, as that battalion experienced its Black Friday. The Canadian Black Watch (Royal Highland Regiment of Canada) had arrived in Normandy generally recognised as a 'crack' battalion. An officer of another regiment said of it that it was 'a bloody good regiment, extremely efficient, everything done by the book'. In several actions it justified that reputation. Then on 25 July 1944 it was directed towards a particularly difficult objective, the village of Fontenay, hidden on the reverse slope of one of the Verrieres Ridges.

While preparing to advance, the unit lost its outstanding colonel, S.S.T. Cantlie, and two coy commanders to m-g fire. The junior coy commander, Maj Philip Griffin, took command. He was given the option by his brigadier as to whether to advance or cancel the attack, knowing that delays had thrown the artillery programme out of gear and that the supporting tanks could not venture on to the wide open slopes, ringed by enemy anti-tank guns. He chose to continue with the plan.

Griffin and more than three hundred riflemen walked out across exposed slopes under the fire of enemy guns on higher ground left, right and centre. The ranks thinned out as men fell along the way. Eventually Griffin and about sixty men breasted the slope and disappeared from sight. He was found dead among his men just short of the enemy lines. Of the whole force only some sixteen men returned unscathed.[11]

That was in Normandy. In the meantime LOB (left out of battle) troops, men returning from hospital or courses, and reinforcements from Canada combined to reform the battalion. By the time it arrived in the Netherlands the unit was almost up to strength, but not quite up to the extremely high standard of training which it enjoyed prior to D-Day. Most other units had suffered similar losses and dilution of skills.

'Friday the 13th' is regarded by superstitious people as being a day of ominous portents. For the Black Watch it would become 'Black Friday'. Because the high command was still focusing its attention on other areas, the Canadians beyond Antwerp were being asked to fight a war of numerous minor battles of attrition without the necessary resources. Again and again Canadian battalions advanced into 'forlorn hopes'. Already within the previous week the Black Watch had lost 119 casualties in one battle and 81 in another. Their front-line battalion 'rifle' strength would normally be not much in excess of 300.

Now they were ordered to cross flat, open, muddy fields to capture the junction of a high dyke and a railway embankment. The onus was on the PBI (truly the Poor Bloody Infantry). Tanks could not cross the mire. Bad visibility hampered artillery accuracy and prevented air support. The trudging advance across beet fields would arrow into a tangent between the two high earthworks on which rapid firing m-gs were located, and in the sides of which defenders, with their sniper rifles, automatics and hand grenades, were deeply ensconced. All could see the impossibility of the task. None could object to the word of command, although battalion COs vigorously protested.

One young officer, Alan Mills, wrote home describing his experience:

We formed up behind a dyke and advanced over open ground. When we got practically to our objective the machine guns and mortars became too hot and we began to drop right and left. Somehow a few managed to get to the objective. Those of us who were hit lay out in the open field with no cover.

Another account said that those who reached the objective found themselves 'pinned against an embankment twenty feet high. As the men tried to dig in, grenades were lobbed over the dyke at them. Most of these men were subsequently taken prisoner, many of them with shrapnel wounds'.

The battalion commander, Lt Col Ritchie, was not himself responsible for the battle plan. He could only obey higher orders under protest. He further commented on what he saw happening:

The calibre of the enemy was completely misjudged at brigade HQ . . . we had no idea the Germans [paratroopers] would be so good. We were really up against the crème de la crème. They taunted our guys. They would jump out of the slits on the dykes, taunt our guys, and as soon as we started to fire, they'd get down.

It was a funny sort of a battle plan – crazy. We were instructed to take four posts forming a rough square with 1000 yard sides. We went in with a dawn attack supported by tanks which were quite useless at the time . . . owing to the flooding and heavy ground fog. We were pinned down by heavy machine-gun fire right from the beginning; our forward troops had to fight their way *to the Start Line!*

All the coy commanders were wounded, and the intelligence officer, watching from a high viewpoint, reported 'the companies are being annihilated'.

One of the coy commanders, Major William Ewing, remembered:

The concept of the attack was fundamentally cockeyed. We had to cross something like 1200 yards of beet fields with no cover other than beets. There was a watercourse that crossed our front; we couldn't get over that except on a narrow bridge which was under enemy machine-gun fire . . . crossfire, and there wasn't the hell of a lot we could do.

We had a bad time. My company strength initially was in the order of ninety men and there were only four who weren't either killed or wounded in the bloody thing . . . you lose all your key people, all your senior NCOs, even down to corporal.

As the inevitable evacuation from the untenable lodgement continued through the hours of darkness, the cost was counted by sad officers left out of battle. One casualty total was reported as 145, another as 183. Tragic enough, but what was unusual was the high proportion of dead and prisoners compared to the tally of evacuated wounded, 57 per cent being totally lost (39 per cent killed and 18 per cent prisoners).[12] In an average battle the proportion of those killed would have been very much lower. As a point of comparison to the 39 per cent of Black Watch who died, in the main Arnhem actions 1st Airborne lost 13 per cent, 10th and 11th Para Battalions 16 per cent, and the highest cost unit, 9th Field Coy RE, 23 per cent.

Black Friday was typical of so-called 'minor' battles fought by many units over a period of two months to clear the flanks of the Arnhem road. Battles made necessary by the fallibility of the Arnhem strategy. Battles exacerbated by the failure to give immediate priority to clearing the port of Antwerp. Battles whose stories of heroism, courage and catastrophe have been overshadowed by the epic of Arnhem, the 'bridge too far'.

CHAPTER THREE

Arnhem – the Sore Thumb

A strange shape was appearing on the battle maps of the Low Countries in mid-September 1944. It looked more like a child's doodle than a general's design. If submitted to the Dutch Staff College it would have elicited the comment 'must do better!'[1] A Washington source called the shape 'a dangling appendix'. Another saw it as a snake crawling up the main road from the Belgian border to Arnhem.

A more apt simile might have been an extended left hand, the thumb outstretched and somewhat bent to the right, the base of the thumb around Valkenswaard and the tip at Arnhem. The index finger would be extended horizontally pointing left to Antwerp and the Scheldt estuary. This was the impact on the map of the first few days of Montgomery's attempt to capture the Arnhem bridge by an airborne drop coordinated with an armoured rush up the exposed road from Son to Arnhem – Operation Market Garden. Again the Dutch Staff College might have commented 'Is this really a project devised by a genuine military student?'

Montgomery, now a field marshal, took several risks and ignored a number of warning lights, including the Dutch Army's long history of studying the precise problem. The outcome is well known. What perhaps is not so well known is the huge distances involved. From Bareel, south of Valkenswaard, to Arnhem was all of 68 miles, up which the armoured divisions were expected to advance virtually unhindered on a single exposed main road. The snake of that advance would be widened into a protruding thumb on the map by supporting flank attacks.

The 68 miles along that road were not the only factor of distance.[2] The leading British tanks had entered Antwerp, but that was 106 miles back down the road. The town of Westkapelle at the mouth of the Scheldt was 140 miles from Arnhem, all country needing to be liberated. Ominously, reverting to the thumb simile, the fingers pointed horizontally back to the west signified other coastal areas not yet cleared of an obstinate, highly skilled enemy. Breskens, Dunkirk, Calais and Boulogne were still being besieged by Allied troops. Boulogne was 230 miles remote from Arnhem. Cap Gris Nez, that dominating Channel cliff, was not attacked by the Allies until twelve days after Market Garden commenced.[3]

Because Market Garden is now known to have been a failure it is easy to criticise Montgomery. In regard to terrain the advance to Arnhem was in some ways even more difficult than in the notorious Normandy bocage or in the wide open Caen plain dominated by the Germans' 88 mm guns. In the Low Countries the map was dominated by watercourses, large and small. The engineering of canals and dykes around polders had thrown up ready-made embankments as further defence opportunities. Even the smaller streams were usually impossible for tanks to cross once the bridges had been blown.

Major obstacles included the Wilhelmina Canal, 27 to 33 yards wide; the Maas at Grave, 270 yards wide; the Maas-Waal Canal, 67 yards; the Waal at Nijmegen, 283 yards; and the Rhine at Arnhem, 100 yards.[4] The relatively narrow canal at *Depôt de Mendicité* was impassible for tanks and difficult for infantry unless a bridge was left intact. A ship canal across South Beveland was 64 yards wide, 21 ft deep and with banks rising 5 ft above the water. Moreover it had 20 ft wide drainage ditches on both sides of it.

Montgomery was under tremendous pressure, some of it the result of his own optimistic predictions about an early end to the war. One of his biographers explains:

In Britain, a desperately war-weary nation anxious to see the war finished quickly, the claim of the nation's most famous soldier that he could be in Berlin by Christmas fell on receptive ears. This was exactly what people were looking for – the avenging sword flashing and cleaving across north-western Europe.[5]

The opportunity for sensational advances appeared to exist. On the day when the Allies entered Antwerp, General Student was made commander of the front in the Netherlands and Belgium. It was known that he had only about 100 tanks with which to confront the 2,000 of the Allies on the same ground. His available aircraft totalled 570 against 14,000. And his reinforcements consisted of elderly reservists and under-age boys.[6]

Another authoritative commentator observed that, although Supreme Commander Eisenhower 'now had 52 divisions under his command, his sole chance of retaining the initiative, of recreating conditions of mobile warfare and dealing a decisive blow at the Wehrmacht in the West that autumn, rested with the three airborne divisions waiting at their airfields in England, and the three divisions of XXX British Corps standing at the Dutch frontier'.[7]

Given the problem, the imperatives and the opportunity, Montgomery, usually the most cautious of generals, decided to jump the waterways by dropping airborne troops behind them or on strategic bridges, while directing XXX Corps to dash post-haste along the one main road to Arnhem.

From Arnhem, Montgomery would then proceed to set up a firm line to the Zuider Zee via Apeldoorn. Side thrusts to Deventer, Zutphen and Doesberg would prepare a solid base from which to advance into the heart of Germany. The expectation appears to have been that all the German troops in that 230-mile tranche of France, Belgium and the Netherlands, back to Boulogne, would either run away or stay and surrender.

Whatever his own private thoughts, Montgomery compounded the high expectations in an Order of the Day, celebrating the rapid advance from Normandy to Antwerp and predicting victory with almost religious zeal. He told his troops:[8]

Such an historic march of events had seldom taken place in history in such a short space of time. You have every reason to be proud of what you have done. Let us say to each other 'this was the Lord's doing and is marvellous in our eyes'.[9]

Now the allies are closing in on Nazi Germany . . . Nazi leaders have ordered the people to defend Germany to the last and dispute every inch of ground . . . but the mere issuing of orders is quite useless. . . . No human endeavours can now prevent the complete and utter defeat of the armed forces of Germany. Defeat is certain. The defeat will be absolute. The triumphant cry is now 'Forward into Germany'.

The general outline of Market Garden is well known and needs only a brief revision. It has been described as 'laying an airborne "carpet" of paratroopers along the main axis of advance' to the Arnhem road and rail bridges while XXX Corps drove up the road.[10] The airborne fleets took off with high hopes on 17 September and the first landings were reported to German HQ at 1.30 p.m. The Anglo-Polish corps landed in the vicinity of Arnhem, the US 101st Airborne Division around Eindhoven and the US 82nd Airborne Division at Nijmegen.

The German strength in the area had been underestimated or ignored by the Allied generals. The 9th and 10th SS Panzer Divisions were reforming after their Normandy traumas but had a backbone of very experienced officers and NCOs. The 59th and 245th Infantry Divisions were well located to counter-attack as the snake salient started to widen into the thumb. And just as important, Field Marshal Walter Model, impassive and implacable, was eating lunch at Oosterbeck as the first parachutes descended. As the British 1st Airborne had been parachuted more than 6 miles distant from the Arnhem bridge, Model was nearer the objective himself and immediately ordered the forming of an extemporary battle group gathered from twenty-eight different commands.[11]

These factors set the scene for the historic but fruitless action of Colonel Frost and his men at the Arnhem bridge, the rapid build-up of superior German forces and the inevitable surrender of many of the attacking troops, as XXX Corps failed to reach and cross the river to their rescue.

The other air drops lower down the road had drawn on the maps a shape like a python with bulges of undigested prey. German counter-attacks cut the vital main road again and again, threatening an even greater catastrophe.

As the last Allied paratroopers were evacuated from the Oosterbeck bridgehead on 25/26 September, the fight was on to widen the slim snake salient into the more solid thumb shape. And in all the wide lands around and behind the Market Garden adventure German formations were being reinforced and would fight ferocious delaying actions in Channel ports, the 'Breskens pocket', the causeway into Walcheren, the 'island' itself, the towns and villages of North Brabant and the damp marshes of Limburg. Defeat might be certain but Montgomery's 'triumphant cry' was now sounding more like flatulent bombast.

On 17 September, as Maj Gen Maxwell Taylor's 'Screaming Eagles' (US 101st Airborne Division) dropped around Son, at the base of the 'thumb', soldiers of the Herman Goering *Kampfgruppe* (KG) were already guarding vital bridges. Immediately a battalion of the excellent heavy Panther tanks, forty of them, entraining for the Eastern Front, had been turned around and sent to counter-attack the Americans. Maxwell Taylor's men soon found themselves defending 20 miles of the main road on both sides.

Farther up the road the thin snake of Allied troops became even more vulnerable to the machete of German armour.

There was confusion for both sides for, while front-line German troops rallied to the counter-attack, there were still hordes of second- and third-class German troops escaping from the main Allied advance across Belgium. Andrew Horne of 1RTR saw some of that German rout:

The Germans were running away with horse-drawn carts and everything they could get their hands on. We had been shooting them all morning and the squadron leader thought we should get on to the road and stop them altogether. I was in Troop 5 and we got the word to go forward.

Before we got to the road we were hit by a shell, 'BLAM!' and we baled out, into the ditch. But our tank engine kept running. So tank commander Sgt Smart shouted 'Back on the tank!' We clambered on to the rear deck but straight away they got us again on the track. So we had to bale out again! [The Sherman tank was notorious for exploding instantly into flames.]

I was a bit deaf by now and realised I had got a bit of blast in the head. I was taken to a Field Dressing Station, on to a hospital in Brussels and then flown straight back to Hereford in England. On the plane we saw they were towing the gliders the other way to go into Arnhem.[12]

Further up the main road, beyond and isolated from the US 101st, would be the US 82nd Airborne Division, responsible for capturing the great bridges at Grave and Nijmegen. In the Arnhem area itself the British 1st Airborne Division would go in accompanied by the Polish Airborne Brigade. All these were elite, tough, well-trained troops but very lightly armed. They would not be able to withstand attacks from masses of Panthers and later Tigers unless support could be rushed up that long road. The onus was therefore on the Guards Armoured Division and the 43rd Wessex Infantry Division to make the links along the road and succour the parachutists at the far tip of the air drops. The Irish Guards had started boldly from the Belgian border towards Valkenswaard and would hand over to other Guards battalions along the way.

However, the entire operation ignored the reality of the terrain as the road continued to the north-east. Lt Harold Lander was on the road commanding a reconnaissance troop. He had heard of the Dutch Military Academy's stock answer to exams on the subject of advancing along the same Arnhem road. He quotes:

'You do not attempt to go that way because it stands for miles in full view with huge ditches on both sides. Once you're on it you can't get off it.'
   That was the road which the British Army was sent up. Consequently the Germans on either side could easily knock out vehicles. Later when we came back down the road we were amazed at how exposed it was. All we could do was hide our tanks behind hedges.[13]

And, of course, behind the British tanks, which were extremely vulnerable to the German 88-mm gun and the hand-held *Panzerfaust*, were long lines of closely packed 'soft' vehicles of all kinds, strung along hundreds of yards of road which could not be defended by static positions.

The advance also depended on German lack of ability or willingness to counter-attack along the ever more extensive snake of soft vehicles. This attitude ran counter to all that had been learned about German tactics, especially in Normandy. The brilliant Canadian general, Guy Simonds, who was not involved in the airborne operation, had no illusions about the German reaction in similar situations:

> Fighting at the present time is not confined on a continuous front. The essence of German defence is the counter-attack. You should never be surprised when he counter-attacks. You should be surprised if he fails to counter-attack. . . . We must always bear in mind that the Boche keeps very still in daytime. When, for instance, all movement has ceased in a village we can accept that the Boche is there.[14]

So in the Arnhem area, FM Model, having eaten his lunch and sent his emergency group, *KG Schleifenbaum*, to defend the main bridge, went into counter-attack mode. Ably aided by his subordinate, Gen Student, he had all the British drop zones under *Nebelwerfer* (mortar) fire by evening. He also concentrated effort on counter-attacking along the line of the snaking road with 59th Infantry Division and 107th Panzer Brigade. Hitler released 170th and 180th Division to assist. To the forty Panthers redirected from the railway sidings were quickly added twenty of the even heavier Tigers. And the hitherto invisible *Luftwaffe* assembled seventy aircraft in a rare bombing attack down the road.[15]

Knowing nothing of these developments, men of the Guards Division were in high spirits as they raced along the good road towards Grave and Nijmegen virtually unhindered as yet. The long miles rolled quickly under the tracks of the tanks and the tyres of the motorised elements. Major H.F. Stanley of 1st (motor) Bn Grenadier Guards had no reason for doubt or false modesty as he reported:

> Charlie Rutland (No 2 Coy) and Alec Gregory Hood (No 3 Sqn) were in the lead. Their battle group cracked off at 0600 hours and I was in

the rear company with John Trotters' Sqn behind me. They fairly brought the whip out that morning; the speed we were travelling at the back end of the column was terrific – just full throttle the whole way. All went splendidly. The bridge over the Wilhelmina Canal had been blown by the Hun, but REs had worked all night and got it fixed by first light.

On to ST OEDENRODE – VEGHEL – UDEN – GRAVES, where the first really big bridge was taken by American paratroopers [82nd]. Those fellows really did a splendid job of work. We would never have made that all-out 40 mph run up if it had not been for them.[16]

At the end of their exhilarating run Stanley saw prisoners being taken in considerable numbers, 'an extraordinary assortment, old and young – SS police, Wehrmacht, Marines, some temporarily arrogant (but only for a very short time)'. He saw masses of captured equipment '88-mm guns, 50 mm, 37 mm, a baby French tank, Spandaus, Hotchkiss MGs, new rifles and old 1916 long barrel and long bayonet rifles, mines and bazookas . . . it was almost a foundation for a War Museum'. For Maj Stanley and his men Montgomery's 'triumphant cry' must still have rung true at that moment.

The moment of disillusionment was not far away. The Allied troops on the corridor were so widely spaced that a determined German attack had been able to cut the main road between Uden and Veghel, held only by light groups of American paratroopers. This halted the long 'sea tail' of supply vehicles upon which the forward units depended. It was a critical situation which XXX Corps commander, Gen Horrocks, countered by ordering parts of the Guards Division back down the road along which they had sped with such high expectations. The units selected were Maj Stanley's battalion, 1st (motor) Grenadier Guards, and the 2nd Armoured Grenadiers. Now, instead of adding their weight to the race to relieve the airborne people at the Arnhem bridge, they were to stem the flow of strong German forces on to the single main road some miles back.[17]

Like most military plans the movement of troops along the single road was based on plans for normal progress at reasonable speeds. Any breakdown at places which did not permit a deviation through the fields (and this road was notorious for its lack of access or egress beyond its flanking ditches) caused the familiar concertina effect of modern motorway traffic jams. When the road itself was cut by enemy troops and had to be fought over, this left battle debris and burning vehicles strewn across the relatively narrow road, the jamming effect fore and aft of the cut being then of much longer duration.

On 20 September, XXX Corps had 20,000 vehicles on that one road, bumper to bumper most of the way. The procession included 34-ton tanks, towed and self-propelled artillery guns, 'funnies' with bridge building equipment and other clumsy vehicles. And the 20,000 count did not include the thousands of American paratroopers already dropped around the road and needing to manoeuvre in its defence.

A further, otherwise welcome, complication was the mass of Dutch civilians coming out on to the roads after the point tanks had passed (or sometimes before they arrived) and causing the columns to halt. Pte D. O'Connell of the 7th Somerset Light Infantry experienced this ambivalent emotion:

> When the Dutch discovered we were British, the barriers went down, hugging and kissing all round, every vehicle in the column had a Dutch fan club . . . I became the front carrier in a dash across the road bridge. At one part of the town was love, kisses, fruit and flowers: on the other there was a barrage of bullets. A motley group tailed behind us, light AA guns, some anti-tank guns, some Pioneers, another tank or SP gun and a few more ragtag and bobtail.[18]

More havoc was wrought to careful plans by communications failures. The lack of efficient radio sets among the Arnhem paratroopers is well recorded. Back down the road, artillery gunners were finding it difficult to zero in on targets because of faulty wireless or phone links. Some ordinary soldiers discovered to their amazement that it was possible to communicate with Arnhem by the normal civilian telephone service. Dutch Resistance men were able to pick up a phone and ask friends in Arnhem or elsewhere what was happening.

Cpl Reg Spittles, commanding a tank with 1RTR, understood that his regiment was to drive on beyond Arnhem and form a defence perimeter there as a firm base for the push into Germany. Instead they found themselves among the American paratroopers, defending the confined corridor of highway:

I was in B Sqdn and we were given areas of responsibility in and around Veghel as initial support to the American Paras who thought they were being pulled out. But it was a couple of days before our infantry came up to take over. The amusing thing was they had been dropping British rations to the Americans but the only things they liked were the tins of glucose sweets, the Churchill cigarettes and the chocolate. They left behind the biscuits and tins of meat and puddings piled up in their dug-outs. . . .

[As the Germans counter-attacked] the fighting was pretty grim. It was the only time we had our turret Besa m-g seize-up because of continuous firing, so we had to swop it over with the co-driver's m-g. We could not get our 75-mm shells up the breech for lack of chances for cleaning. Eventually the whole of B sqdn was withdrawn from action into Veghel itself to do a proper main gun clean-up, with boiling water, cleaning rods, scouring pads – the lot!!![19]

Another tank man, Alex Carder with the 5th Royal Inniskilling Dragoon Guards, had a clear impression of the traffic flow problems and of the narrow, perilous nature of the single lifeline:

Advancing along the Arnhem road, constantly we were told to halt and then advance a bit and then halt again and stop and wait, start and stop. We got up near Graves bridge. We were trying to find out what the hell we were doing, but what was happening, and we didn't then know, was that the Germans kept cutting the line behind us.

So what we did was to fan out on the left-hand side of the road, but we didn't go all that far from the road, the four tanks in the troop. We didn't go much above a field or two away. It wasn't as though we had advanced half a mile from the road, we were just forming a screen to guard the road. But the enemy shells were falling on the road all the time.[20]

Lt Harold Lander was also involved in a screen along the road. It was frightening at night because the enemy were only a field or two away on either side of the road at one time. One night he was woken by whispers of 'Ssh! the Germans are coming!' There were stealthy sounds of bodies swishing through the long grass. The recce men grabbed their pistols and crawled out to defend the road, prepared to sell their lives at a high price to . . . the herd of cows which appeared through the mists.[21]

Not all Lander's comrades were so fortunate. The Germans again broke the line some way from Lander's picket. Their B echelon of supply vehicles was surrounded on the road and destroyed. The Sergeant Major was killed. The remainder of drivers and others were taken prisoners and held in a wood just off the road. Fortunately the advance soon rolled over the wood and the prisoners were released.

In such a mobile situation friends and enemy at times became almost intermingled. Coming up at the base of the 'thumb', men of the 53rd Welsh Division had such an experience. The 4th Welch Regiment had advanced into the village of Reusel against determined opposition. Point men of the battalion had occupied the west end of the church, but the Germans were still inside the east end and refusing to retreat or surrender. At such close proximity the enemy could hear spoken orders. The Welch ensured due secrecy by giving their orders in Welsh.[22]

Capt M.G.T. Webster, commanding a reconnaissance troop of the 2nd Grenadier Guards, had a similar moment of undesired 'neighbourliness'. It was reported to him that Dick Edward-Collins's tank had been hit and that Dick was nowhere to be found. He had, however, sent a handwritten note giving the map reference of the anti-tank gun which had knocked out his tank. Capt Webster went personally to investigate the mystery.

When we got to the outskirts of the village we were told that Dick was in a house farther up the road on the right and that the Germans were installed at the back. Leaving our half-track we walked through the trees, leaving the road, over a ditch into a field. As we got nearer the house someone in the house ordered us to come in and to keep very quiet.

Inside we found Dick being most tenderly cared for by the wife of the house. She had bathed his wounds. She and her husband explained in sign language that the Germans were in the next room! We got Dick, who was in great pain, on to a stretcher [he lost a leg], thanking the Dutch family as best we could by signs and quiet words and as quickly as possible got back to the half-track.[23]

Webster and his men also found that such contiguity led to outbreaks of 'friendly fire'. As the situation became more static along the Arnhem road Webster's troop had to patrol via Nistelrode, Schijndel, Veghel to Uden at dawn and at dusk. American paratroopers were still stationed at strategic points. One evening Webster's troop Sergeant, E.A. Smith, leading the Grenadier patrol, was fired on 'by, it was obvious to me, Americans'. A bazooka shell screamed past Dusty Smith's tank. He took the risk of withholding fire and shouting out that they were British. Quickly an American sergeant and three privates popped out of a hedge. The American sergeant's main response was 'and it was my last f—g bomb as well!'

Men in battle could at times be cheered by a moment of unexpected humour and could prove that their sensitivities were not totally dulled by combat. The Irish Guards, having lost some tanks on the road, remembered:

There was the splendid sight, amidst all the shot and shell, of the elderly (anyway to us – anyone over 40 was really rather old) *Times* photographer, standing on the roof of his van, calmly taking photographs of our burning tanks along the road.

The same unit observed the unusual sight of a German anti-tank gun being towed by a white horse on to the Nijmegen railway bridge. Sgt Cowan, 'Deadeye Dick', commanding the Firefly tank with its large gun, the 17-pounder, was ordered to eliminate the enemy gun. He responded, 'I will that, but I'll leave the horse.' His officer, Eddie Tyler, warned him

'Don't take a chance. Use HE [high explosive]'. Cowan's tank fired. The anti-tank gun disintegrated. The horse stood still – untouched. Later Cowan admitted that he had used solid shot against Tyler's orders, but excused himself with 'a pity to hurt the horse, Sir!'

Cpl Bill Moseley with the Northamptonshire Yeomanry had a good eye for terrain. He describes the differences he encountered compared with the Normandy orchards, woods, bocage and then wide-open, dry plains around Caen. The Dutch countryside was:

Open flat ploughed fields, proving very heavy going for tanks, intersected by numerous streams, rivers and canals with roads carried along the tops of dykes, similar to the Fens of Cambridgeshire and Lincolnshire. Movement was restricted to paved roads, the verges of which were often mined, and separated from the surrounding fields by deep water-filled ditches. Bridges were essential and consequently blown at the last moment by the Germans; the poor old Sappers (Royal Engineers) were hard put to replace them with Bailey Bridges.[24]

Another tank man with the same regiment, Les 'Spud' Taylor, also noticed the change in German tactics from the more massed confrontations of Normandy:

Our tanks were now more often confined to the roads, there being so many dykes, ditches and canals with their countless bridges. In short, 'Water, water everywhere,' as the poet says. The Germans invariably knocked out the leading tank and the rear-most vehicle, trapping the rest of the column in the middle with no quick means of escape.

We did not meet so many panzers but the enemy still had plenty of S-P Guns, anti-tank guns and, of course, *Panzerfaust* teams, with large numbers of Baggy Pants types willing and able to man them. It was NOT 'easy going'.[25]

There is much scope for criticism of Allied planners as regards some of the assumptions made about the Arnhem road. Yet there could be a snippet of sympathy for them as to one unexpected impediment: the decision of the *Luftwaffe* to break cover in considerable numbers. Seventy planes were not a vast armada by Allied standards, but they constituted a quite sufficient force to cause havoc in the relatively restricted 1944 town centre of Eindhoven with its narrow side streets. Some of the *Luftwaffe* pilots had no doubt flown from Eindhoven's nearby airfield and would be able to bomb with good knowledge of the layout of the town.

A lorry driver, Pte Sidney Brown, RASC, went down into an air-raid shelter with civilians as the German bombers arrived. Coming to the surface again after the raid he found his convoy in flames: 'The buildings and the trucks were burning. There was nothing we could do until the trucks had burned out. Then we pushed the wrecks to one side. My vehicle had miraculously survived and I was on the road before dawn.' Most of that convoy would never move again and the survivors like Sidney Brown were delayed. Vital supplies, awaited some 20 or 30 miles ahead, would not be available on time. Dutch workers hurried to clear the rubble and minimise delays.[26]

The air drop and road advance began on 17 September. By the 20th reinforced German troops, supported by the much-feared Panther tanks, were able to strike at Son bridge near the base of the long thumb now sketched on the battle maps. Light American outposts were overwhelmed. This could have caused a major disaster for all the troops committed along the single main road. Prompt reaction enabled the Allies to hold off the German attack. There were reports of panic. Some echelon lorries, having no wireless links and relying on verbal messages, turned tail and drove back the way they had come, causing traffic behind them to halt and succumb to even more delays.

Men of the 43rd Wessex Division were moving up to push through the tanks once the bridges had been captured up to Arnhem, beyond which they would be in relatively open territory. They moved with an immense convoy of 3,300 vehicles. First the convoy was held up by the Son bridge incident. Then on 22 and 23 September another group of German panzers cut the 1,000 yard wide corridor near Veghel, attacking from both sides. Some of the enemy tanks found an unguarded section of the Wessex convoy perched up on the highway as easy prey to the efficient tank guns.

One historian has commented that 'in places the "front" was quite literally the edges of the main Eindhoven–Nijmegen road and defended only by the XXX Corps troops moving along it'.[27] In some cases it was lorry drivers' pistols and co-drivers' Sten guns against *Panzerfausts* and 75-mm Panther guns. As the corridor at widest was only 1,000 yards, say 500 yards on each side of the road, the Germans were able to use their accurate *Nebelwerfers*, with six 'Moaning Minnie' bombs descending in a batch, to cause more damage and casualties. The wonder is that so many of the convoys survived and kept moving at all.

Then on 24 September, in the evening, KG Jungwirth cut the road again at Koevering, with massive destruction of supply lorries halted in a traffic block on the road. That day 4th Dorsets of the Wessex Division were being sent to try to cross the Rhine in inadequate light boats easily sunk by m-g bullets. It was the final attempt to relieve the airborne troops cut off beyond the river. The Dorset attempt failed. The Koevering cut was an important factor in the inevitable decision to call off the attempt to secure the Arnhem bridge.

This left the Allies spread along the main road, with the American paratroopers due to be withdrawn. For a month sections of that road would still be vulnerable. For more than a month battles would rage, all the way down the thumb shape on the map, and back along the index finger line, and away to the coast. The troops on the road, shuffling to thicken and stiffen the defences, were caught in an uncomfortable stalemate. The civilians in the peripheral towns and villages would be condemned to extremes of fear and discomfort by the failure of the much-trumpeted rush for instant victory.

But first occurred the funereal evacuation of the surviving paratroopers, many of them horrified by the experiences of battle but even more by the fact that so many of their mates had been surrounded and taken prisoner, over 6,000 of them from the proud division. Their sad exit took them down the long supply road which they had not traversed before. Only now could they realise something of the destruction wreaked upon those who had sought to reach them.

Those who had fought so hard but unsuccessfully along the road now had to watch the doleful procession of lorries and ambulances heading back towards the coast. Cpl Reg Spittles, a tough but sympathetic warrior who himself had been knocked out in a tank in Normandy, sat on the turret of his tank and gazed helplessly:

> By now we had to witness the very sad sight of vehicles passing *down* the road, packed with men from Arnhem, all looking like zombies, as if they were in a coma. I have to admit to shedding a tear. I suppose we should have shown some sign of our pride in them, but they drove in total silence. And we had so much pride that only silence could show it.[28]

Behind the paratroopers, from that 26 September, the Germans would evacuate the entire civilian population of Arnhem, most of whom had been so publicly sympathetic to the British and Polish soldiers. And the *Wehrmacht* would remain in full control of Arnhem until the last few days of the war.

Few of the 'zombie-like' paratroopers would receive post-traumatic counselling. Even fewer of those who watched, like Reg Spittles, would be treated for the inevitable post-traumatic depression setting in immediately or over the years. There was a certain amount of psychiatric treatment available near the front line for serious 'bomb happy' cases, but the psychiatric staff were far too few to attempt a general counselling programme. On the other hand, the system of treatment for physical wounds had been updated to cope with mobile warfare just in time to meet the requirements of the unique distances involved in the campaign.

Fully efficient armoured divisions did not exist in the American, British and Canadian armies pre-war. Some practices were still based on 1914–18 static trench-warfare conditions. Lessons had to be learned about mobile warfare on the battlefield, and these were quickly assessed, codified and circulated:

> Mobile warfare has presented a new problem to the surgeon. He must put himself, his assistant and the essentials of equipment into vehicles which can move as quickly as the armoured division which he now

serves. He must be prepared to set up his theatre in whatever shelter he can find, and do it quickly. He must be able to disband it rapidly and move forward to another area on short notice, and unfortunately sometimes he must be ready to move it rearwards out of enemy hands when the battle sways against his comrades.[29]

Such lessons had been largely assimilated by the time of the frantic dash up the Arnhem road, and many lives were saved by the mobility of medical staff in the Guards Armoured Division at the front of the race. One worrying factor emerged as a paradox. The farther forward the surgeon operated, the *greater* the reported mortality among chest wound cases. Such cases seemed to die less frequently when operated on well to the rear of the advances. It was then realized that the apparently perverse statistic was due to the fact that most chest-wound sufferers evacuated to a distant operating theatre died *before* they arrived and therefore were not registered on the surgeons' mortality reports.

If the evacuated citizens of Arnhem were demoralised, many villagers and country people along the Arnhem road were both disappointed by the loss of liberation momentum and worried, even terrified by the stubborn proximity of German troops along both sides of the salient. At tight corridor points like St Oedenrode, both during the precipitous armoured advance and in succeeding days of stagnation, a German tank shot fired from one side of the road could be dangerous to German troops on the other side. Civilians still lived underneath this perpetual storm of death-dealing shells and bullets in the air.

Maria van Breugel was a 39-year-old resident of St Oedenrode, a member of a clog-making family. She recorded in her diary the events and emotions of those epic days. First there was the hesitation to believe that liberation was at hand, as the planes passed overhead and parachutes burgeoned in the distance:

Tuesday, September 19th: It's morning, about 7.30. We emerge and look to see if we can find our friends. Then an American appears. He walks around and tells people who understand some English that the first Allied tanks are advancing.

Friendships are soon made with the Allied troops defending the corridor, although the streets remain dangerous from the fall of shot and shell:

Tuesday, October 3rd: I must make many *klompen* [wooden clogs] as souvenirs for the soldiers. The Americans now have to move on. I heard it said that the Germans are more afraid of the Americans than of the British!!!

Before they are evacuated the American paratroopers sign autograph books and write their details in Maria's diary:

Joseph M. Kocsis, Cortland, Ohio.
Wilton A. Driver, Baton Rouge, Louisiana.
James F. Oates, Jr., Tennessee.
Fred A. Palozzi, 1657 Allegheny Ave, East Cleveland.

The Americans go away, but the Germans do not. The situation of the British troops in the town seems fragile, hemmed in on both sides still:

Monday 9th October: We are already in the 4th week of our liberation. We still hear a lot of shooting. It is frightening. I had to try and get some supplies. The road was full of military traffic so I had to come back over the fields.[30]

Maria was not to know that the woods beyond the fields would not be finally cleared of the enemy until 23 October. Young baker's assistant Will Lagarde found the military situation in nearby Oss even more puzzling and worrying. You never knew which colour of uniform you might see next. Will had watched the parachutes open and fall with even more enthusiasm than most local people. Baking bread was a reserved industry, important to the Germans, so sixteen-year-old Will had been allowed to carry on baking in Oss. But now the Germans were gathering up all able-bodied men and youths to work on digging trenches and setting up defences. So, his hands thick with dough, Will happily watched the Americans land on 19 September. And thought the war was now over for him.

He soon learned that partial liberation was more dangerous than German occupation:

I knew that many people from Oss were afraid that the Germans are coming back from Den Bosch to Oss, which many times happens, for short times and there was shooting. Many nights the German soldiers came from Den Bosch with lorries and go to two big factories to steal food. Once it happened at noon. The British soldiers were only in the middle of Oss near the railway at the moment the Germans were coming to steal food. I was just very close to this area. The British tanks were shooting to them and the Germans are driven back to Den Bosch.

There was a final moment of excitement for Will, whose bakery was in the disputed area which neither side had sufficient force to claim, in October, when Oss was finally liberated:

I was working in the bakery for the boss who was a German. It was about 3 p.m. when the British tanks came. They knew the German was in this bakery working with some Dutch bakers' assistants. The Tommies came in and our German boss have to hold up his hands and surrender. My wife of the future, Jo, was evacuated before from The Hague to Nijmegen. When the battle started in Nijmegen she had to shelter in the basement of a religious house. She remembers all the people were afraid the Germans would be coming back and they would be in the front fire.[31]

The veracity of this tale, so alien to 1914–18 trench warfare and even to the circumstances in Normandy, is substantiated by a quartermaster's records.

A huge German food depot existed in Oss (one of Will Lagarde's 'factories'). Although British troops were not enamoured of German sausage and black rye bread, the Dutch storekeeper cheerfully issued stores to Allied quartermasters on signature of his dispensing book. One British QM was astonished to see that the withdrawal before his, that same day, had been candidly signed for by a German captain! For a time opposing QMs were drawing stores from the opposite ends of a vast food complex.[32]

One young lad, serving with the Royal Artillery on OP (Observation Post) duty, riding in his carrier 'Roger Fox', and accustomed to the presence of large numbers of the Highland Light Infantry around him, was astonished by the sparsity of troops in what would normally be called the front line. Wallace Brereton recalled:

On this, and on many other occasions, we advanced with the HLI, but we often found ourselves on our own. Most people believed, as I had done, that the front line was a continuous line of troops facing a similar, parallel line of the enemy, with a strip of no-man's-land in between. In fact, it was quite different. There were perhaps a dozen men in a tight group, with maybe a machine gun, then a huge gap before the next strong point. This may sound dramatic but it worked.

It was into these empty spaces that we of the OP often made forays, sometimes for days on end. It was an eerie feeling, especially when you knew that the enemy also had gaps in his line. You were never quite sure whether or not you were behind German lines. . . . Once we came upon a deserted village and a main crossroads. Here we found just three HLI men. They were crouched down, with rifles at the ready, in a triangular formation and *all facing outwards*.[33]

Many of the infantry, as observed by Brereton, spent the next month in a kind of stagnant jeopardy on a 'dotted line' front, small dots and long spaces. What would have been a good mobile formation became an inappropriate waiting formation. Masses of troops, like the 51st Highland Division and their associated 33rd Armoured Brigade, were still stranded up to 400 miles back because all their own transport had been loaned to XXX Corps. This was to help with the problem of bringing supplies right from the Normandy beaches, still the largest available 'port', to Nijmegen and all depots in between.

As the Highlanders and others moved up and started to fill in the gaps, they found, instead of the heavy artillery and intensive m-g fire of

Normandy, a wilderness situation where the single sniper ruled the roost. In one sector near Olland, Highlanders claimed thirty-eight 'kills' over two weeks by sniping, the main battle activity possible. The enemy positions were few and difficult to identify. One sniper, 'the redoubtable Fraser', was observed in the twilight, cycling across no man's land to do his own reconnaissance.[34]

A colleague of sniper Fraser earned the Military Medal when he came on a German dug-out unexpectedly. A German OP had been pinpointed in a large tree 1,200 yards away. It was nicknamed 'Tarzan's Tree'. L/Cpl Matchwick was one of the small patrol sent out to have a 'look-see'.

Working along a ditch, with frequent use of wire-cutters, they heard German voices, apparently some distance away:

> That was how we got things wrong. The ground sort of muffled their voices . . . they were only ten feet away from us . . . Matchwick poked his head out of our ditch and at exactly the same moment a Jerry poked *his* head out of his ditch, and only the width of the road between the two of them. The Jerry squawked like a hen. Matchwick had a grenade ready, but instead of lobbing it he threw it straight at the Jerry's face. Jerry ducked and the grenade went past him. Matchwick went right after it. There was a Spandau m-g and three rifles lying there. He dived across the road, kicked the rifles out of the way and got down behind the Spandau.

Suppressing his surprise and exercising trained resolve, Matchwick beat off a quick enemy counter-attack by men in field grey 'coming from nowhere'. He then hauled three shivering, frightened German lads out of the ditch and took them prisoner. After another four months of similar bravery Matchwick was promoted and won a bar to his MM. Then fortune turned and he was killed on German soil after crossing the Rhine.[35]

On the German side, with equal spaces to guard but far fewer personnel available, tiredness was an insoluble problem. Jottings from a German 712th Infantry Division sergeant's diary illustrate this:

13 September 44: A convoy has been shot up by fighter bombers. We bandage the wounded and send them back. We have to leave the dead lying in the streets. Some of the dead are so mutilated as to be unrecognisable. . . . One of our mates commits suicide by hanging . . . We are in a hell of a fine place.

25 September 44: We march about forty-five kilometres. Everybody is dead tired.

26 September 44: There is not a dry thread on us.

27 September 44: The men are done. They are all old chaps. We have now been two days without food. . . . Three companies attacked Hees. Only a few stragglers came back. Poor Germany!

28 September 44: We are again fighting tanks with rifles.

29 September 44: I get the order to take an anti-tank section to the road and act as a covering party. It is a suicide order from the start.[36]

In spite of the need to send men like the sergeant again and again into suicidal situations, the incredible German staff work meant that, a month after the end of the Arnhem bridge battle, the thumb shape on the map was still an area of grave danger and concern to the Allies, with reinforced German groups on both sides of the protuberant salient. On 27 October, 9th Panzers and 15th Panzer Grenadiers attacked at Meijel. In two days they advanced 6 miles into the thickness of the thumb.

A very sore thumb indeed!

CHAPTER FOUR

Antwerp: the Generals Forgot

Every schoolchild knows that a port is only a port if it has ships sailing in and out of it. The 1944 generals had long since left school and appeared to have forgotten that fundamental geography lesson.

There was great euphoria among the Allies as they liberated the great port city of Antwerp after that thrilling armoured dash across France and Belgium. The old sayings about battles being lost for lack of a horseshoe nail or because of a broken bootlace were very relevant in September 1944. The nearest considerable port supplying Montgomery's troops was the troubled temporary Mulberry dock off the Normandy beaches, prey to any ravaging Atlantic storm and 400 miles distant from the spearhead troops.

The huge port of Le Havre had been liberated by 49th and 51st Divisions but its harbour installations had been destroyed. It would not be fully operational until after the end of the war. The useful ports of Calais, Boulogne, Ostend and Dunkirk were still being besieged and could not be counted upon for the horseshoe nails and bootlaces. But now, here was the giant of them all, Antwerp, available to bring in the heaviest guns and endless cargoes of ammunition and food. But the generals forgot that, if ships cannot sail into it, it is not a port.

And for a normal heavily laden cargo ship, Antwerp lay three hours' steaming time up the River Scheldt (Escaut), whose close banks bristled with enemy heavy guns. Along the river the thin rusty side-plates of any cargo ship would be within easy range of many m-gs and mortars located on the shores to either side. So all Antwerp's enormous dock capacity would have to stand idle while the vast convoys of lorries themselves consumed thousands of gallons of scarce fuel, making the round journey to the distant Normandy beaches.

This was a tragic omission, for 'the docks of Antwerp could handle all the supplies necessary for a swift and decisive Allied victory *before* the end of 1944'.[1] There were nearly 30 miles of docks, with over 600 modern cranes capable of handling up to 60,000 tons of cargo daily. All idle, because the generals forgot. What made it doubly tragic was that the Belgian Resistance in heroic actions had virtually handed the docks over to the advancing forces without, at that moment, the need to fight for them.

How could the generals have forgotten? The armoured division commanders could perhaps be forgiven for strictly obeying their orders to 'crack on' without giving too much attention to forming firm bases and clearing up odd recalcitrant enemy. But it is unbelievable that the importance of both the docks and the waterway to the open sea should have eluded Dempsey, at Army HQ, and Montgomery, at Army Group HQ. The latter made much play about having 'eyes' at the point of action, in the shape of young staff officers reporting back to him personally. Where were they at that moment?

Montgomery was certainly obsessed with racing on to the Zuider Zee and the German frontier, almost to the exclusion of all else. At the same time he was mounting a fierce battle with Eisenhower about priority of supplies, begrudging his old rival Patton every gallon of gasoline. As in Normandy, it was the Canadians who bore the brunt, being left to slog away in slow attrition battles while the main attention was focused elsewhere – Arnhem and Metz.

The term 'Canadians' is slightly misleading, for while the bulk of the troops under Canadian Army command were the volunteer soldiers of Canada, other nationalities also came within that command – British divisions, the Polish Armoured Division, the Netherlands and Belgian formations and, in the Antwerp area, the so-called 'Belgian White Brigade'. This was largely the creation of a sea captain, Eugene Colson, known to his men simply as 'Harry'. By 1943 he had organised some 600 trusted dock workers as a resistance nucleus, waiting for the arrival of Allied forces. They functioned as part of a wider 3,500-strong Resistance army founded by a Belgian regular army officer, Lt Urbain Remier.

The German Gestapo officers were aware of the existence of this secret army but were unable to make substantial inroads into its web of loyal patriots. Arrests were made and dock workers were tortured. Before liberation, 198 Belgian Resistance men were killed, often after incarceration in a concentration camp at Boom, near Antwerp. But the majority kept their secret, continuing with their training and intelligence work. As the Allied armoured columns approached, they seized vital areas, like the harbour sluice gates, to prevent the panic-stricken German guards from destroying essential dock installations.

Major Bill Close, up front with 3RTR as usual, much appreciated the White Brigade's services in removing mines which they had observed as the Germans laid them:

> We made good progress to Boom but Johnny Dunlop found the main bridge mined. Fortunately a civilian named Vekemans, a Belgian engineer and a member of the Resistance, showed the squadron commander a smaller bridge across the canal which was clear, he himself having removed the mines just prior to our arrival. I learned later that he was awarded the Military Cross for his exploits.[2]

Coming up post-haste were the expert mine destroyers of XXII Dragoons. As tank tracks were susceptible to breakages after high mileage, the tanks were often conveyed on Scammel or similar low-loader trucks when on urgent or long runs. Capt Ian Hammerton's 'Crab', a Churchill tank with flailing chains fixed on a rotor, was perched high on a transporter as they approached Antwerp. They were a little surprised to find that the main Antwerp road tunnel under the river was open and unobstructed, except:

> clearance was minimal . . . our radio aerials bent almost horizontal and scraping along the ceiling. Then I saw to my horror a convoy of three-tonners approaching. Was the tunnel wide enough for us to pass each other safely? It would have been, had it not been for the rotor gearbox on the Crab's jib! . . . there was a series of bangs as [the gearbox] just clipped each lorry, each lorry clashing with each tank. By the time all

the vehicles had emerged, all the flails had suffered damaged rotor gearboxes and all the three-tonners had damaged superstructures. Fortunately, repairs were not too difficult.[3]

Hammerton and his men were pleased with an improvement in their equipment since the Normandy battles. This was in the form of a new system for marking cleared lanes through a minefield. Attached to the Crab was a cable fitted with twelve firing tubes like small guns. The tank driver fired one tube at spaced intervals. The tube shot into the ground a metal rod with a metal flag on the top and a spike at the bottom. The discharge was powerful enough to drive the spike through concrete. The equipment left a neatly marked lane through the mined area.

One of the Canadian battalion commanders left a horrifying account of another use of mines by the enemy: the ruthless construction of booby-traps of all kinds.

The Germans were masters of the defensive art; their imagination and cunning were limitless. They would connect explosives to a corpse — theirs or ours — so that when it was moved, the explosive would be detonated. This stratagem was applied to a myriad of seemingly innocent household objects: doors, windows, even wine bottles left invitingly on bar shelves could become instruments of death. A can of golden syrup was found to be rigged. Cigarette tins exploded when opened.[4]

The same commander, speaking from bitter experience, also described the most difficult problem of all:

Water, even a narrow and placid canal, is a natural and effective anti-tank, and even anti-personnel, ditch. The attacker, forced to cross the water by small boats and rubber dinghies, would immediately become vulnerable to cross-fire from well-entrenched machine guns on the opposite bank. The resulting carnage was to be repeated countless times throughout the Scheldt campaign during the Canadian offensive.

The Germans, essentially, retreated, or were shoved back, canal by seemingly endless canal.[5]

To the left or west of Antwerp and south of the big river the Germans still held a water-bound and water-latticed area which would be known to the Canadian 3rd Infantry Division as the 'Breskens pocket'. To the right or east of Antwerp, the Canadian 4th Armoured and the Polish Armoured Divisions would be pushing into a heavily populated hinterland with cities like Breda, Tilburg and Bergen-op-Zoom. In the centre the Canadian 2nd Infantry Division, with the task of clearing the north bank of the Scheldt, had first to tackle a complicated dockland zone whose name would, for many soldiers, produce long-enduring, post-war nightmares: Merxem.

Bill Close knew about Merxem, perhaps before the Royal Regiment of Canada did. After the Vekemans episode with the mined bridge, other Belgians came to advise and guide, their task made more difficult by the thousands of their compatriots who wanted simply to drink the health of Bill and his troopers. A Resistance worker 'in a rather dirty old mac with a sten-gun looped over his shoulder', fought his way on to Bill's tank and pointed out to him the easiest route to the central railway station. The man in the dirty mac spoke excellent English and gave his name as Gaston de Lausney. He stayed on the tank while the troop 'brassed up' the station, subduing the enemy who still remained there.[6]

Unfortunately the main canal bridge ahead of them had been blown up and this 'put the suburb of Merxem out of bounds'. At that point, for a few precious hours, the Allies had the opportunity to race on over to Merxem by one means or another, which would have left them free to rampage along the north bank of the Scheldt with very little opposition. Close was a mere major commanding 19 tanks and had carried out his own orders to the limit. Maj Gen 'Pip' Roberts, commanding Bill's division, 11th Armoured, might have used his discretion and sent Bill's accompanying Herefordshire infantry across into Merxem. He did not, and later admitted it to have been a terrible error.[7] But Roberts had three higher tiers of command looking over his shoulder, responsible for monitoring his every move. Corps or Army or Army Group or all three should, at that moment, have told Roberts to 'bash on' over to Merxem rather than in other directions.

This was all highly frustrating to 'Harry', alias Eugene Colson, and his Belgian White Brigade. They had endured suspicion, arrest and torture for many months before liberation. They had performed heroically at the spearhead of the Allied advance into Antwerp. They had dismantled mines, provided information and saved dock installations from destruction. Finally they had urged the British most emphatically to make an immediate assault on Merxem. From 'Pip' Roberts down through Lt Col Silvertop and Bill Close the British had to respond that they 'had no orders' to assault Merxem.

Instead, within a day or two, the British spearhead, with Silvertop, Close, Dunlop *et al.*, had been withdrawn and despatched towards Arnhem. This left only sufficient troops, in fact less than sufficient troops, to form a defence along the existing lines through the city. The front positions were so lightly held that some civilians were able to conduct normal business, crossing the Albert Canal and moving back and forward unhindered between the German and Allied positions. This state of affairs continued for almost two weeks until Canadian troops began to move in, on 16 to 18 September. And learned about Merxem.[8]

The Royal Regiment of Canada drew the short straw for the Merxem experience. They had been investing Dunkirk with its 10,000-men garrison, including SS officers, who showed no desire to surrender and, in fact, remained dug in there until the end of the war. Dunkirk was surrounded by well-defended villages, including the medieval walls of Bergues. And at Dunkirk it was proved that sergeant majors as well as generals can forget.

In the chaos of ruins and craters the Coy SM had detailed five men to defend a post well forward. When the battalion was unexpectedly ordered to pull out during the night in profound darkness, the message did not reach the five privates. They, Ptes Boccaccio, Clauessen, Gormley, Lagacy and Slauenwhite, were reinforcements who had been with the battalion less than a month. They were captured by the Germans and kept in Dunkirk prison until the war ended. The Coy SM himself was killed by a mine a few days later.[9]

It took the battalion 'most of the bright warm day' to do the 100-mile journey from Dunkirk, before 'threading its way through the old streets of Antwerp' to the docks. If the men had any ambitions towards heroic deeds they were disappointed for, after relieving the Ox and Bucks of the British Army, they were required to sit tight in their defences, doing nightly patrols across the Albert Canal into Merxem. The period 16 September to 1 October was recorded as the 'most intense patrol activity of the Regiment in the entire war'. Patrol activity may not sound very onerous but the Royals' records paint an unusually clear picture of what was involved.

A typical patrol took place on the night of 28 September. The Scout Platoon's leader was Lt Colin Ross, former full-back of the Ottawa Rough Riders football team, described as 'hard-nosed'. With him was Sgt Alan 'Tommy' Tomlinson who had served in Iceland and fought in Normandy.

The men of the patrol were hand-picked: Cpl Carl Teichman, L/Cpl J. Webster, who had been wounded in the shambles of the Verrieres Ridge in July, Pte Buddy Jones, Pte W. Garnham, and 'Andre' and Eugene, the latter two still deliberately anonymous men of the Belgian White Brigade, who were in fearsome danger of torture and death if captured.

R.W. 'Buddy' Jones was one of those soldiers of extraordinary racial background who seemed to turn up in the Canadian Army from time to time. His great-great-grandfather had been a black slave, who had escaped in 1850 and travelled the 'underground railway' escape route, as it was known, to Montreal. He had originally been trained as a tank man, but rebadged as an infantry reinforcement. He was a boxer who had won 141 out of 143 fights, became the dominion bantamweight champion after the war, and was runner-up at the 1948 Olympic Games. Later he served in the Korean War and in 1975, at the age of fifty, completed the Boston Marathon in 3 hours, 27 minutes – a formidable man to have as number 5 on the patrol. The rookie Pte Garnham was taken along for the experience.

The patrol assembled on the Sports Platz, a short way from the canal. Sgt Tommy handed out boot polish for blackening of faces 'all except Bud Jones, of course, whose natural complexion needed no enhancement'.

The orders were simple: cross the canal and bring back a prisoner for identification. The patrol would stay clear of the destroyed bridge because it was constantly under fixed crossfire of m-gs. A partially sunken barge to the right enabled them to launch a small assault boat and a rubber dinghy.

In the dark night it would now be the discipline of total silence. They would remove their boots before climbing over the 5 ft high concrete wall of the canal and crossing the cobblestone street running alongside the canal. Nothing was visible beyond about two or three yards away. The practised patrol would now rely on their hearing . . . and smell. Bored sentries were inclined to whisper, at least, both to relieve the boredom and to reassure themselves of the presence of their comrades.

Also, a German tended to smell different to a Canadian. This is not a reference to aftershave or body odour. New battledress was impregnated with horrid-smelling chemicals to prevent infestation. British and Canadian troops found this offensive and repellent to girlfriends. They often resorted to illegal cleaning methods in order to remove the stench. German battledress was treated with chemicals of a notably different odour. So one could, if possessed of sensitive nostrils, smell the enemy from a few feet away in the darkness.

But the great betrayal of German sentries was the tobacco which they used and which they frequently, if furtively, smoked on duty. Their cigars and cigarettes burned a strong Turkish tobacco which emitted a distinctive, pungent, almost sickly smell – quite distinct from the weed produced in the Americas. A slight stirring of a night breeze was enough to waft a whiff of Turkish through the darkness. And now it alerted the Royals patrol, pressing on in stockinged feet, towards their objective of the Merxem power plant.

As frequently happened, there was no solid front line but only scattered strong points at strategic places. The Royals were able to crawl right up to the power plant. There Ross with Teichman, Jones and Andre veered to the right, while Tommy and the remainder moved to the left of the main building. Although guided by the tobacco smell, in the dense darkness Tommy's group suddenly literally fell over a sentry who instantly jerked an alarm cord. Like a louder echo of the alarm, m-g fire shattered the silence, the air became alive with tracer fire, and hand grenades started spewing out flame and shrapnel on all sides.

'It was all reaction to sound. Nobody could see anything,' except blinding explosive fire. Webster was hit and killed. Eugene was hit and died quickly. Garnham was hit and wounded. In the confusion the German sentry was also hit by his own side and lay wounded. The enemy seemed to be concentrating on firing without risking movement. Tommy could only abandon the two bodies. Grabbing the sentry, he forced him to crawl back with them, while also helping the wounded Garnham (whose brief war career was ended). Arriving at the place where they had split up earlier Tommy decided to wait. In the meantime he applied first aid to the two wounded men, friend and enemy.

It was a nervous hour before Ross and the others returned from their recce. Apparently the enemy were just as nervous, for Tomlinson's little group was not assaulted. Silently they withdrew to their tiny boats. Ross stayed on watch at the canal wall while the boats pulled over to safety. Then he jumped into the canal and swam the forty yards through filthy water, stinking with bilge and ship's oil.

'Covered in mud, head to foot and soaked to the skin', the lieutenant reported to his CO, Lt Col R.M. Lendrum. The prisoner was handed over to intelligence sergeant W.R. Bennett who fortunately recorded all the details for posterity. Bennett further commented that this type of patrol continued nightly along a too-long front which the companies could not adequately cover. He added 'the bravery of Lt Ross and Sgt Tomlinson almost every night, became legend, yet neither was awarded a decoration. Most regrettable. The Army should have inaugurated a de-briefing system similar to the Air Force, so that worthy recipients were not so habitually overlooked'.[10]

It is quite easy to cite cases, like that of Ross and Tomlinson, where bravery awards should have been made.[11] Other such instances occurred within the 'shadow of Arnhem'. It may be that the responsible authorities were reticent to issue too many awards, thus debasing the currency of valour. Such an attitude was unfortunate for worthy individuals and, for some, caused half a century of resentment. However, where awards were indeed authorised the recipients were undoubtedly very brave soldiers. One soldier called upon to accomplish the virtually impossible was Sgt Ken Crockett of the Calgary Highlanders. They were about 4 miles to the east of Merxem and, as the static period of patrols was phased into more direct action, the Calgarys were ordered to set up a bridgehead over the Albert Canal, ready for a major attack later on.

It was the night of 22 September and a shattered footbridge linked the 'home' bank with a small island. Beyond the island stood battered lock gates. Beyond the lock gates on the far bank the enemy were well dug in and had been using their m-gs very actively. Three m-g pits had been identified. However, rather than a noisy artillery-supported attack it was decided to send a silent patrol over, but with the purpose of staying on the far side and forming a quick defensive perimeter behind which the entire battalion could begin to cross.

Sgt Crockett was to lead a ten-man patrol and he chose to do this in every sense of the word 'lead'. First he crawled silently over the remnants of the broken, unstable footbridge, to check the island. Finding it to be clear of the enemy he returned to lead the patrol across, swinging like monkeys, hand over hand, underneath the remnants of the bridge and over the murky, menacing waters. His next endeavour was to climb over the lock gates to the far bank. In the darkness, moving mostly by sense of touch, he came to a place where the lock gates were partially destroyed and all that continued on to the shore was a thin, rusty pipe. Crockett again went forward alone in the obscurity, hand over hand on the sagging pipe.

At the far bank he found a barbed-wire obstacle too heavy for him to move. He returned and took Cpl Harold along with him to move the barrier, which they were able to do. Meanwhile the patrol continued their monkey progress, some of them weighed down by a Bren gun, a clumsy PIAT mortar bomb projector and spare m-g ammunition and bombs. Still no sound!

Inevitably the swinging patrol soon heard the shouted challenge of a sentry. Crockett replied by pressing the trigger of his Sten gun. This set off a chain reaction of all the guns which the invisible enemy could muster. One m-g was close to the landing site. Sgt Crockett was seen walking coolly towards it, firing his Sten gun. The enemy gun ceased firing. Crockett crawled with the PIAT operator to a position where they could fire a bomb at the muzzle flashes of the second m-g. Two bombs sufficed to quieten that gun. Crockett used the PIAT to finish off number three. He then guided his men individually into places of advantage where they could maintain a continuous fire to prevent an immediate enemy counter-attack.

Behind this fragile shield the rest of the platoon crossed over, stiffening the tiny bridgehead. The remainder of the company followed. Then the rest of the Calgary Battalion. By the time the enemy had formed up for a significant counter-attack, Crockett's lonely bridgehead had become a solid little fortress with the sister regiment, the Maisonneuves, also making their way across the canal. Crockett was recommended for the highest of honours, 'for valour', the Victoria Cross. But the eventual award would be the Distinguished Service Medal, not too frequently issued and still a justified recognition of his achievements.[12]

For front-line troops there is little which breeds more trepidation than knowing one has to attack but being kept hanging around, viewing the objective, waiting for orders which never arrive. The objective tends to loom ever more menacing day after day. Capt George Blackburn, opposite Merxem, knew the feeling:

> For some time, perhaps from the first hour sixteen days ago, when you occupied that OP in the attic of that abandoned furniture factory and peered across the canal for the first time into Merxem, you knew that one day you would have to accompany an infantry attack to clear it of the enemy. Still, as the moment approaches, you are filled with dread.[13]

Back in Normandy, when physically exhausted, George had suffered nightmares about falling asleep at his post and causing the infantry to be slaughtered because he failed to provide artillery support in an emergency. He carried a bottle of rum in his pocket as a 'wake up' aid if he felt himself driven beyond endurance. He was still keeping awake at Merxem, and did not resort to his rum. He won the Military Cross.

George could see plainly, and the Ross patrols could investigate gradually, the geography of Merxem. Beyond the Albert Canal, about thirty yards wide at this point, ran the main canal road, lined with factories and other large buildings on the far side. The demolished bridge near the Sports Platz had led to a street entering the town and then veering left towards the docks. Farther to the right another bridge led to a main street. Some way along at a five-way road junction lay the town centre. To the right of the town, as the Royals viewed it, there lay open country, watched by a scattering of White Brigade volunteers. To the left of the town lay the great maze of docks, watched over by the Essex Scots Battalion.

A particularly notable street at a Y junction just up from the Sports Platz bridge was quickly named 'Green Street' by the watchers. It had rows of houses with a vacant lot in one place. Grass grew between the cobblestones, giving the street 'a greenish hue' from a distance, hence the name. The Canadian watchers were able to discern that a German platoon was billeted in houses on the left side of Green Street. Strictly on time, in true German Army discipline, at midday every day the off-duty men (duties were mainly nocturnal) appeared with their mess tins, crossed the street and the vacant ground, entering another house which was obviously their cookhouse.

George Blackburn was well aware of this and decided to do something about it. He took some time firing occasional apparently random shots to fall in Green Street. The Royals always remembered:

One day Capt George Blackburn, a FOO [Forward Observation Officer] from the 4th Field Regiment, RCA, very casually began to register his guns on the gap the Germans crossed. The following day, just before noon, he called for the target. When the unsuspecting Germans appeared in Green Street, Blackburn shouted 'Fire!' and eight guns pumped shells into the midst of the unfortunate enemy platoon.[14]

The days of waiting, temporising, patrolling and registering guns ended at 0300 hr on 2 October with the orders to attack Merxem at last. The Royals were to go straight over the canal, while the Essex Scots came in from the west. The infantry were to make a silent crossing of the canal but the artillery opened up in full blast.

> As you approach the dark and deserted Sports Platz stadium where Caldwell's company has been ordered to assemble for the crossing, the guns in the docklands, northwest of the city, are pouring shells into Merxem, where several fires are burning fiercely, their ugly glow in the smoky sky reflecting disturbingly in the waters of the canal, turning it blood-red.

Maj Paddy Ryall was to lead the way with C Coy of the Royals. Royal Canadian Engineers brought up small rubber assault boats to cross the canal which, of course, was deep enough to take large ships. Under cover of darkness and the artillery noise, Ryall's men crossed between the demolished bridges and Lock 16. The brilliant flashes of shell explosions tended to make the darkness even more obscure to human eyes. Strangely enough, darkness was easier to see through if the eyes could become accustomed to its uninterrupted minimal content of starlight. In those conditions Ryall's group crossed unmolested.

Maj Bob Suckling took his D Coy over the canal to the east of Lock 16. Both groups had White Brigade guides who contributed greatly to the advance through main streets, side streets and gardens. The Canadian riflemen looked askance as they saw the first aid workers who attended the fifty Resistance men. The 'ambulancemen' were all women nurses, resolutely advancing under fire.

Fighting was uneven and sporadic but not as costly as many had imagined. Street fighting was not an infantryman's favourite hobby. Maj Caldwell's coy made their way over and more White Brigade men, with the 'eyes of the artillery', George Blackburn accompanying them and savouring the experience of crossing a canal under enemy guns. The fragile rubber assault boats used by Ryall and returned to the 'home' bank had been riddled by mortar fire. A report is made to Caldwell:

> that all but two have been sunk and that the two survivors are half full of water . . . you really start to 'get the wind up' . . . You fill your

pockets with hardtack and bully beef, and advise [driver] Gnr. Bob
Stevenson to do the same since there's no telling how long it will be
before you see your carrier again.

Suddenly you realize that all the painful anxiety and tension
affecting you only a moment ago have disappeared, and when you and
Stevenson go down to the boats with Hank Caldwell, you paddle across
a canal which is as silent as a country night, the only sound the swirl
and gurgle of paddles dipping and pulling at the water. Even the fires
that earlier seemed to be consuming Merxem, have calmed down.[15]

Bob Suckling had reached the local Tramways office and decided it was a
useful coy HQ. He settled in there with his Belgian guides. Battalion CO,
Lt Col Lendrum, had occupied the principal's office of the Stedelijke Girls
School and was supervising operations from there. With him was
intelligence sergeant W.R. Bennett. First reports were not too
encouraging. The attackers were making steady progress and sixty-nine
prisoners had already been captured. But intelligence officer Maj Don
Cornett quickly discovered that their opponents were not 'cannon fodder'.
They were units which had been diverted when on their way to the
Russian front and were reinforcing the original garrison. They included
twenty-five men from a Belgian SS unit (Fascist sympathisers were
recruited into the SS from occupied countries) and sixty-four German
grenadiers from the 1018 Regt, all likely to be very aggressive troops.

Sgt Bennett was able to jot down the story of an unusual street
skirmish. Two of D Coy platoons, numbers 16 and 17, were heading along
a main street. Like many Canadian units they were under-strength, with
only 18 men in each. Sgt Arnold King of 17 Platoon observed an entire
company of Germans moving towards them down the wide street. He
took Cpl Eldridge and eight men into the buildings on one side, while
Cpl Carl Teichman and his section were sent into the houses on the other
side. An 18 Platoon section was farther back. King ordered his men to go
upstairs but first to bolt and bar all the downstairs doors of all the houses.

As the enemy came nearer the Royals counted more than eighty
infantrymen, some of them towing an anti-aircraft gun (which could be
used in an anti-tank or anti-personnel role) along the street. The

Canadians were vastly outnumbered but they waited patiently in silence. As the enemy came into the ambush area, the Royals opened fire and started lobbing grenades from the upstairs windows. The men in the street 'scattered "every-which-way", in instant panic, hollering and shouting commands'. But there was nowhere to shelter in the street. All the doors were shut and barricaded. The Germans retreated, carrying their wounded but leaving sixteen dead in the street.

The incoming reinforcements enabled the Germans to counter-attack. Suckling's small group was being attacked from all sides. Suckling himself was an imperturbable character who had seen this kind of situation in Normandy. What was worrying him most, as it worried Lendrum at battalion HQ, was the poor quality of communications. The portable no. 18 wireless sets, normally adequate, were proving to be either useless or only sporadic in the built-up areas. Suckling needed artillery support but how could the precise cyphers of location be discerned amid the crackles and fadeouts of the faint radio signals?

Incredibly, Lendrum's phone rang in the principal's office of the Girls School. He picked it up rather dubiously. It was Bob Suckling loud and clear. One of the White Brigade men with Suckling was a telephone technician. He had connected the line in Suckling's Tramways office with a secret line maintained by the Resistance throughout.

With no obvious technical failing Suckling's voice began to fade. It became quieter and quieter. Lendrum barked, 'Bob, why are you whispering? Speak up!' Cornett, Bennett and the rest are astonished as Lendrum broke into 'gales of laughter'. Bob Suckling had whispered hoarsely, 'The frigging Germans are just outside the door!'. Quickly the artillery came to his aid, driving off the immediate attackers.[16]

Often the close approach of danger failed to diminish the front-line soldier's sense of humour. Neither did it affect his powers of observation or surprise. George Blackburn and Hank Caldwell reconnoitring side streets and 'traversing endless backyards' were astonished to find themselves ducking under many, many 'fluttering lines of laundry – the war having interfered with the Merxem ladies' traditional washday'. An even greater surprise awaited Blackburn, who had not crossed the canal with the spearhead Belgians:

Ryall's company headquarters turns out to be a tiny cramped cellar dimly lit by a candle on a table in the corner, and in the shadowy light you could swear that just there on the floor a pile of sheepskin coats is moving up and down as though breathing. For a moment you think you're going batty, but when you bend over and lift one of the fluffy skins, the tousled head of a beautiful teenage girl appears and as you stare in disbelief a husky voice says 'Eh-low'.

She was one of the Belgian 'ambulancemen', not actually a trained nurse but a university student working with the White Brigade after taking crash courses in first aid. Her stock in trade consisted of a few bandages and a bottle of iodine. She is in tears at the sight of the terrible wounds which her friends had suffered. She gained some solace by discussing with George Blackburn (himself a composer of popular songs) the latest hit tunes with which the Belgian youngsters had kept up to date on illegal hidden radios, dangerously retained.

Unfortunately, most of the brave Belgian White Brigade fighters had never received adequate training for the sort of pitched battle in which they now found themselves. Maj Ryall had noticed that, on the canal bank, under mortar fire with the batches of six 'Moaning Minnies' falling around them, the volunteers tended to bunch up for reassurance, rather than instinctively fanning out as trained infantry would do. Even to the hardened Ryall's eye, 'it was terrible – so many wounded'.

It takes quite a time to clear out all the enemy from the buildings of a town, and even as elements of the Royals arrived at the limits of the built-up area, German troops were still prowling some streets. Still accompanying Caldwell and men of his company, Blackburn was amazed to see a German patrol tramp unconcerned across a street intersection ahead, oblivious of the noise their boots were making on the cobblestones. The Canadians automatically froze into the shadows and, before they could begin to shoot, the Germans had disappeared down another route.

Another counter-attack was foiled by an artillery concentration of 4th Field Artillery, guided by Blackburn. Almost as though a switch had been operated, the enemy fire seemed to diminish and they were found to be quietly withdrawing from streets and strong points.[17]

At about that time George Blackburn's interest in Merxem came to a slightly bloody halt, but not through enemy agency. Drama dissolved into a kind of comedy. George and Hank had met a Royals patrol consisting of a sergeant and a private who had a Sten gun hanging by the sling from his shoulder:

Fortunately the gun is pointed down at the pavement for suddenly – BANG! – and you feel a thump on the calf of your left leg. A torrent of expletives from Hank tells that his knees have taken the brunt of concrete bits dislodged by the bullet ricocheting off the sidewalk. He pulls up his pant-legs and starts picking cinder-like bits out of his kneecaps. Your leg is wet . . . you pull up your pant-leg and see two little holes where the bullet passed in and out.

'That's the third time this morning it's done that' says the soldier in wonderment, pulling back the cocking-lever of the Sten now pointing directly at your stomach. Pushing the muzzle away from you, you tell him, 'For God's sake, man, put it on safety!' In obvious bewilderment he asks, 'What's that?'

Hearing this, Hank demands, 'Where the hell did you get your weapons training, soldier?' Says the soldier apologetically, 'I never had any weapons training, sir. I was a cook until I was sent up to the Royals.'

This incident was symptomatic of the problems of reinforcement with which Canadian commanders had to contend. Each soldier was a volunteer who had enlisted in Canada. He then had to volunteer again before he could be sent overseas. So adequate reinforcements were always in short reply, especially in the French-speaking battalions where it was not so easy to plug the gaps with 'odds and sods'. At the very time of the Merxem battle the Canadian government was being forced into the recourse of conscription into the forces and compulsory overseas service. Meanwhile trained infantrymen were in some peril from cooks, clerks and mechanics coming up as reinforcements, not always unwillingly but almost always lacking in specialised infantry training.

While the Royals had been driving northwards through the town, men of the Essex Scots had come from the dock area, across the Groenendaal

Laan bridge, and formed a pincer from the west. As the enemy retreated from the possible trap they yielded some 153 prisoners. Conspicuous among these prisoners of war were two Gestapo men, whose capture was particularly heartening to the Belgians. The White Brigade had lost a disproportionate number of men, but no women nurses, having thirteen killed in action and ten badly wounded. Their sole compensation was the discovery and occupation of an enemy store with what appeared to be Russian front equipment, vast quantities of long white sheepskin or fur coats and jackets, some of which ended up warming Canadian bodies during the winter.

As the Germans evacuated Merxem the battle became more mobile and the intensity of firing much less. On 4 October the Essex Scottish were able to occupy Eekeren and then advance more than six miles to Starboeck, capturing intact a bridge over the next canal. The Essex war diary reported rather gleefully: 'a most successful day for the battalion . . . On more than one occasion the Jerries had been seen hot-footing it down the road trying to keep ahead of our advance.'

The Arnhem airborne operation had been called off on 26 September. The 'sideshows' at Merxem and Starboeck had liberated those areas in the first few days of October. But it was not until 15 October that Montgomery finally conceded that his cherished drive towards the Ruhr was not to be achieved in 1944. And it was not until 16 October that he issued the directive, now insisted on by Eisenhower, that the opening of the waterway to Antwerp should be the prime and most urgent objective of his armies. That was just a month after the issuing of the final orders for the Arnhem adventure which, even with a captured bridge at Arnhem itself, would have been fruitless without a seaway into Antwerp.

The Royals recorded the operation to open up the Scheldt as finally completed on 28 November and the first cargo of supplies arriving in the Merxem docks on 1 December. The liberation of northern Belgium and the southern Netherlands continued with many minor skirmishes intermingled with days of frustrated waiting. The casualty statistics revealed no catastrophic losses like those at Arnhem. Yet such times provided no relief for the infantryman in his apparently endless plodding with under strength-numbers towards meaningless objectives. And it did not require major battles to continue the bleeding white of the Merxem battalion.

A reflection of this factor is that the Royals' no. 17 Platoon, nineteen men strong, lost no casualties at all in the epic liberation of Merxem. In the following three weeks, with no significant battle to wage, they lost thirteen out of those nineteen.[18]

The men at the front of the battle were now under no illusions about the toughness of the German defence. Troop leader Bill Bellamy, of 8th King's Royal Irish Hussars, had been told about the 'low medical category soldiers' of the Stomach division but found that 'they fought extremely well. Perhaps their dyspepsia helped them to hate us'. However, Bill found that the most aggressive soldier around at the time was the colonel of 1/5th Queens, who was organising training in house-to-house fighting. The colonel's war chant echoed in Bill's ears long afterwards, and aptly illustrated the nature of street battles:

Grenades through downstairs windows – Sten through the door – Door down – Grenade top of stairs – Rooms to right and left – Sten through the ceiling – up the stairs – Grenades through the doors. . . .[19]

CHAPTER FIVE

A Pocket of Small Change

Destiny spared some sister units from the fiery nightmares of Merxem, but presented them with an alternative name of similar sinister portent and sodden reality: Breskens.

The Breskens pocket: to the supreme authorities just a dime sideshow. Lt Gen Simonds's idea of dashing along both banks of the Scheldt to cut off the German 15th Army had been rejected by higher authorities. The Breskens area was not a priority. Even the Plans Section of the Canadian Army thought that the area would tumble into Allied hands easily enough in three or four days.[1] Consequently, in the words of one historian, 'The Canadian Army was treated as a kind of odd-job organization and given a very low claim to supplies'.[2] So, deprived of resources and encountering exceptional resistance, the Canadians would fight 'one of the grimmest and longest battles'[3] experienced in north-west Europe.

A brief recapitulation of chronology will put Breskens into context and highlight the fatal delays in opening up the port of Antwerp.

September 4: Allied troops in Antwerp centre.

September 8: Canadian Argylls attacking the south of Breskens pocket with totally inadequate resources.

September 13: Crerar briefs Simonds on the minor Breskens role coupled with the waste of troops to capture far smaller Channel ports.

September 17: Arnhem airborne operation commences.

September 21: Simonds rejects the doctrine that Breskens will fall easily.

October 15: Eisenhower belatedly insists on the prime importance of opening Antwerp port.

October 16: Montgomery orders top priority for the same.

November 1: German guns on Breskens fall silent.

Meanwhile, from Hitler down, the German High Command had grasped the importance of resisting in the Breskens pocket and along the north bank of the Scheldt. As one historian put it, 'With his usual mania for having men die where they stood, Hitler had designated these two areas protecting the approaches to Antwerp as "fortresses".'4 The 64th Division consisted of 10,000 experienced regular soldiers with roots in the pre-war Hitler Youth movement, and was to be the nucleus of the resistance to Allied attempts to open up Antwerp. The division mustered nearly 500 machine-guns.

The commander on the spot, Gen Knut Eberding, was also a distinguished soldier. He had fought in the First World War. During the wars he had been prominent in sport. He was later the coach of the national handball team (a battalion team) which won the gold medal at the 1936 Berlin Olympic Games. Although the division itself had been assembled only during June and July it had been formed of first-class men on leave or convalescent from other fronts, and had not yet been subject to the huge casualties which had affected other front-line divisions.

Other units were not so formidable, like the 'White Bread' division further north which was composed of chronic invalids still able to pull a trigger. The German authorities considered it necessary to threaten potential deserters, or men who failed to fight in obedience to orders, with dire penalties. One order dated 14 October stated that 'in cases where the names of deserters are ascertained these will be made known to the civilian population at home and their next of kin will be looked upon as enemies of the German people'.5 The order went out in Eberding's name, although he later denied that he was the author.

Indeed orders in a similar tone went out to all German units coming to rest on static defences after the hectic retreat from Normandy. It was necessary to combat the panic and fear afflicting so many who had suffered the humiliation of that defeat. Other commanders attempted to offer the carrot as well as the stick. One division was offered autographed pictures of FM von Rundstedt for soldiers who did their duty well. The divisional commander concerned was very cynical about the idea, responding, 'the troops can only be induced to shoot better by the creation of more equal fighting conditions'.[6] It is unlikely that the idea came from the staid and aloof von Rundstedt himself.

Allied intelligence had estimated that only 4,000 German troops stood in front of the Breskens attackers, an error of 250 per cent. However, even if the defenders had been so few the Canadians did not enjoy the minimum three-to-one superiority generally regarded as necessary for a successful attack. And the men on the ground could see how the terrain would favour the enemy. John A. Marin, of the Queen's Own Rifles of Canada, could see the hazards clearly enough:

The conditions of war were different from what we had been accustomed to in France. The roads ran across high dykes. The Germans had all the crossroads zeroed in by their mortars and artillery so the poor footslogger had to stay off the roads and slog along through the flooded fields where at times the water was four feet deep. The Germans had blown up some of the dykes.

You could see just two or three infantrymen going up the fields to take out machine gun and mortar posts one by one. It took a lot of guts to keep going. A large number of troops advancing would have been mowed down by the enemy guns. To make things worse the Germans had their guns dug in on the rear of the dykes and we were unable to see them from our lines.

It was a tough job, just a matter of taking one crossroads after another, one dyke after another, one canal after another, with many casualties. In this case a corporal and six or seven men would be all that could be deployed in an attack. If they stayed too close to the roads they would be blown up on anti-personnel mines so they ended up wading through the flooded fields.[7]

Marin's sergeant-major, the much-decorated Charlie Martin, DCM, MM, CM, was impressed by the skill of the veteran survivors from Normandy as they tackled the new terrain:

There was no cover. It took courage for the men to move along the dykes. It was what we called a section job . . . a corporal and a few

riflemen would leapfrog forward . . . from farmhouse to farmhouse . . .
five or six times a day – tense, stressful manoeuvres . . . we saw men in
action at a speed that was unbelievable. Nobody moving straight
ahead. It was left and right. Up and down. Down and roll right. Fire.
Then up again. Roll left. Fire. The action was perfect in its timing.
Our men supporting each other in clever coordination of movement,
fire and flanking fire.[8]

Two of the youngest generals now pitted their energy and initiative
against all the odds. Lt Gen Guy Simonds, the youthful corps
commander, would have to double up on the duties of army commander
while his superior Crerar was ill. Simonds ordered 32-year-old Maj Gen
Dan Spry to send his 3rd Canadian Infantry Division into the attack on
the Breskens pocket. Simultaneously the Canadian 2nd Infantry would
attempt to clear the north shore of the river, while their 4th Armoured,
together with the Polish 1st Armoured, would seal off the right flank.
But even before this main attack could be coordinated, Canadian troops
had been slogging up the Channel coast unheralded.

If some German troops were having to be bullied and bribed back into
action, the advancing Canadians, volunteers all, were having to grit their
teeth over a new commitment. Many of them thought that the war had
been won in Normandy. They felt they had shed blood enough to win
two or three wars. Twenty-year-old Cpl Cliff Brown, with the Lincs and
Wellands, remembered that, one night on a bloody cornfield outside the
tiny village of Tilly-la-Campagne, he and his mate Bill Chawrun had
been the only survivors of the thirty men in his platoon. The men of the
Algonquins thought about their two companies from which not a single
man walked away when their armoured column was wiped out. It was no
fault of their own they had been surrounded by the *Hitlerjugend SS* and,
after a fierce battle, all had either been killed or, a relatively few, taken
prisoner.[9]

At last light on 8 September the Argylls approached the first of the
great canals, the Canal de Gent, through an area of interlinked villages
on the outskirts of Bruges. Their objective was Moerbrugge, menacingly
translated as Swamp Bridges. All the Argyll companies were still under

strength from their Normandy casualties, and the regimental history states pithily that, when counter-attacked, 'they found themselves fighting a determined enemy for their very existence, rather than to capture new ground'. The Lincoln and Welland Regiment then moved forward to cross the canal.

At this point a bottleneck developed which was to affect supplies throughout the battle. There was only one boat available for crossing the canal. By the time it had ferried the front rifle companies across, it was reported to be 'something less than sea-worthy' due to shrapnel and m-g bullets in profusion. Under the weight of heavy equipment the boat sank slowly lower and lower. At the same time, as the Canadians dug in on their tiny bridgehead over the canal, the Germans 'threw everything they had: small arms, mortars, Oerlikons, 75s, 88s and 105s'.[10]

One of the Cinderella units came into its own in this situation. The New Brunswicks were a heavy m-g battalion who rarely functioned as a whole but were normally farmed out to support rifle battalions. At Moerbrugge the massed guns of the New Brunswicks caught and halted masses of the enemy advancing incautiously over the open fields to counter-attack the bridgehead. This support inspired riflemen like Cpl James Alexander, of the L&W A Coy. Twice wounded and using a Bren m-g, he found it difficult to fire from a prone position. So he rose and walked up and down, firing the gun from his hip, inspiring his comrades. He was awarded the Military Medal.

The riflemen then became embroiled in street fighting through the villages. It was slow and dangerous work, clearing house after house of skilled defenders who were well armed. An indication of the perils is seen in the award of three Military Medals to NCOs leading these forays. Everyone was tightly packed into a tiny space on both sides of the water. The Medical Officer, Capt McKenzie, found himself at the tail of the leading platoon of some twenty-plus men. He personally helped to evacuate the wounded and, on return, took charge of the ferrying of food and ammunition, as well as medical supplies, across the canal on the boat whose flotation potential now seemed to depend on angelic intervention. McKenzie earned his Military Cross as did the artillery FOO, Capt Griffin, who was sometimes even farther forward than the doctor.

Fragile as the bridgehead may have appeared it permitted the divisional engineers to bridge the canal during the remainder of the night. Next day tanks of the South Albertas were able to barge over the bridge and assist in rounding up 450 prisoners. Numerous dead were seen across the fields beyond the canal as the tanks and riflemen hurried forward towards the next obstacle.

By 11 September the Polish 3rd Brigade was in position to launch an attack around Ghent. It cost them a two-day battle to break the enemy defences. They then encountered a series of ancient frontier forts, all of which bore the names of saints. There was nothing holy about the assault of the Poles on the German 712th Division infantry who were relying on the strength of the saints. By 16 September the Poles had disposed of the saints and collected many prisoners. They would still have another four days of fighting before they reached their own immediate objective at Terneuzen on the River Scheldt.

The Poles had been nicknamed the 'Sikorski Tourists' because, in order to join Gen Sikorski's Free Polish Forces, they had had to undertake vast journeys from Poland, some trekking right across Russia, others finding routes through the Balkans, many joining the Allies in time to suffer the debacle of Dunkirk. Their divisional general, Stanislaw Maczek, had been in action since the first day of the war in September 1939. So they combined both enthusiasm and impatience in their quest for victory. Some of them exceeded the brief.

The 9th Battalion of Chasseurs had advanced to the edge of a wide flooded area. They had no 'ducks' (DUKW amphibious carriers) or assault boats. Their Lt Col Zgorzelski had been wounded at Axel and was temporarily absent. A man described tactfully by Maczek as 'a young but impudent officer' launched an unsupported infantry attack, wading and swimming across the floods. The attack seemed successful at first but, in typical manner, the Germans counter-attacked with heavy weapons and armoured vehicles. The Poles had no such weapons. Two officers and twenty-eight soldiers were lost before they could withdraw. Maczek ordered 'a more considered' style of advance.[11]

By the time they had reached their Terneuzen objective on 20 October the Poles had suffered 75 killed, 151 wounded and 63 missing, but had captured 19 enemy officers and 1,154 other ranks, as well as great quantities of material. The 'Sikorski Tourists' would be called to more adventures yet.

On the left of the Poles, and still some miles from the Scheldt in the bulge of the Breskens pocket, the Lincs and Wellands' next assignment was to provide a boat party to assist the Algonquins in another canal assault at Moerkerke. Lt R.F. Dickie and his party of eighty men were provided with more than the one 'unseaworthy' boat on this occasion. The small portable boats, although heavy were extremely fragile and easily sunk, either by overloading or by enemy fire. At this crossing the boats needed to be portable because it involved not one but two stretches of water. First came the Canal de Derivation de la Lys, then an island only thirty yards wide, followed by the main majestic Leopold Canal.

Meanwhile the Lincs and Wellands were being assailed by the delirious local population, so that free drinks became almost as lethal a danger as enemy bullets. The history speaks of soldiers 'being weaned from their refreshment'. The whole area was still under heavy German mortar fire, so battalion HQ was set up, sensibly enough, in the crypt of a church. Lt Col Cromb had just returned after a bout of malaria, suffered in the mosquito-infested swamps of Demouville in Normandy. He took over from Maj Young who himself went back to hospital to be treated for another frequent complaint of front-line soldiers, dysentery.

Safe from enemy shells, Cromb was not too happy when, that night, his HQ was invaded by hundreds of local people who, apparently, used the crypt as a communal air-raid shelter. Then it appeared that a part of the communal evening events was a prolonged religious service at which 'a well-fed religious gentleman in a brown cassock', presumably a Franciscan friar, preached long sermons and followed on with endless patriotic diatribes. Cromb, trying to issue orders, was not impressed. It is not recorded if prayers were said for the frail unseaworthy boats about to be launched.

For the Algonquins, still grieving for their lost companies in Normandy and not yet totally reinforced, this was to be another episode of horror, their own 'Black Thursday'. Maj George L. Cassidy, the Algonquins' historian, took part in the battle, was blown up on a mine, survived miraculously and lived to tell of the agonies his men endured. The Canadians were still working on intelligence reports that they might expect 'an enemy weak and demoralized, with little equipment, who would show little or no fight'. Cassidy calculated that 350 Canadians 'were pitted against a large well equipped force, many times their number' and with adequate reserves available from 50,000 Germans waiting in the area to cross the River Scheldt as their army withdrew.

The 350 Canadians included reinforcements hurried up, many of them with no infantry training. Cassidy saw that 'it was barely possible to take down their names, assign them to companies, give them the briefest of briefings and show them what an assault boat looked like'. Darkness, smoke, mist and incessant artillery fire from both sides made it almost impossible for the majority of the Algonquins to make contact with their paddlers from the Lincs. So they had to haul the boats themselves.

There were forty awkward boats made of wood and canvas and seating eighteen men. The carriers had first to haul the boats through the narrow alleys of Moerkerke, then up the first bank. Having paddled across the Derivation then they had a twenty-foot climb amid brambles up on to the island. At that point they became clearly visible to the enemy guns. There was still another bank down which to drag the boats, then climb in, paddle across the Leopold, and at last the struggle up the far bank deep in mud. Exhausted, they had not yet started to fight. Those who had not made contact with the paddlers from the Lincs had no way of returning the boats to fetch ammunition and other supplies.

The wireless connecting Maj A.K. Stirling of C Coy with HQ failed almost immediately. B Coy lost the equivalent of a platoon before beginning the advance. Two of Stirling's platoons, led by Lt Butler and Lt Hunter, had pushed on some 200 yards beyond the canal, but were now cut off from all signals. Enemy patrols were already infiltrating between units. One German patrol set up a gun on the island between the two canals.

Farther back the situation was almost as bad. The wounded were being cared for at a first-aid post in Moerkerke village. A well-targeted mortar barrage came down on the post, killing the Roman Catholic padre and wounding the medical officer and the Protestant padre. The surviving wounded were carried back to battalion HQ. Instantly the barrage switched to that house, which was hit several times and caught fire. All survivors moved again to another house. As if by magic it too was an immediate target. But it was not magic. A German sympathiser had been watching and reporting back to the enemy mortar commander by radio.

German snipers were still lodged in various houses short of the canal. The battle became reduced to fights between two or three soldiers. Lt Dan McDonald and Sgt Marshall had become surrounded and were holding out from a chicken coop. The platoon rallied and drove off the enemy, while McDonald and Marshall emerged unscathed but leaving behind them a 'mass of scrambled egg'.

Few though they were, the Algonquins were making an impact on the enemy. The corps commander, Gen von und zu Gilsa came up the line to confer with Lt Gen Sander of the German 245th Division, and committed the corps reserve in order to drive the Canadians back over the canals. The result, in Cassidy's words, was that 'enemy attacks reached a new crescendo. He sent wave after wave of men, heedless of casualties, against our battered forward positions'. With front-line casualties at 75 per cent the Algonquins were at last withdrawn, still fighting their way along ditches and over dykes.[12]

Those who had still to cross the canals encountered the continuing problem of shortage of boats and paddlers. In an incredible gesture several German prisoners being herded back with the Canadians volunteered to row wounded men back to safety. The Germans rowed across the canals several times under fire, underlining the empathy between front-line troops, especially where the wounded were concerned. Some Algonquins still had to swim the muddy waters. Lt Hunter 'and his brave little crew' did not return.

A particularly poignant example of the extreme lack of reinforcements concerned Lt T.C.W. Byrne, no doubt a staunch and ambitious young Canadian volunteer officer. He arrived, accompanied by fifteen other ranks, at battalion HQ during the battle. He was sent straight out to join a forward company. Within half an hour he was ordered to take a patrol to try to contact the missing no. 17 Platoon. Under cover of darkness the patrol went out. It never returned. Byrne's body was found eleven days later, caught up in a tangle of barbed wire.

Pte Ted Gale was also having his first day's experience of battle as a member of that missing no. 17 Platoon. Trained as a tank man he was sent to the infantry with no infantry training. His section was holding out in a farmhouse. The enemy brought up a tank which began to blow the house to pieces, brick by brick. Gale's group had no anti-tank weapon. The farmhouse roof collapsed. Enemy infantry were dropping grenades through the windows. Having used all their ammunition the platoon was surrounded and had to surrender. By that time Ted was unconscious with twenty-two wounds, mainly in his legs. A twelve-hour soldier! The only bright moment in the sordid story was when Germans gave the prisoners a good supper at their command HQ. After that it was a journey in box cars for seven days.

These experiences led Simonds to call off any more serious attempts on the Leopold Canal for about three weeks. They did not result in any increasing of the priority given by higher commanders to the Breskens pocket or to any particular concern about the numbers of Germans who were able to make their way across the Scheldt away from the threat of encirclement. All eyes were on Arnhem and the apparent fervent hope that Germans in such locations as Breskens would run away once the Arnhem bridge had been captured.

Activities in the pocket continued but on a reduced scale. On 18 September the Lincs and Wellands were ordered to move against Philippine, one of the ancient border fortified towns, just inside the Netherlands. Capt Ian Hammerton was with the British XXII Dragoons offering flail support to the Canadians (as units of the 79th Armoured Division, the 'Funnies', did across nationalities). He remembered taking part in a school play where the ghost of Julius Caesar appears to Brutus (Ian's role) warning him that he will meet his death at Philippi. Ian was not reassured.[13]

However the danger which Ian encountered at Philippine among the low-lying polders was that all the roads were submerged under water. The tank commanders and drivers could proceed only by following the lines of trees at the roadside. So deep was the flooding that, where Bailey bridges had been erected over streams, the flooring of the bridges was under water and only parts of railings were visible to drivers.

The Lincs and Wellands men were particularly concerned because, as they waded through two feet or more of water, they were aware that wounded men, if not observed, could be immersed and could drown in those conditions. Indeed B Coy sergeant-major, in a brand new carrier loaded with ammunition and mail, suddenly disappeared entirely under the floods. Without being aware of it, they had been crossing a submerged bridge which collapsed under the carrier's weight and sank them in the bed of a stream.

Sometimes anticipation was worse than reality. Cpl Cliff Brown had been one of only two men of his platoon to survive an attack on a Normandy village. Any attack on fortified buildings tended to resurrect the ghosts of Tilly-la-Campagne in Cliff's mind. Now ahead of his platoon, the large village of Eeklo loomed and Cliff was to lead his platoon and company of the Lincs into the streets. Approaching cautiously in open order of attack they were relieved as yard after yard passed under their boots with no enemy response. The Germans had made a strategic withdrawal. Cliff was able to march upright, leading his men in Indian file along the streets. The greatest problem was the wild joy of the liberated inhabitants who thronged out of the houses and made Cliff's job of setting up a counter-attack position almost impossible.[14]

During the relative Breskens lull on 23 September the Ultra radio system in England, which could read German coded messages, picked up an alarming piece of news which even then failed to alarm anyone at the various higher HQs. From the German Group West HQ it read:

West Europe- From Gruppe West stamped 1600/23/9:- ARMY THE SITUATION MORNING 23/9: Crossing of 15 Army over the Wester Schelde carried out except for Bridgehead. With the energetic help from the Navy over 82,000 men, 530 guns, 4,600 vehicles, 4,000 horses and much valuable equipment of all kinds brought over.[15]

The Army form (AM form 1479) on which the transcript was issued is headed 'to be kept under lock and key and never to be removed from the office'. In a strange way this almost reflects the Supreme HQ attitude to such news, or what has become known as 'masterly inactivity'.

Be that as it may, the main part of the German 15th Army, except for garrisons in Channel ports, had escaped from the pocket which dangled as far down as Boulogne, although now that force was still moving in the area of Walcheren and Beveland and susceptible to Allied counter-attack. The Allies had already lost nineteen days since arriving in Antwerp, during which time the 15th Army might have been eliminated or very severely damaged. It is also of interest that Simonds's four under-strength divisions (including the Poles), ostensibly attacking, totalled less than a third of the forces either opposing him or moving around his left flank, a complete reversal of the minimum ratio needed for attacking.

Patrol activity now became the main concern of those lodged in the muddy banks of the canals. Capt Dandy of the Lincs and Wellands was sent on a raid into Moershoofd village, with the objective of taking prisoners and perhaps obtaining a lodgement in the houses. Moving in the misty dawn it was here again that the sense of smell came into prominence. This time it was the enticing odour of frying bacon. Following the scent like furtive hungry beggars, the Canadians came on an enemy soldier concentrating on his frying pan. They took him prisoner and ate his bacon. Capt Dandy radioed 'Gathering in the harvest. 15 PW.' By 0630 hr Brig Moncel had ordered the raid's withdrawal as the forces available could not have withstood the inevitable counter-attack.

On 3 October it was Sgt Clifford Skelding's turn to go looking for a prisoner. He and his three men spent an hour watching across the canal at Krabbe. At 1140 hr, under a brief smoke screen, they crossed the canal, knocked out an m-g post, shot up an enemy patrol of six men, brought back three prisoners, and were back on the home side of the canal by 1147 hr. Quick work, but good value for the Military Medal which Skelding earned. But still a dime sideshow.

It was 6 October before Simonds had completed his careful preparations for a final assault across the canals towards Breskens. The previous day was a very busy time for two groups who were preparing what was still somewhat experimental aid to the advancing riflemen. In military terms there could be smoke without fire. But for Operation Switchback there would be both smoke and fire of a very special kind.

Brig J.G. Spragge, planning the attack, requested smoke to cover the initial attack. Smoke had been used in many battles in both world wars but was still something of a hit-or-miss system. A Canadian smoke unit under Capt Jim Bond had been able to mount a kind of full dress rehearsal during an attack on Cap Gris Nez on 22 September. This taught Jim various lessons, the main one being the need for a meteorologist in the forward positions. The smoke screen has been described as a double-edged sword, able to inflict confusion and sufferings on those who release it if the wind changes. In Normandy there had been smoke problems because the prevailing southerly winds generally blew away from the Germans and towards the Allies.

Jim Bond and others had noted that wind speed was also a factor in smoke screening as too high a wind would quickly shred the screen. Humidity and air turbulence also affected the laying or motion of the screen.

Smoke was available in portable pots or through large Esso generators mounted on a four-wheel low-bed trailer and using a mixture of fog-oil, fuel oil and water. For Switchback the group assembled forty-eight of the Esso units plus a platoon handling smoke pots and smoke floats. The Met Office forecast southerly (favourable) winds.

At 0300 hr on 6 October, with all smoke resources assembled and located, Jim Bond's forward meteorologist informed him that the wind was about to shift to the unfavourable north. Within a few minutes the gods of war had fulfilled the meteorologist's adverse forecast. Much of the smoke preparation was wasted and the screen was only of limited use. Jim Bond and his smokers would have to wait a while yet before the day of perfect accomplishment.[16]

Another man busy with late experimentation was Capt Norman Mould. The Chemical Warfare Branch had devised a way of mounting flame-throwing projectors on Bren gun carriers, which were then called Wasps. Two days before the Leopold action Mould held a trial with the Wasps. They found that their idea of raining fire from above the enemy positions would not work as the fire tended to disperse in the air. They then discovered that the jets of flame could be shot at the front of the dykes and that the fire stream would ricochet over the dykes into the enemy positions behind.

As the infantry went into the attack at 0530 hr on 6 October, Mould went forward to direct the Wasp fire personally. In spite of a counter storm of enemy fire of all kinds his Wasps either eliminated or drove off all the enemy lurking behind the dykes. The Wasp flame lasted only twenty seconds but the 1st Canadian Scottish Regiment, following closely, were able to cross the canal and occupy the positions beyond the dyke with no casualties to themselves. A remarkable feat, 'attributable . . . to the skill, bravery, coolness and disregard for personal safety of Captain Mould', according to the citation for his Military Cross.

The Regina Rifles, a D-Day battalion, known to all as the 'Farmer Johns' or simply 'the Johns', were not quite so fortunate, although eventually successful. One of their high casualty companies had been transferred to HQ guard duties for a rest, and the original guard, a company of the Royal Montreals, was functioning as a company of the Johns. Lt Col Matheson of the Johns had been impressed by the Montrealers' part in the assault on Calais. He offered them the vanguard of the attack across the canal. Their Capt R. Schwob was happy to accept and would attack with 6 officers and 112 other ranks up front.[17]

An artillery barrage of 326 guns had opened up and 16 of the Wasps were supporting the Reginas, staggering the twenty-second bursts of flame through a period of five minutes. One German pillbox survived and its guns wiped out no. 1 Platoon of the Montrealers in the water. Other attackers crossed the canal and disappeared over the high dyke banks. The German concrete pillbox defied all attempts to silence it, so Capt Mel Douglas was ordered to take his company across and deal with it.

His men carried a couple of PIATs, heavy, clumsy anti-tank bomb projectors usually fitted on to a stable tripod for firing. While the remainder of the company provided what covering fire they could, Mel Douglas and his PIAT men would have to find their way along the bank on the far side of the dyke. They would then have to hold the PIATs up to the slits in the pillbox, fire the bombs and immediately throw hand grenades after the bombs. The ploy worked and the crossing was clear, but Douglas's company lost all its officers, and only twenty-seven out of more than a hundred men remained in action.

C Coy of the Johns lost its commander, Maj L. Gass, killed early in the action. As more men fell, the company was merged with the only eleven men from the Montreal company who could be found still active. German counter-attacks were repelled, but the assaulting Johns found that the country beyond the canal was a wide, open, bare stretch of fields dominated by German guns from a distance.

In the frequent mêlées and confusion of battle, a group of attackers were surrounded and Lt Bergin and Lt Black with four others were taken prisoner. They were ordered to act as stretcher-bearers for wounded enemy soldiers. Bergin and Black were concerned because they still had their maps, marked aerial photographs and written orders with them. After a whispered consultation they contrived to trip with a stretcher and accidentally fall into the water. While the other Canadians prisoners rescued the wounded German, Bergin and Black managed to lose their documents in the muddy, opaque water, which was more like thick soup.

One of the Johns, A.J. Gollnick, noticed that the front line of the attack now consisted simply of a single line of rifles strung out as far as the eye could see along the southern face of the far bank of the canal. The enemy could shoot at them from three sides. German mortars and artillery were accurately zeroed in on every feature of the ground. Evert Nordstrom had noticed that the big shells were arriving in threes with an interval of five seconds between each shell, and the first two straddling the point where the third shell landed. He was in an m-g post, a hole in the bank. Suddenly he noticed that two heavy shells had landed, straddling his hole. Instinctively he jumped out of his hole and was almost blown on his way by the third shell which landed directly in the pit. Crawling back he found that his gun had disappeared.[18]

Incidents of that kind were sometimes treated by veteran soldiers as a kind of humorous happening or a superstitious augury. Rifleman F. Court was by the canal when a German sniper put a bullet through the tin hat of Court's mate Bill Sutherland. Court suggested he get rid of the helmet and borrow one from a casualty. Sutherland replied that he wouldn't wear a dead man's helmet and that his own was now definitely 'lucky'. Court replied, 'or maybe the guy who did it was a damn poor shot.'

Court and Sutherland were still laughing amid the horrors at the thought of their misadventures with loot. The had taken from a German officer a briefcase crammed with banknotes. Although they had seen various types of money on the continent these were a different design which they decided was fake money, about which they had been warned. In their progress towards the Leopold Canal they had liberally donated handfuls of notes to astonished civilians along the way. Only when they were down to the last few notes did they discover that it was real, valuable cash.

Court was not so lucky with his acquisition of the German colonel's cap, a prized and rare souvenir to take home to Canada. He was suddenly summoned to the awful presence of his own colonel, Matheson, and ordered to surrender the cap in question. The German colonel had complained. The Canadian colonel then, in Court's words, 'explained the Geneva Convention in no uncertain terms'.[19]

At 2300 hr on 6 October the Royal Winnipeg Rifles, like the Johns and the Canadian Scottish, a D-Day battalion, also crossed the canal successfully. But it was three days before the three battalions could finally link up and consider that they had secured the bridgehead over the canal. Throughout this operation men of the North Shore (New Brunswick) Regiment also performed heroically. The North Shore men had landed on D-Day but in August had lost an entire company when they were accidentally bombed by the US Army Air Force. Now stoically they paddled the boats back and forward across the totally exposed waters of the canal.

Another often unsung unit was rewarded by a Military Cross for one of its members, Lt Edwin Eperson of the Royal Canadian Army Service Corps. He was responsible for delivering bridging equipment to the banks of the canal in order to enable the Royal Canadian Engineers to construct the vital bridges which would accommodate tanks and trucks. One of Eperson's vehicles was destroyed and another set alight, drawing enemy fire from all directions. Eperson led his men to extinguish the fire in the vehicle which silhouetted them clearly to the enemy only a hundred yards or so away. He then carefully unloaded all the equipment at the places and time as required by the engineers.

Reinforcements began to arrive to fill the gaps in the three forward battalions. Evert Nordstrom, now lacking his gun, was directed to guide reinforcements along a cleared path marked by white tape up to the canal banks. He commented:

it was unbelievable how many were raw green men without training that we were escorting to the front lines. Through no fault of their own after a couple of hours of this intense battle we would be escorting some of them back to the rear, too afraid or hysterical to be of use up front, being more of a hindrance and needing help.

Gollnick of the Johns was worried in case his gun would not fire in a moment of emergency:

A special difficulty was the fact that the wet and sandy soil caused small arms to jam, which meant that every weapon in the battalion had to be employed in the bridgehead . . . the carrier and anti-tank platoons took turns at maintaining posts at the crossing point. Working in a pillbox, they were constantly busy stripping and cleaning weapons which were brought to them.

Capt Ian Hammerton's crew encountered a similar problem in their tank.

Unfortunately the rain had rendered the track very muddy and within a minute our periscopes were blocked. The co-driver and wireless-operator were both kept busy swopping the driver's, the gunner's and my periscopes for clean ones . . . I found it necessary to travel with the front half of my cupola lid closed to keep mud out of the tank. Every man in the crew was covered with mud. . . . We engaged and knocked out an anti-tank gun . . . I climbed out of the tank and immediately slipped on the inches of slimy mud covering the tank. I tumbled without stopping from the top of the tank to the foot of the dike, landing in front of an amazed Canadian. I was unhurt but smothered from top of helmet to toe of boot in wet mud.[20]

Lying out in that all pervading mud were many undetected wounded and even more unburied dead, now becoming bloated and adding to the stench of explosions and human defecation. Wounded Germans had been heard screaming in pain throughout the night. Several Reginas remembered the welcome truce which was arranged. Lt Robert Gray arrived on 8 October, had a word with the colonel and was then led to the front line:

> We didn't know what to do with our dead; they could not be moved because of sniper fire. Eventually we pushed them up on the canal bank in front of us and left them there. It was the Germans who helped solve the problem. They arranged a noon truce . . . supervised by the Red Cross . . . extended well beyond the original half-hour. The German officers who had supervised were an arrogant well-turned-out group and we must have looked quite grubby by comparison. We were never dry. It rained almost every day but we could light no fires to dry out.[21]

Others were not too happy about the presence of German officers. Lt Jim Cameron stated, 'A German officer all trimly dressed, came right up to our position to recce. I told him to leave or be likely to be shot. He left but had easily figured out our tenuous position before he did.'[22]

Even in this saga of sacrifice and endurance the story of Sgt A. Gri of the Canadian Scottish was exceptional. Gri's platoon of less than thirty men were guarding the battalion's left flank when they were rushed by about 150 enemy soldiers. For an hour the little group of defenders fought on until only Sgt Gri was left on his feet. The house in which he was standing had been set on fire and Gri himself caught fire before being overwhelmed by Germans. Eventually survivors of the other platoons, together with Gri, were marched back to the German HQ for interrogation.

The Germans unsuccessfully tried every legitimate trick to extract details of information from the prisoners. The interrogators were confounded by one factor, inexplicable to them. Some of the captured men were wearing a shoulder patch saying 'Rocky Mountain Rangers'. Apparently the Germans had never heard of that regiment. Those Rangers were actually reinforcements into the Canadian Scottish and had never had time to take off their old patches. They did not disabuse the enemy of the idea that a entire brand new battalion might have arrived on the battlefield. And during the interrogation Gri, who had hidden a knife in his clothing, fought his way out and escaped.[23]

On the night of 7/8 October another extraordinary initiative was launched as a result of the combination of 'youthful' brains, as Guy Simonds ordered Brig John 'Rocky' Rockingham of Dan Spry's 3rd Division to get into Breskens by the back door. 'Rocky', a lieutenant-colonel in July, had already gained praise for an unusual attack with his battalion on the vital village of Verrieres in Normandy. During that battle a German Panther tank had halted unawares on top of the trench where Rocky was directing the battle. Rocky and his staff coolly loaded a PIAT and blew up the tank at a range of a few inches.[24]

Simonds had observed the German concentration on the Leopold Canal to the south of Breskens. He also assumed that they would think that the port of Breskens was safe from the rear where their big guns across the Scheldt would beat off any seaborne attack. So Rocky's 9th Brigade would invade via the apparently impassable mudflats of the Braakman Inlet. And while the Germans had considered the canals ideal for defence purposes, Rocky would use one of the canals as an artery for his attack.

An important contribution to the details of landing areas came from a Dutch engineer, Peter de Winde. He had been appointed commander of the Resistance in West Flanders, although only nineteen years of age. He had also noted the gap in German defences offered by the mudflats and had reconnoitred them in depth. From a crashed Canadian plane he had obtained a tunic, an identification card and a rubber dinghy, and would pose as a Canadian airman, to fool the Germans if he were captured and to convince the Allies if he reached them.

He embarked in the dinghy in the dark. Before he could paddle into the open river, defence stakes in the shallow water had ripped his dinghy beyond repair. It was blowing a gale and the water was almost at freezing point, but de Winde's only option was to dive in and swim the river. Against the tide and heavy waves he covered some four miles in eight hours. Landing on the far bank he found refuge in the house of a loyal dyke worker.

After two hours' rest to restore circulation he walked to the nearest Canadian outpost. After giving his initial report he was posted to the 3rd Division intelligence section at a crucial moment in planning the new offensive. He later remained with the Canadian Army as an interpreter.[25]

Rockingham's task was to convey his three battalions along a 19-mile stretch of canal from Ghent to Terneuzen, and then to move into the Scheldt and along the Braakman Inlet. The men would be conveyed on a 'fleet' of ninety-seven amphibious Buffalo carriers, along roads, over dykes, down into canal waters and then along rough tidal stretches before reaching the mudflats. As the brigade would be in an isolated position almost all the way it was necessary to proceed at night in absolute secrecy, with a top speed of 5 miles per hour. As the extraordinary convoy set out they were accompanied by cheering local civilians on bicycles who found that they could easily outrun the bumbling Buffaloes.

John A. Marin of the Queen's Own Rifles described his first encounter with a number of strange amphibious beasts:

The next day we saw the arrival of some strange vehicles called Weasels. These were small amphibious carriers designed to accommodate 4 men with a wireless set. Other larger carriers were called Buffaloes. These could carry a Bren gun carrier and its crew of 3 or 4, or a dozen armed men, over land or water. I think it went about 4 mph which wasn't fast enough later when the Germans were shelling us.[26]

Spr Kenneth McKee of 79th Assault Sqdn, RE, in his engineering role, was more intimately concerned with these water-bound creatures, including the Terrapin:

There were problems with the Buffaloes. By 10 October they had been worked to death. It was mainly a problem of the aluminium grousers [spinners], the main cause of failure. They became worn to such an extent that their speed in the water was insufficient to counter the tidal flow. So at full speed against the tide they would go backwards! This obviously affected navigation!

The Terrapins on the other hand had managed to maintain their voyages to and fro. But they required the assistance of 'cheese-pailing' carpets to enter and leave the water because of both the slippery, deep mud and the angle of the beaches. The amphibian Terrapin was used because the DUKW was not available in sufficient numbers. The four-ton Terrapin had eight rubber-tyred wheels, and two rear-mounted propellers provided water propulsion. Two Ford V8 petrol engines were mounted side by side. Bilge pumps removed any excess water which came over the front due to the shallow freeboard when loaded.[27]

Progress along the canal was slow and it was not possible to hit the target by dawn next day. So the convoy buttoned up and lay still. Men of the North Novas, Highland Light Infantry, and Stormont, Dundas and Glengarry Highlanders (SD&GH) spent a long night of silence, cramp, damp, fear and impatience. When the grinding, thundering, splashing, floundering armada moved on again, early on Sunday (9th), North Novas' Maj Morris Clennett 'wondered if every German in town knew you were coming'. Surely some fifth-columnist would betray them. But an RAF raid in the distance caused every German gun to blast away at the skies and conveniently drowned the sound of the approaching fleet.

As the hundreds of vehicles turned into the river waters, Lt Cdr Robert Franks of the Navy was waiting in a small motor boat with two red lights astern, to navigate the host safely to their appointed landing place. As light increased, smoke was discharged from special storm boats and smoke floats were dropped in the water. The uncomprehending enemy could only fire blindly and with no great concentration on the dark apparition looming to their rear. The marker boat located a convenient groyne and many of the leading infantry were able to attain the beach dry shod.[28]

Capt Reginald Dixon was with his colonel of the Glens (SD&GH) on what he calls that 'miniature D-Day':

We made our way across. The vessel rode low in the water and seemed to go far too slowly. A smoke screen was being laid. The enemy knew we were on the water but could not bring down direct fire on us. Shells were landing on the beach and in areas 'Daffodil' and 'Violet'. Our Signals Officer was killed when the vehicle he was on [and on which Reg was originally listed to ride] was hit by a German naval shell. We crawled up the beach and across the dyke to a farmhouse, now in a sea of mud.

The companies had landed and were deploying. Some enemy had infiltrated between companies of the HLI. It was difficult to estimate the enemy strength. As 'A' Coy advanced some snipers were giving trouble. They had been passed by at the start line and then came to life. We turned to recce a farmhouse we could use for a command post. The basement was filled in the most part with women and children seeking shelter from the shells. At one place we had stopped and a damaged German military vehicle was beside the road. I went over and looked inside. In the dark interior I saw bodies, covered with a thick blanket of maggots. There was no time to dwell on such thoughts.

We were still harassed by the big naval type gun fire, big naval guns at Flushing, in heavy concrete bunkers, could reach fifteen miles to the point where we were. Fortunately the ground was soft so the big shells buried themselves in the mud before detonating. 'A' company was having some difficulty along the dyke. Ahead of them there was a big bunker at the [Breskens] harbour entrance. 'C' company were told to move over to help them. A fire in the village, by the church on the corner, proved to be an enemy ammunition truck. At 19.00 hours the CO ordered companies to push out patrols and 'B' company to contact the North Novas on our left. Capt Medhurst was killed as was Lt Fisher. Capt Smith and Lt Annabel were wounded. 10 ORs wounded and one missing. 20 prioners collected. Each time one of the naval shells came in from Flushing the ground would shake.[29]

Both around Breskens itself and down at the bottom of the pocket the Canadians, still low-priority, small-change troops, continued to wear down the enemy in unrelenting strife, just as nature itself was unrelenting in its donations of rain, gales and chilling temperatures across the swampy fields where the sheltering ditches were now choked with decaying bodies.

By 12 October the Reginas' medical officer had counted about 300 casualties through his aid post, although he knew that the normal front-line strength of rifles would have been only about 300. Reinforcements kept on appearing, firing, dying. Many of the Johns had now fought through five virtually sleepless nights. The CO ordered each platoon to send two men at a time back behind the line to rest. The tired men were so close to their enemies that an order was given to cease throwing grenades because with the three-second pause the enemy could catch the bomb and throw it back. Robert Gray recalled that lighting a cigarette could attract an enemy 'potato masher' grenade.

By now the troops were taking pride in their new nickname 'The Water Rats'. As the Johns counted the cost, with fifty-one fatalities, the list threw an interesting sidelight on the racial variation among the men. Sgt Harvey Dreaver, killed in action, was one of the many Cree Indians in the regiment. His death led to a court artist painting his picture to hang in Buckingham Palace as a tribute to all 'Canadian Native' soldiers. Also dead on 15 October was Rfn R. Riel, a relative of one of the most famous Natives, Louis Riel. Another Cree, Rfn S.J. Letendre, was awarded the Distinguished Conduct Medal. A different but incredible statistic was that the battalion had used up a calculated six months' supply of no. 36 grenades in two days.

As the campaign drew to its close George Cooper saw the unbelievable sight of German troops drawn up with kits neatly packed, ready to march into captivity. Instead of guns they were holding 'at the present' their wrist watches, having heard that the Allied troops would loot these and hoping by this gesture for better treatment. Cooper's company was roused during the night by the sound of a horse-drawn vehicle. This proved to be an enemy mobile field kitchen with mashed potatoes warming in the pot. The driver ran away but the Canadians took the kitchen and its contents prisoner. 'Lovely mashed potatoes!' chortled George, 'but I don't know what happened to the horse!'[30]

On 25 October, a bullet at last found Lincs and Wellands B 138453 Cpl Cliff Brown, one of the company's two survivors from the Tilly-la-Campagne massacre. He was safely evacuated. His surviving mate, 4118091 Cpl Chawrun, lasted until 26 January 1945, when his wounding wiped out the last of his company who had landed in Normandy only six months before.

Denis Crockett was knocked over by the explosion of an 88-mm shell and then 'a sniper worked me over'. He was only occasionally conscious as he was operated on and evacuated. When he came to his senses he was greatly astonished to find himself in St Margaret's Hospital, London – a maternity hospital![31]

As more resources were diverted to the Scheldt area some tired Canadian infantrymen were able to raise a grim smile. They were to be relieved by a Scottish unit, the 52nd Division, a specialist outfit trained for mountain warfare, but coming to fight on polders that were below sea level.

Relief would only be relative and temporary for the troops. Life anywhere near the front line could be dangerous at any moment. John A. Marin found one incident of 'friendly fire' almost comic – after it had happened:

The captain had given an order for our mortars to fire on some barns and houses while we advanced. All of a sudden I hear a peculiar noise, and somebody shouted 'Duck!' The fins had come off one of our own mortar bombs and it was tumbling end over end, back down at us, making a hell of a noise. It landed only fifty feet away but, because of the wet ground, all we got was a lot of dirt thrown over us.[32]

Other incidents of 'friendly fire' did not have that comic element. One tragic incident caused men literally to disappear and has remained something of a mystery for nearly sixty years. Ian Hammerton in his flail tank heard a single horrendous explosion, and found out that some RASC lorries had simply 'disappeared in the enormous blast'. The redoubtable CO of the Glens, Lt Col Roger Rowley, preparing to attack Breskens (for which action he was awarded an immediate bar to his DSO), found his plans shattered when the explosion occurred and 'blew the whole squadron to kingdom come. There was nobody left alive who was not either blind, or deaf, or both'.[33]

Martin Reagan was within range of the vast blast. He survived and was able to research the incident over many years, arriving at a conclusion somewhat less sensational than the Rowley version, but equally terrible. A sergeant in 1944, he commanded a specialist Churchill tank called an AVRE (Armoured Vehicles Royal Engineers) in the 79th Armoured Division. AVREs could be used carrying fascines, huge wooden bundles, to fill in anti-tank ditches, cross craters or small streams, and climb up obstacles. They were part of a whole repertoire of specialist vehicles. One variation was the 'Conger', an adapted Bren gun carrier towed by the tank.

The Conger was towed to the edge of a minefield. The tank's demolition NCO got into the Conger. He fired a rocket across the minefield. The rocket pulled 60 metres of hose behind it. The NCO used compressed air to pump nitroglycerine into the hose. He lit a time fuse and then took shelter in the tank. The resulting explosion was intended to set off any mine within 3 metres of the hose, thus leaving a cleared path 6 metres by 60. But Conger work was not popular, for nitroglycerine is perhaps the most temperamental and violent of substances.

On 19 October, near Philippine, Reagan's tank became stranded and fell behind the rest of the squadron. Eventually they found the way to the rendezvous at Isabellaweg Farm near Ijzendijke. The squadron was preparing to support the attack of Lt Col Rowley and the Glens. Reagan's tank, 3 Fox, approached the squadron on the morning of 20 October. It was not possible to pull right up to the remaining vehicles because the huge tanks had caused a culvert to collapse and 3 Fox was on the wrong side. A convoy of Service Corps vehicles arrived with routine supplies which included petrol, food, mail, and on one lorry the squadron's supply of nitro glycerine. Just before 1300 hr the squadron leader, Maj Bloomfield, came back from a mission and stopped to talk to Reagan.

Then there was a tremendous explosion, so deafening as to be indescribable. Massive sheets of flame shot up from the convoy. Reagan's driver, Ginger Hall, collapsed in terrible pain from a shattered leg. The empty petrol container on which the sergeant had been sitting had a huge shrapnel hole through it. Maj Bloomfield called out 'Good God, what was that,' shouted down to his driver and drove off at speed towards the inferno.

Reagan continues his story:

> Once our driver had been made comfortable I crossed the culvert on foot and made for the scene of devastation. The force of the explosion must have been that of a fireball; there was wreckage everywhere. Men had been out in the open, some on top of the tanks, probably re-fuelling . . . There was stunned confusion everywhere . . . When night began to fall we were called together and taken to a nearby farm. We learned that fifteen of our colleagues had been killed and over fifty wounded. Our Canadian colleagues had also suffered casualties.

Later figures were seventeen killed and sixteen missing, or simply blown to pieces and untraceable. Fifty-one were evacuated seriously wounded. Some of the trucks had totally disappeared. Next morning the squadron could crew only six tanks instead of the normal eighteen. The horrors were not ended for Sgt Reagan. As they stood next day about thirty metres from the farm barn which had been destroyed, 'I saw three horses running across the field and alongside each other; as I watched the horses an explosion erupted underneath the middle horse, killing it, and the other two galloped away. The explosion I saw was what you would expect from about five pounds of Guncotton [explosive] or an anti-tank mine'.

Over many years Reagan was unable to trace any official explanation for the event. He could not find any reports of an official enquiry. He returned to Ijzendijke and talked with local people. They told him that twenty years later a bracelet belonging to Canadian Cpl Edwin Larkin (reported missing) was found at the site. His relatives were found and his bracelet was returned to them. Martin Reagan collaborated with local people in order to raise a suitable memorial at that place. Remarkably Edwin Larkin is remembered in Manitoba, where a lake has been given his name.

Reagan's own theory is that the unstable nitroglycerine in the truck had had 'a very, very rough passage over the collapsed culvert' and was prone to explode. Having seen the horse killed in the next field he thought it most likely that there was also a rogue mine where the trucks were unloading and that a vehicle or even the weight of a human body set it off as a primer for a load of a most dangerous explosive which should not have been there in one quantity in one place. He was sure about one thing: if his tank had not been delayed, and if the culvert had not been smashed, he would not now be telling this horrific story.

It lends gruesome significance to the old adage: 'Those who play with fire . . .'.One Canadian padre, exhausted from consoling the wounded and burying the endless lines of dead, wrote a tribute poem entitled 'Strange Harvest'. He was Stanley E. Higgs who, like Canadian padres everywhere, held the rank of honorary captain. He had no doubt about the validity of the 1944 soldiers' task, 'that men may live in a world set free from guilt by their blood atoned'. His last stanza read:

> Dip gently your scythe, good reaper now,
> O'er the field of the hallowed dead,
> For young men fought and young men died.
> Nearer the sea, where the earth is red.[34]

CHAPTER SIX

Chill Ghost of Autumn

Much has been written about Allied tactics of deception: how the enemy was persuaded that a second 'Second front' would follow the Normandy landings; how the Ultra readings were acted on without betraying the source; and so on. The Germans also had their methods of deception. One of them was called 'Chill'.

A great tactical advantage which the German Army enjoyed was its ability to form battle groups (KG or *Kampfgruppe*) at a moment's notice and of all shapes and sizes. The group would be led by an experienced front-line officer with considerable authority and discretionary powers. As the Germans tried to stem the headlong flight of their battered Normandy troops in the region of the Belgium border with the Netherlands, they played a trump card.

As the Allies swarmed around Antwerp, Lt Gen Kurt Chill had gathered what forces were available and welded them into a battle group, KG Chill, which quickly impressed the Allies by its adaptability and dour resistance. At one time Chill was defending a front of more than 30 miles with only twenty-five tanks and thirty-five batteries of 88-mm guns, a most flimsy bulwark.

As German reinforcements moved in, Chill continued to command his 85th Division, but German radio message continued to refer to KG Chill. This led the Allies to believe they were still dealing with 'bits and pieces' defenders.

KG Chill, which had 'long generated respect in its enemies, was to serve a new and fruitful purpose as a ghost battalion'. Lt Col F. von der Heydte, who commanded the defence of Woensdrecht, himself stated that 'Battle Group Chill was merely a camouflage name to disguise the stength and location of my battalion' of elite paratroopers.[1]

Allied intelligence was sadly lacking in its ability to read the war at this point. One report optimistically assumed 'definite indications of an enemy withdrawal', noting that enemy prisoners were of low category and drawn from many varying units, not front-line infantry. A corps summary on 7 October assumed that the enemy 'had given up any plan he might have had to stand on the approach to Walcheren'. The same day German 15th Army commander, Gen von Zangen, was telling his troops that their defence 'represents a task which is decisive for the further conduct of the war.'[2]

At lower levels the Germans also revealed great ingenuity in deceiving Allied attackers. Some deception was not entirely in line with the normally respected conventions of war. Maj McCarthy, an anti-tank officer supporting the South Saskatchewans, when out on a 'recce' was ensnared by such a trick as the regimental history recorded: 'They encountered a patrol dressed in camouflage jackets and British steel helmets, complete with nets and shell dressings. Believing the patrol to be Canadians, McCarthy and his companion [junior officer] approached, only to be taken prisoner by what turned out to be Germans in masquerade.'

Other tactics were more despicable. Again it was the South Saskatchewans who were involved. Two Germans had stood up during an exchange of fire and shouted 'Kamerad!' Two Canadians responded by rising to wave the prisoners forward. Immediately enemy fire deluged the Canadian position thus exposed, causing nine casualties, although none fatal.[3]

The fluid nature of the front lines enabled the enemy to infiltrate spies, according to one report, and also to liaise with a few civilians with German sympathies. On 3 October, British I Corps put out the following warning:

Two German agents posing as American war correspondents driving a German car with USA painted on fender and American flag flying . . . carrying a camera and yellow briefcase. Speak good French with definite German accent. . . . Agent A, 25 years old, fair hair, blue eyes, slim, dark blue coat over open neck yellow shirt. . . . B, older, taller, partly bald, dark hair, plump build, dark clothes.

Another unique German idea seems to have failed because of their extreme shortage of supplies at this period. Lt P.H. Dixon, of the Royal Engineers, came across this ingenious weapon on one of the many canals. He described it as a 'kamikazi boat'. It was a high-speed craft with space in the bows which would have been filled with explosives. These boats would have been driven at the Bailey bridges put up hastily by the Royal Engineers, and would have been capable of destroying the relatively fragile temporary structures. Fortunately the boats had not been used because they had been emptied of their explosives. These were needed for the more urgent task of blowing up existing permanent bridges as the Germans retreated. And there were no more explosives in reserve.[4]

Canadian troops were now pushing to the right or east of the Antwerp area, and northwards from Merxem. Their main immediate objective was Woensdrecht, the key to the causeway which linked Walcheren 'island' with the mainland of the Netherlands. The majority of infantry companies were below half strength. A full battalion attack at this time, with large numbers of untrained or poorly trained reinforcements, was probably about one-third of the fighting effectiveness of that same battalion in its early Normandy battles.

It would be fair to point out that the Germans had even more worries than the Canadians and Poles. Orders of the day verged on hysteria. FM von Rundstedt was relatively restrained when saying 'I expect you to defend Germany's sacred soil with all your strength and to the very last'. FM Model became more strident. 'The enemy shall know that there is no road into the heart of the Reich except over our dead bodies . . . whoever retreats is a traitor to his people . . . the lives of our wives and children are at stake.'[5]

Goebbels's Propaganda Ministry menaced soldiers with visions of German prisoners working as slaves in Siberia, their wives married off to members of the occupying forces and their children separated from the parents to be educated by the Allies. Himmler, more direct, simply threatened deserters with the promise that their families would be summarily shot.[6]

Montgomery's continued concentration on Arnhem had left wide spaces on the Canadian right with very little defence. Divisional commander Maj Gen Foulkes was acting corps commander as Simonds stood in for the sick Crerar. Foulkes felt he had to leave a substantial force guarding those open spaces on his right. Consequently his main attacking force consisted only of six weak battalions of infantry with a squadron of less than twenty tanks of the Fort Garry Horse. The platoons and sections found themselves engaged in a series of tiny, vicious but vital fights along another Via Dolorosa across flooded polders into insignificant mist-shrouded villages with, for the troops, unpronounceable names like Ossendrecht, Huijberge, Hoogerheide and Kalmsthoutsehoek.

Thankfully leaving Merxem behind them as a receding memory on 4 October, the Royal Regiment enjoyed a quick advance of twelve miles and by dawn on Friday 6 October found themselves a little unexpectedly on the outskirts of Ossendrecht. Lt Col Lendrum decided to attack immediately without the usual preparation. The defenders were taken completely by surprise and during the day the town was occupied and Lendrum was sitting in the town hall as his HQ. Eighty-three prisoners were taken.[7]

As might be expected, the Germans quickly found men and guns for a furious counter-attack, putting the leading Royals in a situation of some danger. Capt George Blackburn was the artillery FOO on the spot and witnessed an outstanding example of coolness and obduracy in action. Once again it involved Bob Suckling, he who in Merxem had whispered 'The frigging Germans are just outside the door'.

Blackburn and others stood studying maps in Middel Straat. Men from several platoons had been sorting themselves out at the street junction. Suddenly a very high velocity German gun, unseen, fired at the back of a row of cottages. There was no interval between the 'wham' of its firing and the 'crash' of its landing. Virtually simultaneous explosions! Somebody yelled 'Tank!' A troop of recce armoured cars had driven up, but their 37-mm guns were virtually useless against 88-mm guns. Now they turned tail, skidded round the corner and made off at full speed.

Infantry subaltern Bob Suckling now took matters into his own hands:

pounding on locked doors of the row of houses where an upstairs back window could provide observation of the field where Suckling says the gun is. When at last a door opens, he unceremoniously brushes aside the bewildered woman standing there, and leads you thumping up the stairs two at a time to a back bedroom window. 'There!' he yells pointing down a broad, grassy slope to a tree-lined ditch.

And there indeed it is, the spurt of smoke that jets from its muzzle as it fires, its vicious *wham* coupling with the instantaneous smash of its shell on the back of a house just a few doors to the right. Panic blinds you as you glance from map to gun and back again, trying to establish a map reference.

The gun begins to traverse along the line of cottages, trying to smash them down one by one. Scribbling down a six-figure coordinate, George Blackburn dashes into the front bedroom, throws up the window and yells orders down to his man Hiltz standing in the street. It is now a race of fate. Orders being passed back by radio, gunners responding to the plot, Blackburn calculating the delay, two, three, even four minutes. He goes back to Suckling, who is leaning at the window watching the remorseless progress of the shell bursts along the neighbouring back walls. It is a heart-stopping situation.

The problem is, you can't leave Suckling up here alone. With all your heart and soul you want to say right out: 'For God's sake, Bob, let's go downstairs. To stay up here is plain suicide.' But something in the eyes of this resolute man as he looks at you makes you clam up. There is even a slight smile of amusement on his face as he waits to see if you will silence the German gun. Then he asks coolly, 'How long should it normally take them to get something up here?'

CRASH! a particularly awesome concussion, followed by the sound of glass and debris cascading down out back, ends your imaginings. That's it. They've started on the house next door. You're next. God — what are they doing back there at the guns.

As the sound of demolition next door continues, and Suckling obstinately refuses to leave his window, the Canadian guns crash, shells roar overhead, explosions spout around the enemy gun which disappears. But Suckling is shouting 'Look! Look! Don't you see them?' By a fortunate coincidence the enemy had just launched a massed counter-attack up that same grassy slope. A quick adjustment of the map reference and the shells are falling in the enemy ranks. The attack goes to ground. A single soldier stands and runs back down the slope. Twos and threes and then larger groups follow. But when Suckling reports back to Maj Tim Beatty he makes it sound like a comic opera instead of a moment of supreme crisis.[8]

On 8 October Maj Beatty formed a miniature battle-group based on his D Coy with Dutch Resistance men, engineers, mortars, artillery FOO, medium m-gs and all the 'etceteras'. This force fought its way over massive dykes, amid polders flooded eight feet deep and obscured by thick ground fog. The renewed surprise and speed of advance enabled them to avoid major interference from German guns on the ridge behind Woensdrecht which overlooked the entire area. The next day they captured the main sluice gate of the drainage system. Lt Pleasance in the lead won the Military Cross, Sgt Foster received the Military Medal, and the reward for D Coy was a hot meal. They had not eaten for thirty-six hours but morale was high and complaints were few.

Morale was even higher on 10 October when Maj Whitley's B Coy, passing through their comrades, captured the locality where rail and road squeezed together through the narrowest part of the 15-mile neck of land linking Woensdrecht to the main bulge of South Beveland. While casualties were few relative to their achievement, 'Moaning Minnie' mortar fire was always a danger. One man, B143428 Pte Reginald L.Parnham, wounded in Normandy on 18 July, was fit to fight again on 13 August when he was wounded for the second time. Returning to unit, in the thrust towards South Beveland on 9 October he was wounded for the third time in just twelve weeks.[9]

Brig Megill's 5th Brigade set out on 7 October with the twin objectives of Hoogerheide and Huijbergen. The Calgary Highlanders and the Regiment de Maisonneuve moved parallel with the Black Watch marching behind to consolidate. The enemy's defence was becoming more stubborn, and as the infantry advanced there was a transition from flooded polders to more wooded country amid low sandy dunes and with shrub land and open spaces intervening. Again it was largely a matter of platoon fights with victory or stagnation being dictated by actions of individuals.

Fortunately outstanding individuals were available. One of the Calgarys, Lt Alex Keller, displayed good sense and bravery in a difficult moment. His men had emerged from the shelter of woods into a larger clear area swept by enemy fire. Keller carefully observed the location of enemy guns. He then pinpointed them for the four tanks of the Fort Garry Horse which accompanied him. While the tanks opened fire on the identified gun pits, Keller led his men at a fast steady walk across the perilous area. The enemy kept their heads down and were surprised by the Calgarys, who took sixteen prisoners without suffering a single casualty themselves.

Lt Charlie Forbes of the 'Maisies', the Maisonneuves, had already established a reputation as a bold and innovative leader. In the confusion of movement two weeks earlier he had borrowed a priest's cassock, walked through the enemy lines, obtained vital information and then did his holy stroll back. Now his men encountered a heavily armed post in an anti-tank ditch. Charlie worked his way to the flank and charged at the ditch, firing his Sten gun and calling to his men to follow. By the time they had caught up with him he had driven the enemy out of two gun pits and captured five prisoners. The immediate effect of this act was to clear the Maisies' way forward for several hundred yards without further hindrance.[10]

The 'ghost battalion' of Chill was now resisting the advance with considerable skill and élan. The force had varying reinforcements including grounded air crew and technical staff, but 'it was larded with well-trained and highly motivated survivors of parachute regiments and the remains of SS units that escaped the Falaise pocket'.[11] The experienced and long-suffering Black Watch of Canada in their war diary described their opponents as 'definitely the cream of the crop . . . fine physical specimens, keen, with excellent morale'.

Such expertise required equal quality of soldiering from the Allies. Again it was George Blackburn who was present at a demonstration of such a response. George was also able to see the humorous side of an event which left him soaked in icy water. He was in the dubious shelter of his lightly armoured carrier, trying to range on a large enemy gun about 2,000 yards away in the woods. Reluctant to leave even that frail shelter he suddenly sees his colonel, Mac Young, unconcernedly standing in the road. He joins his commander out in the open and Young asks for a compass.

At that moment you hear the gun *THUNK!* and the tone of its whine clearly indicates it's coming directly this way. The Colonel seems to realize this too and leaps for the water-filled ditch. Instantly you follow. Too late, you realize he doesn't mean to jump into the ditch, but over it. You land floundering in icy-cold water up to your hips. Struggling to regain your feet you see him unconcernedly kneeling, squinting into the compass, outlined against a flashing geyser of black mud and smoke spouting up with awesome roar no more than fifty yards in front of his unflinching face. . . . He points a finger at a clearing in the bush, and in his calm drawl says, 'Try plastering around there'. With that he turns away and starts back down the road as casually as he'd come.

The leapfrogging of battalions continued as platoons and companies borrowed men to make up to some kind of battle strength: Essex Scots through the Royals, and Royal Hamilton Light Infantry (the Rileys) through the Essex Scots. The Royals listed 'minor skirmishes' at Krabbendijke, Yerseke and Gravenpolder, places never heard of before and not likely to be heard of again. Along the Royals' route seven men are killed and twenty-four wounded. The Calgarys lose two majors and a captain, not easily replaced. Back at 5th Brigade, constantly trying to eke out woefully inadequate resources, the war diarist comments in frustration: 'Cannot understand why they do not put more troops in the area and finish the job once and for all instead of playing about, shifting first one battalion and then the other. This is beginning to look like a winter campaign unless something breaks soon.'[12]

The main objective was now Woensdrecht from which the Germans had evacuated 800 people. Behind the town was a well-fortified slope with a wide view across the countryside, while to the left dykes and polders were inconveniently located for attacking infantry and often were impassable for tanks. The Canadians did not yet know that the 'ghost battalion' of Chill had been swollen by 4,000 first-line reinforcements led by von der Heydte's tough paratroopers. Attacking once again with low-priority resources the Black Watch suffered their Black Friday.

Next on the list for the short straw were the Rileys. Their commander was Lt Col Denis Whitaker, veteran of the 1942 Dieppe raid. Whitaker had refused to commit his battalion to the attack tactics ordered for the Black Watch. This gained his men a day or two of respite while Whitaker himself was instructed to prepare a plan for the taking of Woensdrecht. At the same time von der Heydte had arrived in his motorcycle sidecar ahead of his troops. From the north ridge he could survey every aspect of the eventual battle. As the town had been evacuated it was now a well-defended fortress.

The Rileys would not need any incentive to battle the enemy because the catastrophe of the hopeless Black Watch attack had been visible to everybody. Black Watch casualties were still being evacuated to aid posts and their dead brought in for burial wherever possible. The Rileys were looking for vengeance.

Whitaker's first response to the domination of the guns on the ridge was to plan a night attack.[13] This involved the danger of men getting lost in the darkness. Whitaker intended to repeat on a smaller scale Simonds's Normandy tactic of Operation Totalize, when he sent in massed columns of tanks guided by coloured phosphorescent tracer fired overhead and directed on the objectives. He also 'intended to lay on a dense concentration of shellfire on the German positions to allow our men to close with the enemy under its protective cover', a resource which had not been available to the same extent for the Black Watch.

Partly because of the danger of units losing their way Whitaker took the risk of having his two lead coy commanders accompany him in an aerial reconnaissance over the enemy positions. They flew in the small, slow but extremely manoeuvrable Austers piloted by Royal Artillery officers who were accustomed to 'hedge-hopping' as observers. Other commanders studied a sandbox model. Previous unhappy experiences led Whitaker to give high priority to the laying of sufficient landlines so that dependence on radio would be as brief as possible. Faulty wireless sets had produced tragic situations in Normandy and at Arnhem.

At the last moment the local Resistance reported as many as 2,000 German paratroopers in the woods beyond the town. This information was largely correct, except that a proportion of the enemy were not actually paratroopers. It meant that the defenders enjoyed a ratio of five to one over the attackers. Yet normal attacking tactics prescribed a five to one ratio in favour of the attackers. This was once again a total reverse of appropriate resources, or as Whitaker himself said, 'it made the hope of winning a long shot'. But as a 4-oz tot of rum was served to the troops, the date was 15 October and the Canadian front was suddenly becoming the priority focus of Allied strategy. 'Free the Scheldt seaway!'[14]

The weather gave no encouragement to the shivering soldiers for whom the rum ration was not simply a morale boost. It was 'grey, cold and miserable . . . the cold wind, with the smell of approaching winter in it, had begun to gust strongly'. Artillery FOO Blackburn noticed that as the gunners fired their more than 37,000 shells (in 17 days), they were piling both the empty cartridge boxes and the spent shell cases in high windbreaks to gain a modicum of shelter. For the average infantryman the only resort in that bare plain was to crouch low in a slit until it was time to rise up and walk to the pace of the falling shells. The signallers had at least managed to commandeer a large pigsty which they had to share with the legitimate residents.[15]

As the infantry heard the first shells overhead, saw the flashes just in front of their holes and scrambled up to follow, it was the gunner again who so sensitively portrayed their traumatic task:

Shivering and sweating at the same time – half-intimidated and half-stimulated by the raging linear inferno of blinding flashes and hot concussions, seemingly erupting just before their faces – they plunge into the sour fumes and stumble over steaming gashes left by the violence that just passed, desperate to keep up, but at the same time dreading the moment when they will confront the enemy.[16]

In typical fashion the Germans had pulled back from the worst of the barrage and prepared to counter-attack the moment the infantry reached their objectives. Some of the advancing men, recent reinforcements with little if any infantry training, found it difficult to brave the appalling curtains of fire. Sgt Pete Bolus looked on these 'rookies' with great sympathy.

> We had had a few reinforcements come up; I didn't even get to know these guys' names that were hit. The older fellows were all in one piece practically; they knew how to look after themselves. It was a skill that you seemed to develop. Some of the kids didn't have more than their basic training. Some of them hadn't even had that. I had a kid who didn't know how to detonate a grenade. We lost a lot of good kids that way.[17]

In the darkness and confusion some of the leading troops did not land precisely on target and gaps tended to open up, discernible only as dawn shed some light on the ravaged countryside. Capt Lyn Hegelheimer leading his company decided to rectify his directional error by ordering a quick backtracking march down the road. They met two Germans walking towards them, deep in conversation. Hegelheimer drew his pistol and took them prisoner. The Germans were astonished having assumed that the marching men, coming from the direction of the German lines, were their friends.

In the chaos and cacophony comprehensible only to those who experienced it, strange things happened. One coy commander went to sleep and could not be wakened. Later he was found wandering in a daze, totally oblivious to danger. He then went missing. This coincided with a fierce enemy counter-attack. Lacking orders a number of the Rileys began to move back. A disorderly retreat could quickly become a rout, a panic, a disaster. Maj Joe Pigott, with the neighbouring coy, recognised the imminent peril and promptly planted himself in the middle of the road with a drawn pistol. A moment later he was joined by Whitaker, also with revolver at the ready. The situation was quickly restored as enemy paratroopers and tanks moved into yet another attack.

Whitaker was never one to underestimate the enemy. He admired the skill and toughness of the best of their soldiers, like those now defending Woensdrecht. But even he was due for a surprise as he tried to interrogate the first prisoners:

> I was deeply concerned to note that all of our prisoners bore the insignia of the 6th Paratroop Division, whom I knew to be specially trained and skilled infantrymen. They already had the reputation of being an elite, hard-fighting battle group who were only committed to major trouble areas. As I leaned over one wounded prisoner to question him, he glared up at me . . . and spat in my face. Even in captivity, the beast could snarl.

One of Whitaker's commanders, Maj Welsh, had a more pleasant kind of surprise. After days of confused struggle between the two sides, Welsh's men were at last clearing the main crossroads in the small town. As they approached the church they saw three men of his company who had been reported missing. They came from behind the church 'grinning through soot-streaked faces'. Their leader, nineteen-year-old Sgt Harold Hall, told how they had been cut off while on patrol. They slowly retreated into the shelter of the church until they were 'just about ten feet away from the Jerries'. Overwhelmed by the numbers of enemy they found refuge in a large coal bin. Fortunately nobody tried to open it and after three days they were able to emerge as the enemy retreated.

Battle was sometimes lightened a little by moments of grim humour. Sgt Bolus was with Capt Bill Whiteside during an enemy barrage on a farm nearby. There were pigs running about in the open. One of the pigs was hit by shrapnel. Whiteside stopped his carrier, jumped out and expertly bled the pig.

They intended to keep the pig and eat it when possible. A day or two later, the men gathered around as the captain dissected the pig prior to cooking it. It was only then that the men learned that their captain had studied at a veterinary college.

Other casual incidents helped break the continual routine of interchanging tedium and terror. John A. Marin, of the Queen's Own Rifles of Canada, together with one or two mates, was invited into the house of a civilian. Apart from the usual gestures of hospitality and gratitude, the Dutchman proudly wished to show the soldiers how the family had defied the occupying enemy by listening to the BBC news every night, a highly dangerous pastime. It gave the soldiers some idea of the perils of civilian life under the Nazis.

They had a large open fireplace, four feet wide by three feet six inches high. The Dutchman reached up the chimney and brought out from a shelf in the flue a small crystal radio set. It was a piece of board three inches by six inches with a piece of galena [lead ore] mounted on it. It was attached to an aerial which ran up the flue. On one side of the crystal a wire ran to an earphone. A second wire was attached to a small flat spring which was mounted so that one part was over the crystal.

On the end of this flat piece was fastened a needle. To receive, all he had to do was to move the needle point to various parts of the crystal and this would pick up the music and news from the BBC in England.

When the family had listened to the news they passed on the truth about the progress of the war to reliable neighbours. This apparently innocent entertainment could have merited the death sentence if they had been caught and accused of being Resistance workers.[18]

The civilians were now free to listen to Dutch broadcasts containing Dutch government pronouncements. As long as they stayed under cover there was a good chance that they would not suffer personal injury as the battle raged on. Material loss was another thing, for after the battle had ended the Woensdrecht authorities found that 427 civilian homes had been totally destroyed, while another 235 were badly damaged but repairable.

For most of the troops for most of the time, the pleasure of intermingling with liberated and grateful civilians was rare. Once the soldier was caught up in the front-line whirlpool of battle on the

Woensdrecht slopes, it was an infuriating succession of attacks and counter-attacks which seemed to be producing no significant progress at all.

Cpl 'Jimmy' James of Vancouver found an apt metaphor for his experiences in the huge rollers of the Pacific Ocean:

It was like trying to stand up against the biggest ocean rollers and the undertow sucking you off balance and all. You had just reached your objective when a great ocean roller of enemy men and guns rushed you back up the beach staggering all over. Then your own artillery opened up and it was the turn of the tide, rolling over the enemy and washing him away up the slope. But the tide turns twice a day and that's how it was, first us thinking we had won a few yards and then him crashing back all over us. Day after day the same.[19]

Another corporal, ordered time after time to force his men up the forlorn slopes against overwhelming firepower, found himself rebelling against his orders, cursing his superiors, but unable to do anything except obey. He became what he called 'battle mad' and kept his sanity by shouting insults as he advanced.

You see, it was alright on the maps. But when they said 'Go!' you couldn't really see anything to go at. And these paratroopers up there had their burp guns that fired so much quicker than our m-gs. You could imitate our Brens that went duh-duh-duh-duh. But their Spandaus were too quick, sort of brrrrrrrp! They called them burp guns. A thousand rounds a minute.

So I was running across this field with no real objective in view and all their guns burping, and I was shouting 'Bloody captains! Bloody majors! Bloody colonels! Bloody generals!' and pulling my trigger as if firing at them 'cos I couldn't see any enemy anywheres. And then their Moaning Minnies came down and all we could do was lie down and hug the grass until they had stopped.

And so my mate Harry, who was lying beside me and had heard me, says 'But Whitaker's OK. A good colonel. Doing a job. And braver than any of us. And he didn't start the so-and-so war, did he?' So when the Moaning Minnies go home we get up again and this time I'm running faster and yelling 'Bloody Hitler! Bloody Goering! Bloody Krauts!'[20]

Summing it up, Jimmy James thought that if you had to describe Woensdrecht battle in one word it would be 'Again. And again. And again.' He remembered wryly that towards the end of the battle he said to another man 'God knows what day it is. It must be Wednesday.' The other man replied, 'And you must have slept a whole day away. It's Thursday already'. An officer who overheard the chat grinned and announced, 'You're both wrong. As yet, it is only Tuesday.'

Maj Joe Pigott, who had stopped possible panic by drawing his revolver, described how close and confused the fighting became. Pigott was using a room in a cottage as his HQ. His driver, Pte Harry Gram, had been wounded by a piece of shrapnel. Pigott tried to persuade Gram to go to the aid post but Gram refused. Pigott then gave him a direct order. Little was happening behind the cottage but chaos rained in the front street. As a gesture of disobedience, instead of using the back door, Gram stormed out of the front door and got into the jeep which was standing there.

He tried to start the jeep but it was riddled with bullets and shrapnel and would not function. Harry Gram was cursing so much that he did not observe a mighty German self-propelled gun standing a few yards in front of the jeep. In the narrow street the jeep was effectively blocking the bigger vehicle's progress. Suddenly the turret of the tank opened and the German commander waved in a supercilious manner for Harry to move the jeep out of the way. The commander may not have realised which nationality Harry was. As little impressed by German authority as by Canadian instructions, Harry got out of the jeep and walked away down the road. Immediately there was a tremendous crash, and the tank began to burn. It had suffered a direct hit. The commander had disappeared.[21]

Harry Gram had been able to walk away, relieving his shock with a medley of swear words. Many of the wounds seen around Woensdrecht were of a much more horrifying nature. While the shock of some severe injuries, such as amputation, could for a time assuage the worst pain, other types of injury induced agonies beyond comprehension.

George Blackburn was a veteran in tending to wounds and had just been pushing a soldier's brains back into his head as he applied dressings. He was horrified by the wounds to gunner Harold Wiens. Wiens had seen a Dutch civilian carrying an unexploded phosphorus bomb. He took the bomb away from the civilian and went to dispose of it, but it exploded in his hands. It covered him with globules of burning phosphorous which could neither be easily extinguished nor detached from the skin.

Wiens would be in hospital for over a year before he could walk out. Blackburn described his treatment at the first hospital. He was: 'Stripped of his clothes. His bandages and his stretcher [were] kept soaking to prevent his body from smoking, they scraped off the phosphorus, shot him with penicillin and painkiller and shipped him on to a civilian hospital in England.'

As ever in a war zone, danger was everywhere. It was not necessary to be leaping out of the front-most slit trench and charging towards the enemy to suffer death or wounding. Men released from those duties for a day or two were being treated to a visit to a mobile bath unit just behind the lines. It was a place of brief fun and relaxation, until it was hit by a rogue flying bomb intended for London. Of the naked front-line soldiers enjoying the jollity of the showers, nine men were killed outright and twenty-seven were wounded.

A ray of light on a dark horizon was the fact that, during the Woensdrecht battle, the Allied Supreme HQ was at last directing more priority in troops, materials and petrol to the clearing of the Antwerp seaway. The fresh 52nd Scottish (Lowland) Division arriving from Britain was allocated to the Canadian Army. There was even the promise of an American infantry outfit which rejoiced in the spectacular name of the 'Timberwolves' (104th US Infantry Division). But for the most part it was a story of Canadian units leapfrogging each other.

However, Les Fusiliers Mont-Royal (FMR), their own ranks still too slim, were reinforced by 200 men from the Belgian White Brigade under Lt Edouard Pilaet. Similarly the Canadian Camerons were joined by the renowned Col Colson from Antwerp docks, with 150 Belgian enthusiasts who, as the Camerons' diary commented, 'set a fine example of courageous and unstinting service'. Even so the Camerons had to use all arms, anti-tank gunners, clerks, cooks and drivers as replacement infantrymen, in view of the extraordinary length of front which they had to cover. The Highland Light Infantry fared even worse as one small batch of reinforcements included half a dozen butchers from a rear supplies unit.

As Woensdrecht was made secure, the Essex Scots were sent off to the left to secure the isthmus towards South Beveland. This was one of the wettest areas of polders and the Essex Scots had to advance along the narrow railway embankment towards a junction code-named 'Mary'. Understandably advancing along such a narrow front swept by German m-gs made progress slow and painful. The position would only be occupied after a raid by Spitfires with bombs, another raid by Typhoons with rockets and artillery firing both at the remnants of the target and providing air bursts above the target. Maj Carr, directing the attack, brought a little humour to the occasion by reporting on the radio 'Our Mary is turning out to be a very tough broad'.[22]

A further touch of unconscious humour was provided by the first officer of the fresh Scottish division sent to cooperate with the Canadians. The long-suffering veterans of the Royals were astonished by what they saw, as one of their officers recorded.[23] They had borrowed Dutch bicycles in order to patrol the dykes:

All our men were desperately tired and in a filthy, wet, muddy condition. On our way we were terribly surprised to find a party of what were obviously Allied troops landing in a small boat. Then forth from the boat on to the shore stepped the finest soldier I had ever seen, a fine figure of a Scottish gentleman, carrying a shepherd's crook. He had a small pack neatly adjusted on his back. His gas cape was neatly rolled. He had his pistol in a neatly blancoed web holster. His boots were neatly polished.

He was a Colonel and I was a Captain. I did manage to salute, although I think it must have been haphazard. He politely enquired if

1. Jack Harper VC, 'the quietest man you could ever wish to know'. (*John Brown*)

2. The memorial to Jack Harper at Hatfield Woodhouse, inspired by local Rotarian John Brown. (*KJT*)

3. The paupers' dormitories at *Depôt de Mendicité* (1940s), indicative of the vast size of the settlement. (*Karel Govaerts*)

4. The vital 2-in mortars: crew man drops bomb on to striking pin in the tube. (*IWM BU1420*)

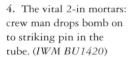

5. Westkapelle civilians being issued with coupons for wooden clogs under German occupation. (*Mrs Flipse-Roelse, per Zeeuwse Bibliotheek*)

6. Infantry cross an open polder which is easily covered by enemy m-gs; canal is impassable for tanks. (*IWM B11720*)

7. Main roads in 1944 were not constructed for two-way armoured traffic, a hazard of the Arnhem Road. (*Tank Museum, 2121*)

8. Ammunition exploding from burning vehicle blocking the single Arnhem Road with no way of passing by. (*IWM B10124A*)

9. FM Walter Model (right), fast mover at Arnhem, with Maj Gen Walter Bruns of the reconstituted 89th Division destroyed in Normandy. (*Lt Kol Gevert Haslob*)

10. After Arnhem many Allied escapers were saved by the Dutch Resistance; here an escaping RAF pilot, Eugene Haveley, has a Resistance haircut.
(*Illegal wartime photo, Ger Schinck*)

11. Numbers of prisoners were taken around Antwerp, and the lions' cages at the zoo had to be used as temporary lodgings. (*IWM BU559*)

12. An anonymous nurse representing many women who served in danger, including George Blackburn's 'ambulancemen'. (*IWM B7946*)

13. An apparently indestructible Cpl Cliff Brown leads the Lincs & Wellands into Eeklo, happy to avoid street-fighting this time. (*Eeklo Civic Archives*)

14. A Buffalo, 'an iron box with an outboard engine', crosses the river ferrying about twenty men. (*IWM BU2449*)

15. The impossibility of tank manoeuvre amid flooded polders and rain-saturated embankments (Shermans queuing). (*Tank Museum 2727*)

16. Canada's Lt Gen Guy G. Simonds, one of the youngest and most brilliant of Allied generals, decided to sink the island. (*National Archives of Canada*)

17. The crew and ground staff of Lancaster ED 888 (576 Sqn), piloted by Flg Off Jim Bell (extreme left, back row), illustrate the huge dimensions of the plane which bombed Westkapelle at about 1435 hr. (*Jim Bell*)

18. P/O Vernon Wilkes looks out through the bomb sight of his Lancaster: while over the target shrapnel from anti-aircraft fire damaged the landing gear and necessitated a perilous landing at an emergency airfield. (*Flt Lt Vernon Wilkes DFC*)

19. Spitfire PL 850 of 541 Sqn photographed sea wall gap at 1515 hr. The sea was already flooding in. 'A' indicates lighthouse strong point 1 km inland at end of Westkapelle main street; 'B' indicates battery of six British guns captured in 1940. (*Keele University, Crown copyright, MOD*)

20. Col Reinhardt, German CO at Flushing, measures the flood waters; the impact of the 'land mattress' rockets would be even worse for him. (*Zeeuws Documentatiecentrum*)

21. Willy Paugstadt, shot at Middelburg in front of ten-year-old Jan Wigard: Paugstadt, a prisoner, was too tired to keep his hands up. (*Jan Wigard*)

22. A little space in the Netherlands for Paugstadt who could never have returned to his home in East Prussia, which was occupied by the Russians. (*Jan Wigard*)

23. Mine-flailing 'Crabs' coming ashore at Westkapelle; Cpl Himsworth's tank just leaving LCT737. (*IWM B11632*)

24. Polish Maj Gen Stanislas Maczek talks to war correspondents as Col K. Dworak and Capt T.A. Wysocki pay attention. (*Ken Bell, National Archives of Canada PA129140*)

25. Bedraggled infantry trudge yet another mile through yet another devastated village. (*Ger Schinck*)

26. A defended farmhouse outside Den Bosch is flamed by a 'Crocodile' from Joseph Ellis's unit; a stalled train is on the railway to the left. (*IWM BU1242*)

27. Infantrymen of 53rd Welsh Division advance through Den Bosch while Resistance man Martin Suiskes watches along a side street; in the British newspaper photo three days later, Suiskes' face has been blanked out by the censor. (*Peter Handford, per Luc van Gent, IWM B11376*)

28. 53rd Welsh Division veterans return to Den Bosch in more comfort (with Dutch lady driver) on the fiftieth anniversary of the liberation. (*Bill James, 53rd Division Association*)

29. Tanks of 1st Northamptonshire Yeomanry carry 51st Highland Division men forward in the drive towards the last bridge over the Maas. (*IWM B11458*)

30. Men of the Scottish Black Watch line up the two workhorses of Allied infantry battle, the very accurate Bren m-g and the not always so efficient Sten sub-m-g. (*IWM B8912*)

31. The smoke of battle still obscures a ditched 1NY Sherman (on right), a wrecked Kangaroo and two knocked-out German S-Ps as the Raamsdonk battle ends outside St Lambert's Church. (*NY Association*)

32. Recce sergeant Kenny Jack, MM (1NY), used an old cartwheel as a traverse turntable for his heavy m-g. He was the first man to walk into the ruins of Caen from the north. (*D. Purchard*)

33. Civilians evacuate a disputed village near Overloon as infantrymen move up, a familiar sight in the fluid fighting. (*Ger Schinck*)

34. Sgt George Eardley VC, MM, after being presented with his Victoria Cross by FM Sir Bernard Montgomery near Overloon. 'Monty' himself was not a tall man, illustrating the VC hero's own slight build. (*King's Shropshire Light Infantry Museum*)

35. The good news telegram must at first have caused some worry in Mrs Eardley's mind, for the yellow forms were also used to convey the news that the next of kin had been killed in action. (*Roy Eardley*)

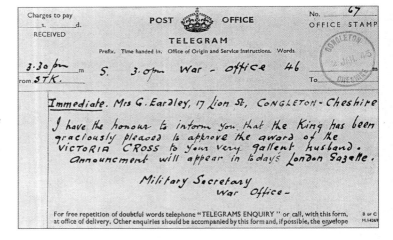

Charges to pay

s. d.

RECEIVED

POST ✠ OFFICE

TELEGRAM

Prefix. Time handed in. Office of Origin and Service Instructions. Words.

No. 67

OFFICE STAMP

CONGLETON

2 JUL 45

CHESHIRE

3.30 pm ....m S. 3.0pm War - Office 46

from STK. ....

To ....m

Immediate. Mrs G. Eardley, 17 Lion St, CONGLETON - Cheshire

I have the honour to inform you that the King has been graciously pleased to approve the award of the VICTORIA CROSS to your very gallent husband. Announcement will appear in todays London Gazette.

Military Secretary
War Office -

For free repetition of doubtful words telephone "TELEGRAMS ENQUIRY" or call, with this form, at office of delivery. Other enquiries should be accompanied by this form and, if possible, the envelope

B or C
M.14269

36. Gerhard Stiller (*circled*) and SS panzer comrades rest behind the lines, listening to a portable gramophone first looted from the staff car of a Russian Commissar on the Eastern Front. (*Stiller*)

37/38. Taking shelter in the cellars of the Santa Anna psychiatric hospital: patients, orphans, villagers, Resistance workers and escaping Allied servicemen. (*Photos illegal when taken – Ger Schinck*)

39. An underground weapon repairs workshop of the Dutch Resistance hidden in a picture-framing workshop near Venlo. (*Ger Schinck*)

40/41. Evacuees from the Schink family village set out in a snowstorm on their two-day walk to the cattle trucks for an unknown destination, baby Ger Schinck in pram. (*Illegal wartime photos – Ger Schinck*)

42. The end of the road for wounded German prisoners. (*IWM B6008*)

we were Canadians. I assured him that we were. He asked if I could direct him to battalion HQ. I did better than that. I escorted him to battalion HQ. I was taking no chances on losing such a beautiful specimen to the German army.

Tough or not, the possession of the 'Mary' area snapped tightly shut a trap on all the enemy around Walcheren, Beveland and back down the Channel coast. There was now no easy retreat for the walking German soldier. Heading north he must cross the Oosterschelde (the 'Eastern' Schedlt, which actually ran north of Beveland), then the Grevelingen inlet, and after that the Haringvliet inlet, each of those water obstacles from two to four miles wide. Even so, there would still be the intricate pattern of waterways around Rotterdam and Dordrecht to pass over.

A longer retreat route which led more directly into the heartland of the Netherlands would be across two remaining bridges, one at Moerdijk, over the Netherlands Diep. The other, the Keiser, lay a few miles farther on at Geertruidenberg where it crossed the Bergse Maas, a rather narrower river but still not a waterway to be swum by tired soldiers in full battle kit. But there was no sign that the Chill 'ghost battalions' were about to undertake a phantom-like disappearance into the night.

All veterans returning from the wars had an impression of which battle had provided their worst moment. For some Canadians it was Merxem, for others Breskens, and yet others Woensdrecht. The horrors of Woensdrecht are well reflected in the experience of one young lieutenant, a recent reinforcement, during Maj Carr's attack towards position 'Mary'. The young officer

collapsed in a dead faint when he learned that he would have to lead his platoon through a gap in the dike covered by a German machine-gun, clearly perceiving that he had been condemned to die. When he came to, he alerted his platoon and they took off. He was the first man around the end of the dike. As he anticipated he was met by a burst of Spandau fire. He died instantly with a bullet in his forehead.[24]

CHAPTER SEVEN

A Dutch Krakatoa

In about 1500 BC the island of Santorini sank beneath the waves. In 1833 the island of Krakatoa exploded and disappeared into the waters. In 1944 it would be the turn of Walcheren island.

At the beginning of October the island of Walcheren still crouched along the low sea coast like a defiant porcupine, its erectile quills pointing in all directions. Or perhaps, more appositely, like an armadillo sporting porcupine quills. And those quills were big guns, pointing out to sea, up into the air, along the beaches and over the river towards Breskens. A local Dutch historian says of it: 'The island Walcheren grows during the war to the most fortified coastline in the *Atlantikwall*'.[1]

The same source describes Walcheren as having the shape of a saucer with sand dunes and sea walls around the rim, and measuring about 15 km north to south, about 18 km west to east:

Walcheren was a beautiful island called 'The Garden of Zeeland' and was frequently visited by English tourists by the mailboat Vlissingen [Flushing]-Harwich. Most of them stayed in Vlissingen hotel 'Brittania' on the seafront . . . before the war a good spot to live or stay in. . . . In Westkapelle lived most dikers who had a job on the huge seawall.

The guns of Walcheren were formidable. Sixty were directed towards the sea and were weapons capable of taking on the largest battleships which might approach. The guns were embedded deep in concrete.[2] There were also some lethal quick-firing guns which had been captured during the

British retreat to Dunkirk in 1940. The guns were in turn defended by permanent hides for infantry.

However, if the guns could be eliminated the quality of some of the defending troops did not match up with the images of *SS Panzergrenadiers* or parachutists as perceived in Normandy or at Woensdrecht. A unique division known as the 'White Bread Division' awaited an Allied attack. It has been defined as 'one of the most curious collections of men ever assembled together to represent a fighting unit'.[3] 70 Infantry Division was composed of 10,000 men who were suffering from, or had barely recovered from, stomach problems.

This was the harvest of years of war with poor rations, severely tortured nervous systems and physical deterioration. It was not practical, given the German manpower shortages, to 'discharge this huge flood of groaning manpower from military service'. They needed special nutrition and the 'Garden of Zeeland' was able to supply fresh foods, vegetables, milk, eggs and fruit. There was even a ration of white bread, visible nowhere else on the continent except on the tables of the ruling elite. Appropriately they were commanded by Lt Gen Daser, a tired, elderly, meek man, bald and bespectacled, the antithesis of Chill or von der Heydte.

If the stomach ulcer division as an active unit defies the imagination, an even more inexpedient class of men formed the *Ohren* (Ear) battalions. These were men who were either deaf or physically deprived of parts of the ears. Most orders had to be given to them by gestures and sign language. Night was perilous when guards could not hear anyone approaching. Day was dangerous as men could not hear artillery shells until they exploded among them. On one occasion two sergeants of the guard, encountering each other at night, shot and killed each other as instantaneous reaction to the unheard apparition.

These foibles were of little encouragement to Lt Gen Guy Simonds on whose capable and willing shoulders fell the responsibility of breaching the impregnable defences of Walcheren and opening the seaway to Antwerp. Simonds was a man of boundless imagination and sterling will. It has been said that if Simonds had been there when Hannibal marched his elephants over the Alps he would have been looking for a way of moving the mountains.[4]

In Normandy, where the finest British brains had sent 800 tanks across the open Caen plain to be slaughtered by the German 88s, Simonds solved the problem by lining up columns of tanks in four, like old-time marching infantry, firing coloured directional tracer over their heads, directing them on compass bearing, sitting his infantry in newly invented Kangaroos and sending the entire pageant to drive right through the immensely strong enemy defences to set up armed camps in the enemy's rear at night.[5]

His ideas did not always receive immediate commendation from others. For the Goodwood catastrophe the British general had banned armoured infantry carriers as likely to reduce the fighting spirit. However, in Totalize Simonds greatly reduced infantry casualties. His chief of staff, Brig N.E. Roger, recorded:

> Never have I worked for anyone with such a precise and clear and farseeing mind – he was always working to a plan with a clear cut objective which he took care to let all of us know in simple and direct terms . . . he reduced problems in a flash to basic facts and variables, picked out those that mattered, ignored those that were side issues, and made up his mind and got on with it.[6]

While many officers had a similar confidence in Simonds, and were equally aware of his facility for developing quite eccentric ideas into organised practice, there was general amazement and incredulity when he announced his simple system for winning the battle for Walcheren: 'SINK THE ISLAND!'

As the inner 'saucer' shape of Walcheren was below sea level, Simonds proposed to breach the sea walls by air bombing, flood the interior and then sail his troops in behind the defences. They could then attack up newly formed beaches not on the enemy's maps.

His critics were as outspoken as Simonds himself was wont to be. Several people labelled the idea as 'crazy', or 'a brainstorm', or 'half-baked', and commented that the airmen would not agree to such a plan. More seriously, the army's chief engineer, after considerable study, advised Simonds's superior Crerar that hydrographic engineers, intelligence staff, local residents and seamen all considered the plan to be impractical.[7] Although a general, Simonds was two tiers of command down from Montgomery and each tier of command imposed certain restraints on its subordinates.

Fortunately for thousands of Allied troops who might otherwise have been killed or disabled, at that point the courteous but cautious Crerar himself became disabled. In quick succession he was ordered into hospital for treatment and Montgomery was cajoled by Eisenhower into giving top priority to the Antwerp seaway problem. On 27 September Simonds became acting army commander with licence to innovate and the political ability to persuade Montgomery to approve a plan which otherwise, still smarting from the Arnhem debacle, he might have vetoed as too risky.

Simonds prevailed on his 'doubting Thomas', Chief Engineer Brig Walsh, to call in a second opinion in the form of Capt 'Spot' West of the Royal Canadian Engineers. Walsh asked West if the bombing proposal was feasible. West collected a mass of aerial photographs and a stereo viewer on which, by viewing pairs of photographs, he would obtain a three-dimensional impression. For forty-eight hours, almost without rest, 'Spot' viewed hundred of pairs again and again. Then he marked up a map and forecast that by bombing the sea walls at certain phases of the tide the island could be flooded.

The solution was not that simple. Normal bombing methods would not suffice as the sea walls had foundations running deep into the solid ground. Then there was the question of civilian casualties and permanent damage to property on this fertile stretch of reclaimed sea bed. Queen Wilhelmina, resident in London, was consulted and agreed that the alternatives were too horrific to contemplate.

Once convinced, Bomber Command specialists hurried to translate into feasible action the brilliant but vague idea Simonds had propounded, to use delayed fuse bombs which would, by the power of their descent, burrow through the sand dunes and earthworks to explode in the depths of the foundations. At the same time more classic methods of bombing would deal with some of the enemy's armaments. Major warships would stand out at sea and match the power of the remaining

German guns. The landing ships would be accompanied by small craft designed to move close up to the beach with fire support.

A three-fold attack would develop: the main seaborne invasion around Westkapelle coming from England and Ostend; an amphibious attack across the river from Breskens to Flushing; and the forcing of the land causeway on the east near Woensdrecht, an advance which would menace the main town of Middelburg.

Especially important would be two tactics which were still in the process of refinement, the sophisticated use of smoke and the firing of the oddly named 'Land Service Mattress'. The latter was simply the First Canadian Rocket Battery, firing groups of long-range, heavy rockets from a base near Breskens and controlled by an officer in the tower of an abandoned lighthouse. Its effect on the morale of the enemy in Flushing would be enormous. The First Canadian colonel, Eric Harris, remembered that when the enemy commander surrendered 'he was still jittery about the rockets and [at the receiving end] couldn't figure out just what they were'.

The experts of the smoke operations, Maj Stewart Bastow and Capt Jim Bond, who had been refining their system, were now challenged by an ambitious directive from the infantry brigade commander. He wanted two screens laid across the Scheldt from Breskens to Flushing. The attackers would cross in this corridor out of sight of enemy eyes, but there was to be no smoke in the corridor itself or in Breskens harbour. When convinced that issuing smoke was not quite like piling sandbags, the commander accepted that some smoke might blow into the corridor. He insisted on a direct radio link, so that if the intrusion of smoke was too high he could shut the smoke operation down in an instant.[8]

At last the Supreme Commander's queries were all satisfied and he gave the order to go ahead with Operation Infatuate. A naval force under Capt A.F. Pugsley, RN (reporting to ADM Ramsay), was assembled and Cdr K.A. Sellar of the Support Squadron Eastern Flank (SSEF) was briefed. Brig B.W. Leicester's 4th Special Service Brigade was available for the beach assaults. The long-suffering Canadian infantry 'girded up their loins' once more. But it was over to the RAF to initiate the complex operation which would have to contend not only with heavy enemy anti-aircraft batteries but also appalling conditions of cloud, fog, rain and gales.

The first planes to fly over Walcheren in this operation were medium bombers from the 8th USAAF. They dropped thousands of leaflets to reinforce BBC warnings to civilians about the proposed bombing. It is a reflection of the total Allied domination of the air that its airmen were able to drop messages saying that they would be coming back tomorrow or the next day to carry out the actual bombing. No significant enemy air reaction would be anticipated. The leaflets were even as specific as to warn that 'not only aerial bombardment, but danger of flooding also threatens your lives and the lives of your families'.

The RAF missions commenced with a single Mosquito in Mission Snooper on 3 October. Of 1409 (Met) Flight, crewed by Flt Lt Arthur F. Pethick and Flt Lt N.W.F. 'Gurt' Green, was first of all to check prevailing meteorological conditions and radio the information back to the master bomber of the Pathfinders. After that it could 'stick around' and photograph six waves of bombing and then the results of the bombing. It was able to do this from 10,000 feet through the fixed automatic camera. However, cloud had thickened during the first three bombing waves and Green had to use a hand-held camera at 3,000 feet, in 'uncomfortable flak' and dust clouds, for the remainder of their observations. 'Gurt' recorded this as 'too much like hard work'.[9]

Following closely on the meteorological plane rumbled the full panoply of Bomber Command power, fast circling Mosquitoes guiding the huge Lancaster bombers on to targets. Gp Capt Cribb, an Australian from 582 Pathfinder Squadron, acted as Master Bomber as, from 1300 hr onwards, wave after wave of the heavy bombers aimed for the sea walls at Westkapelle. Crews were drawn from several countries, including Australia, Belgium, Canada, Czechoslovakia, the Netherlands, New Zealand, Norway, Poland, Rhodesia and South Africa. Some of the earlier crews did not see magnificent results because their bombs had been fused at base for delayed explosion. But within twenty minutes second-wave Lancaster PB 427, was reporting 'sea wall appeared to be breached slightly'. Bombers in the third wave, Lancaster LM 257 and others, could see definite breaks in the massive wall and the first leaks of sea had begun to penetrate into the lower polders inside the wall. All within the hour.

Buoyed up by the success of the first attack, the Mosquitoes and Lancasters returned again and again. On 7 October they concentrated on Rammekens and Flushing sea walls on the south of the diamond-shaped island. On 11 October they hit the wall at Veere on the north-eastern edge of the diamond. On 17 October they were back at Westkapelle to widen that essential gap. The Germans reacted energetically, conscripting civilians to try to rebuild the sea defences. But the bombers returned and knocked over the replacement constructions. The sea exerted its mighty power and gnawed away at the edges of the bombed gaps. Each tide pushed more and more water behind the old walls and beaches. The waves built up new landing beaches inside the old defence ring.

This was undoubtedly one of the finest achievements of the RAF. For the sea walls, although so substantial at ground level, viewed from 5,000 or 6,000 feet showed only as a narrow strip of land: a thin thread, sometimes obscured, between the grey-black of the sea and the grey-brown of the land across a vast landscape drifting with shivering mists. This mission impressed itself on the memories of many for a number of reasons. It was an unusual 'hit and run' target with no enemy country to traverse; it called for extraordinary aiming skill; it called for bombs to do what still sounded like a crazy job; and there was great concern too about the fate of the civilians and their meticulously cultivated fields in the conditions of sudden cataclysmic disaster.

Lancaster PA 160 belonged to 300 (Polish) Squadron and its pilot was Flg Off J. Pohoski. He was in the eighth wave and was able to see immediate results: 'Bombs were released visually on the target. Bombing very concentrated on target area. Small fires with smoke seen in town area. Two minute after bombing water started to flood immediate area of the target, spreading towards Westkapelle.'[10]

The Polish squadron commander, Wg Cdr T. Pozyczka, flying in ten minutes behind Pohoski's plane, was even more specific:

Attacked at 15.00 hours in very good visibility. Bombing very concentrated and accurate. Water seen to flood the area around the

Aiming Point, spreading towards the village, half of which was flooded. Sea wall was broken for a distance of 500 yards. Slight accurate light Flak and machine gun fire over the target.

Wg Cdr G.F. Rodney of 626 Squadron, coming in at 180 mph, dropped his bombs from 4,000 feet into the breach and noted 'water was flowing through the gap and the southern part of Westkapelle was already flooded'. Behind him 12 Squadron had bombs fused for delayed explosion of between thirty minutes and six hours, the intention being to keep the breach free from investigating enemy. Lancaster LM 224 saw that 'water was flowing through to the fields', all within two hours of the first bomb falling.

Sgt Danny Driscoll was the rear gunner on Flg Off Markes's plane of 550 Squadron and so had, as it were, a front seat as Markes turned the plane for home. Danny sensed something of the drama of it all as he watched the scene about ninety minutes after the first bomb.

I saw several delay bombs that must have exploded at the same time, causing a large part of the wall to fall away. The sea at the time was at maximum height for breaching. The water around the wall was a mass of white foam with bombs falling in it. All of a sudden all hell broke loose as the wall was breached, with the sea pouring inland with nothing to stop its force, swallowing everything in its path. I was supposed to have said [on inter-com] 'The Germans are going for their gum boots'.

Flt Sgt Frank Petch, wireless operator on the same plane, commented that they had to run in six times, once because another plane appeared underneath them and then because wisps of cloud obscured their vision at the crucial moment of bomb release. Flak was increasing and 'it appeared we had charmed lives'. Their load was one 4,000-lb bomb, eight at 1,000 lb and a smaller long-delay bomb. The impact of their bombs was devastating.

Seconds later, passing over the sea wall, it blew up, sending 'blue metal' high into the air. Buffeted by the repercussion, our Lancaster shuddered but flew on without any apparent defects. Sea water was pouring inland in a great torrent. I glanced at my watch. It was 14.50 hours. The flak was fierce . . . I noticed German soldiers running inland.

Within an hour of the start of the operation the 'rush hour syndrome' began to impact on the traffic of aeroplanes. In neat echelon as they took off, variations of wind, speed, cloud and enemy interference reduced the formations to something less ordered. Evasive action caused some planes to circle several times in the area. The 514 Squadron Lancaster in which WO 'Don' Donnelly was rear gunner had good reason to circle in that way.

There was, inevitably, a great concentration of aircraft on the run-up to the Aiming Point, so much so that we espied another Lancaster directly above us with its bomb doors open. The Skipper [Australian Flg Off R.W. Vickers] decided that this was distinctly unhealthy, did a hard turn to port and went round again. . . . Soon after crossing the coast outbound, I noticed a small trickle of water in the target area, and within minutes it had turned into a flood, which with great joy I communicated to the crew and congratulated Abe Hearn [the crew's bomb aimer].

Although Donnelly experienced a feeling of joy once the plane was well on the way home, other crews had moments of considerable trepidation during the period over the target. Even flying in formation, if it was an incorrect formation, could inspire nightmares as Flg Off Tommy Gummersall discovered over Flushing. He was piloting Lancaster LM 100 in 467 (Royal Australian Air Force) Squadron.

Some bright spark in the planning section of the Air Ministry had decided that it would be an excellent idea if we attacked in a formation known as line astern. I think his mother must have been frightened by an old sea captain for line astern belongs to the Navy. It looked good on paper but in practice it didn't work.

I had a good view of the whole formation until the leading plane reached the target area. The Germans let him have the lot, the poor bugger couldn't hold position and dropped down, his slipstream hitting No. 2 in the formation. No. 2 did some crazy aerobatics and his slipstream caught No. 3, who then dropped down and his slipstream played havoc with No. 4, and so it went all down the line until it got to yours truly. Instead of going through the target at 5,500 feet, I remember most vividly seeing 3,300 feet on the altimeter as we went through the target.

Flt Sgt Eric Baldwin, mid-upper gunner with Gummersall, was more concerned with enemy interference. He spotted an enemy fighter during the bombing run. Both he and the rear gunner opened fire. They observed hits and had at least damaged the fighter badly. In the meantime, with the slipstreaming problems and a need for a second run, the enemy anti-aircraft gunners were concentrating on their flight. On return to base they found that the plane had been considerably damaged by enemy fire but it landed safely.

A bomb aimer, Flt Sgt J.A. Tarran in 115 Squadron, had an unusual worry all the way to the target. The 4,000-lb bomb loaded on their plane was shaped in traditional bomb style and not like the 'blockbuster' modern ones which they had been using in raids on German targets. The consensus was that it was a bomb left over from the First World War, because in 1918 there was no plane able to carry it. Unstable ammunition was always a nagging fret in the minds of those whose buttocks were poised over a huge package of such a lethal mixture. A bomb now at least twenty-six years old was not a welcome partner on a day trip to the Dutch coast. Tarran was doubly delighted to operate the bomb release mechanism and pass the problem down to the enemy.

Flg Off George Meadon, piloting PB 487 in 149 Squadron, felt some satisfaction in the thought that when bombing an inert sea wall away from human habitation they were not, on 3 October, likely to injure any innocent people on the ground, which was always a concern for him. The crew on which Flg Off Donald Fenn of 166 Squadron was flying had more personal thoughts about the people on the ground. The parents of their pilot, Flg Off W.C. Kuyser, were Belgian and might be down there somewhere.

The sight of the breached dyke was unbelievable; from our height the very slow motion of the encroaching sea through the broken dyke made one feel for anybody left behind the dyke. The inward movement of the surging water was the most impressive scene in memory, although we wondered about the people who lived there. How many people, in their lives, have had to witness the flooding of a large area of low-lying land, and seen it happen from a height which made it all happen in filmic slow motion?

Flg Off Jerry Monk (630 Squadron) over Veere saw the sea wall 'standing out like a very thin long island'. Looking down on the 'Garden of Zeeland' he reflected, 'what a shame it was that so much hard work in land reclamation by an ally was being vandalized. I suppose it was a necessary part of things'. In a similar vein Sgt W. W. Burke (207 Squadron) had mixed feelings. The attack on the Dutch coast was a 'soft' target with no tough anti-aircraft fire before reaching the target. But 'I regretted the damage and pain which we were causing for our Allies as a consequence of smashing the dykes'. He had no such regrets when attacking targets in enemy country, for 'they more than deserved what they got'.

Damage and pain were indeed being suffered on the ground by the local residents: vast damage by sea flooding on fertile areas which, it was then thought, might take a generation to reclaim and rectify; sad stories of casualties, dead or permanently disabled. Maternity nurse Jo Theune was most disturbed about her mother, who was ill, and thought of taking shelter in the family's solidly built mill:

My father cut loose a few goats. He opened the doors to the [mill] basement and in the end there were forty-seven people in the mill. I put my mother in a wheelbarrow and brought her to the mill. I put a bucket of water close to the door. There were so many bombs exploding that my mother thought they were trying to bomb the mill. She asked me to bring her a mug of water because she didn't feel well.

I went to the bucket . . . when the mill cracked. It completely crashed. I couldn't reach my father and mother any more. Though I could hear them. I was struck by debris. Everything had come down, bales of corn, the millstones . . . you name it. Then the water came. The men who were trapped in the basement tasted the salt water and called out 'They are demolishing the dyke!'

The neighbourhood started with the rescue work. The men outside saw a little strand of my hair. They pulled on my coat, it was a strong coat. I said, 'Hurry up men, the water is rising.' By now the water had reached my neck. At the end they pulled me out. I was put on a door which served as a raft and was brought to the Zuidstraat.

After some time I was brought to my sister in Serooskerke. One of my brother-in-law's sons was there. His other son was killed in the mill. My brother-in-law said, 'Jo, you were born again.' Even when we were liberated I couldn't cheer. The [air] crews couldn't do any- thing about it. They were sent. When I was not at work I was worrying, why had my parents to die in such a terrible way?

One of the men who came to the rescue, or attempted rescue, at the mill never forgot the experience and did not wish to give his name. He remembered first of all the sky being 'illuminated by coloured balls. It was a so-called "Christmas tree", the bombing marker'. His father then commented 'It's getting serious'. After taking cover in a dry ditch they emerged to find bomb craters up to thirty metres in diameter. But by evening in Westkapelle water had reached the street and was squirting out of the sewers. A local water official, Bram Boone, was organising matters and sent this particular man and his brother to help at the mill of Theune.

We used a hand pump to pump the water out of the basement. It was a huge mess, the beams of the mill lay in it, heavy beams. The corpses were swollen and we grabbed them with our bare hands. I remember a father who stood beside me when we found his wife and two children in the basement. This man even helped us to recover their bodies. There never was any hard feelings with regard to the British crews. We looked at them as liberators.[11]

Altogether 159 residents of the village of Westkapelle lost their lives out of a total population of 2,369. Although air crew casualties were comparatively light on the day, some 120 crew members from the 252 Lancasters involved failed to survive the war. Jan Wigard of Middelburg was only ten during the battle but he well remembers five days and nights of almost incessant explosions either from air raids or from ground artillery explosions. The biggest bang in his young life occurred less than half a mile away from his home when a direct hit blew up a German ammunition ship and the ammunition store in the warehouse beside the ship.

Part of the reason for favourable local attitudes to the Allied bombing was the fact that on 17 May 1940 a German air and artillery bombardment needlessly wiped out the heart of the city of Middelburg, at a time when the small Dutch Army could do little other than surrender. Wigard also relates that only higher places in town and village centres were left habitable by the onrushing floods. Most rural people moved into Middelburg; its population rose from 20,000 to 40,000 in a day or two. In addition there were still 2,000 German soldiers in the locality, so that food and drinking water became almost unobtainable. The population tightened their belts, held their breath and waited.

One positive factor, which was important to the impressionable ten-year-old was to learn that macabre folk tales were often exaggerated. There was a local saying, which Jan believed, that 'if the dykes are broken, the sea water comes as high as the pointerplate of the "Lange Jan" tower in Middelburg'. The plate was forty metres off the ground. So when the flood waters gushed in Jan was terrified of being submerged. Fortunately, while immense damage to property was caused by the initial torrents dynamically driven by tide and gravity, the level of the waters when they settled was not much more than knee-high to a ten-year-old.[12]

Another ten-year-old, Willemina van Sluijs, came early to an undesired state of maturity and understanding of death. The Germans had dug some foxholes during exercises and Willemina's father dug another one alongside them so that the family could take refuge. They saw some wounded and terrified German soldiers running past the foxholes. One

German shouted, 'You must go to the tower. The water is coming'. The family chose to stay in their foxholes.

> Towards the end of the bombardment I noticed debris flying overhead. I thought it was from the dyke but it came from close by and was caused by the last bombs that exploded. These had fallen exactly where my grandfather, grandmother, their daughter, their other son and his wife and their two children had taken shelter. Besides them there was a cousin and her daughter and a maid who worked for my aunt. These people, ten in number, were all killed. We never blamed the Allies, rather the Germans. Because of them the bombardment was necessary.

One thoughtful Lancaster pilot, Fl Lt John Stratford of 166 Squadron, summed up succinctly the ambivalent reaction which many crew experienced to an extraordinarily successful operation which, if it had related to a target in Germany, would have generated wild capers of exhilaration in the air crew's mess at base on return.

> A point very much in my mind at the time . . . whilst a good breach was strategically a blow to the Germans, it was rather tragic for the hard pressed Dutch in that area. It was a contradictory target. No sense of elation on hitting it. I imagine there were [civilian] deaths too, but we wouldn't have been made aware of that, such is war.

New Zealander Flg Off Dick Robertshawe of 57 Squadron had similar thoughts as his crew set off on what was to be their last operation before changing squadrons.

> This was to be our last operation from East Kirby and the target was the sea wall at Rammekens. [Rammekens, almost contiguous to Flushing, was in an area much more thickly populated than the open coast around Westkapelle.] This was one operation which I had some regret as to what we were doing. The Dutch people had been invaded by the Germans and we were breaching the sea walls which the Dutch

had built. We went in very low. People could be seen running in the streets as we passed over Flushing.

The operation was not without its difficulties. While many early crews found good visibility the weather was temperamental. Lancaster NF 914 was able to bomb visually at 1514 hr, but cloud closed over the target so quickly that by the time the bombs had fallen from 7,000 feet the results were not visible. A following Lancaster LL 843 with a Polish crew received the 'abandon mission' signal at 1519 hr. Another Lancaster, JB 138, had 'orbited' for thirty-three minutes. Finding no break in the cloud it heard the 'abandon' signal, turned towards home and jettisoned its four 1,000-lb bombs at sea, sixty-five miles from Skegness.

The Lancaster on which Flt Sgt Jim Davies was crewing as engineer had its port outer engine blow up as it took off. The pilot, Canadian Flg Off Yaxley, at first intended to fly out to the North Sea from Wetheringham and jettison the bombs. Once over the North Sea they decided to push on and try to deliver the load at the appointed destination. They were encouraged when, with smoke trailing from the damaged engine, they saw some Dutch people waving to them. But:

As we crossed the Dutch coast on the return journey the port engine burst into flames. We were now aware that we may have to ditch in the North Sea and we were forced to issue a 'May Day' call. Within seconds there was a terrific bang, the port engine had seized, the reduction gear broke and the propeller spun freely on its axis. Fortunately the prop did not come off and we were able to limp back to base. We landed with a windmilling propeller which lasted about two hours after landing.

Lancaster LM 971's wireless operator, Flg Off Roy Hill of 207 Squadron, was called on to care for one of the RAF casualties. They had seen their bombs straddle the sea wall and had thought the anti-aircraft fire to be not as heavy as on their previous raids. It was in fact a near miss which riddled the mid-upper gun turret and wounded Sgt Jock Sweeney in the shoulder:

The navigator and I carried him on to the rest bed – he was unconscious. We administered morphia and applied dressings to the wound, but couldn't arrest the bleeding. After contacting base I spent the next hour in the mid-upper turret, with a gale blowing through the shattered perspex and never have I been so cold. On landing at Spilsby Jock was whisked away to hospital where he underwent surgery.

LM 971 had good fortune on that occasion and avoided the almost inevitable fate which lurked in wait in the skies. A few weeks later, over Heilbroon in early December, they were shot down by a German fighter ace, Friedrich-Karl Müller, his twenty-seventh victim. Three of the crew were killed, including the wounded Jock's replacement, while Roy Hill and the other three survivors spent the rest of the war as prisoners. However, on release they were flown back from *Stalag Luft* 1. Flying low, with no oxygen, 'I got a glimpse of Walcheren and was amazed at the watery devastation'.

While the air crews were breaching the sea walls and creating a new inland sea for the Navy to sail into, naval men were busy preparing their craft for the final Walcheren showdown. William H. Cheeney was a naval rating, posted to the SSEF group of support ships intended to supply close fire for the landing craft. He was sent to England to commission one of these small boats. They were of a simple wooden structure and were being made in carpenters' shops at boatyards in many different places. Cheeney's craft was being produced in a shed on the Barking Creek, and he had the unexpected pleasure of being billeted on his own at a friendly pub just across the road from the yard. A moment of calm before the storm.

Cheeney discovered that the craft was very small for a seagoing mission. It was ugly with a blunt nose and shallow front draft which would be ideal for moving in shallow water and beaching. It would be 120 feet long and able to mount quick-firing Oerlikon guns. Eventually it would accommodate a crew of fifteen. While Cheeney was concerned mainly with the twin engines he felt that the boat was somewhat fragile for a role at the front of the battle and at close range from the big guns which the enemy were expected to have available, even if some of them could be knocked out by prior bombing or distance shooting from British battleships. Cheeney's reservations would prove to be well founded.[13]

Petty Officer (Motor Mechanic) Basil Woolf was a veteran of seaborne landings in North Africa, Sicily, Italy and then Normandy. In September the SSEF, formed for the Normandy D-Day, was withdrawn to Poole for repairs and refitting. It was being prepared for another operation. A surprise for all was the appointment of a new officer, a full commander, RN, a very high rank for taking charge of a landing craft. The officer already held the DSC. He was an ex-rugby star named K.A. Sellar but known to all as 'Monkey'. What was he doing on such a tiny ship? They learned that he was to command their flotilla which was assembling in Ostend.

On 27 October the SSEF force arrived in Ostend. It was composed of six LCGs (gunships), six LCFs (anti-aircraft), six LCS (support craft firing Oerlikons) and five rocket craft, as well as other miscellaneous vessels. It was some encouragement to be told that ships with the biggest naval guns would support them, *Erebus*, *Warspite* and *Roberts*. However, Cdr Sellar was quickly to disillusion them, that this would not be 'a piece of cake' because, due to the weather, they would have no air back-up. Furthermore, he said, 'we were going in there even if it means with small arms!' On the chart-room walls had been pinned a series of aerial photographs showing that the dykes had been breached in two places, and that the 'flooding had possibly nullified some of the gun positions'.[14]

As the force set sail from Ostend early on 1 November, the weather was dull with low clouds and heavy seas. A gloomy prospect? That question arose in the minds of others not so nautically inclined. Frederick Weston was a Royal Marine commando who was seated in a Buffalo, which might be described as a steel box with an outboard motor in which infantry could be transported through the surf and up the beach. If his LCT (landing ship, tank) was sunk the Buffalo might float. Hardly a thought to lighten the gloom.[15]

Twenty-year-old Cpl Frank Himsworth was no sailor at all, although as a tank gunner-operator he had gone ashore from an LCT on the

Normandy beaches in June 1944. His unit was the 1st Lothian and Border Yeomanry of the 79th Armoured Division. He now commanded Bramble 5, a peculiar armoured vehicle which was nicknamed a 'Crab' but with no particular reference to crawling about on beaches. It was a Sherman tank with flail chains and rotor arms fixed on its front. These beat the ground and exploded mines to clear a path for the walking infantry. Shermans adapted to float and 'sail' on the sea did exist, but if the LCT sank, then Frank's Crab would sink with thirty or more tons of weight driving it down.

Before leaving Ostend the tank crew waterproofed the tank, simply covering or filling in any cracks or orifices up to track level, so that the huge vehicle could disembark in a certain level of water and waddle through the surf up to the beach. Once there it could, in addition to beating for mines, fire its 75-mm gun and two Browning m-gs.[16] Frank Himsworth, Frederick Weston, Basil Woolf and ex-rugby star Monkey Sellar were now ready for the kick off. Operation Infatuate!

CHAPTER EIGHT

Wet! Wetter!! Wettest!!!

'Have you looked between your toes lately, sir,' jested the cheeky little gunner, 'to see if any webbing has sprouted yet? Great weather for ducks, eh, sir?'

Capt George Blackburn could enter into the humour which replaced legitimate complaint as his poorly protected men sloshed around in everlasting floods. These were conditions possibly worse than the more publicised terrain horrors of the First World War. The flooded lands of the Belgian and Dutch sea coast were not considered to be fighting territory in 1914–18, but in 1944 soldiers were sailing them in weird vessels or wading deep, day after day. Fortunately the suffering was only for a few weeks, as against years in that earlier combat. But to the fighting soldier there was never a clear end in sight.

After weeks among the flooded fields, mud, mists and rain of South Beveland, you should be used to the bleak vistas of polder country in these bitter wet days of fall, but the sight of the grim, grey sea of mud into which the guns are ordered to deploy next to the shattered village is appalling. This must surely be the ultimate in miserable living conditions, which no human being should ever be asked to endure.[1]

Out where Basil Woolf was bringing his naval guns towards the battle area, the waters of the sea were even more icy and immediately dangerous than the floods in which the land guns wallowed. The sailors were ever too aware that their crafts were of matchbox strength opposed to the big naval guns on Walcheren. There was, however, expectation that the combination of RAF raids, battleship shells and Canadian artillery from the Breskens shore would have subdued the German naval guns still concreted into the narrow strips of sea wall remaining between the breaches.

At least Basil was a seaman, inured to some extent to the perils of the ocean. Frank Himsworth was a land soldier, cooped up in a 32-ton armoured steel monster called a Crab. And the Crab itself was aboard an LCT, a small, low vessel, which had precious little armour plating, could not defend itself in any way and was not the kind of boat in which to take a trip around the bay even on a calm summer's afternoon. For Frank, with no lifebelts issued, the trip from Ostend seemed as hazardous as the prospect of landing right under the snouts of those enemy guns.

Sellar's little SSEF flotilla sailed from Ostend at 0330 hr on 1 November. Together with the big ships *Erebus*, *Warspite* and *Roberts* they were to support the LCIs carrying Royal Marine commandos to the beach. But things were beginning to go wrong as Sellar directed his ships towards the surf. Basil Woolf was in the middle of the carnage.

About 8.15 am we approached the island under heavy fire from the Battleships. The Germans started to make smoke. The LCGs went into the beach, under withering fire, to engage some of the big batteries. The enemy shooting was fierce and was systematically hitting the small craft approaching the beach. One LCG was hit and on fire. A rocket ship was hit by a shell which caused her to pre-ignite her rockets; two other rocket craft in the smoke, believing this to be their signal to shoot, released their rockets, each rocket craft with twelve hundred rockets. This tremendous barrage landed amongst OUR craft as we had disappeared under a pall of smoke. For a few minutes I held my hands to my ears to deaden the awful sound. This was the most frightening moment of the whole landing.

We threw ourselves on the deck hoping to get out of the line of fire. My short life flashed before my eyes! Our First Lieutenant was killed by a piece of shrapnel that penetrated his steel helmet. Several craft were hit. All around us craft were burning, sinking and exploding. With the heavy fire from the shore we were being annihilated rapidly.

The LCGs were courageously taking on the shore guns, pouring 20-mm fire into the slits of the turrets. The LCIs had reached the gap in the dyke and had successfully landed the commandos.[2]

The concept of 20-mm (about three-quarters of an inch) calibre shells assaulting 14-inch calibre naval guns solidly set in concrete bunkers defies the imagination. It was not intended to be thus. It was not Sellar's fault, nor RN Capt Pugsey's, nor even Lt Gen Simonds's. The Navy had collaborated to traditional standards with its small craft, and the RAF had worked wonders on the delayed explosions inside the sea-wall foundations, yet at this vital moment of landing the senior and junior British services had, to use a nautical term, 'lost the plot'.

Simonds's master plan recognized that breaching the sea walls would not knock out all the big gun bunkers. He therefore relied on the combined power of battleships and the renewed onslaught of aeroplanes, directed on to the guns themselves, to clear the way for Sellar's 20-mm Oerlikons which were intended to be engaging enemy m-g nests and infantry slits. It is hard to avoid the thought that, to some extent, inter-service and inter-Allied rivalry had some influence on the failure of this crucial element of the commandos' disembarkation.

HMS *Warspite* had arrived only in time to chime in with the LCGs, although it was intended that the capital ship should undertake a prior bombardment of the German guns with the objective of knocking them out before the commando assault. In any case, one of the battleships turrets, excessively used off the Normandy coast, was out of action. Some of the guns on *Erebus* had been put out of action in the Normandy assault and had not yet been repaired. *Roberts* could not approach for fear of mines. The spotter planes on which the naval gunners relied had been grounded by fog in England and no alternative arrangement had been made. The naval gunners had to guess, hit and miss, through the all-pervading smoke.[3]

Simonds had no authority over senior air officers and could only make requests. His requirements should have been reinforced by the highest commanders. Unfortunately two senior air officers were positively rude in their denial of support to take out the guns. Bomber Command's

Harris boasted that he could 'capture Walcheren with his batman after all the bombs that had been dropped on it' and refused to bomb the guns themselves. Tedder, whose authority was second only to Eisenhower, also vetoed the bombing, saying that there was only 'a part-worn battery' left. He excused himself by accusing the Canadians of being 'drugged with bombs', implying that their infantry was afraid to move until all enemy targets had been wiped out.[4] Sellar, Woolf, Himsworth and the rest paid the cost.

Basil Woolf was already collecting up evidence of that cost as his ship continued miraculously to survive:

We started to pick up wounded and dead men from the sea. Our well deck was crammed with wounded. Our Doctor was crying as he had exhausted his medical supplies and the hospital ship was anchored a few miles out to sea. We met the hospital ship and transferred the wounded. As we made our way back to the beaches there was a tremendous explosion. We had been hit on our port bow just above the water line. I was in the engine room. The ship veered over to starboard. Cdr Sellar called me and asked if the engines were OK. I replied 'Yes'. He shouted 'For God's sake keep them running and get a damage control up here to the bow'.

The hole was, luckily, just above sea level. We used plywood and all the hammocks we could find to plug the hole, and shored the repair with lumber, while the enemy guns continued to shower us with water from near misses. A fuel tank was ruptured. Diesel fuel about twelve inches deep was slopping dangerously about in the Skipper's cabin area. We arranged a bucket brigade. I ran back to the engine room, looked at our blueprints to find the valve location for a pump out, and then started to pump the fuel overboard. As we pumped, I looked out above deck and could not believe my eyes. Except for us our force was completely wiped out. But the shore guns had been quietened one by one.

The heroic action of SSEF inspired praise and wonder in the minds of journalists who had accompanied the flotilla. One of them, Dennis

Johnstone, was on Basil Woolf's ship, LCH (HQ) 269. He broadcast his impressions in a BBC programme the next day, 2 November:

> In front of us the dawn came up behind the lighthouse tower of West Kapelle. As it got lighter this armada of small craft drew slowly in towards the coast. Our ship was leading. . . . I don't think they saw us for some time. The dawn was behind them and we were backed up by a long line of scudding rain clouds. But as it became daylight the assault craft moved up from behind and passed through, heading for a big gap in the Dyke covering.
>
> There was no question they saw us then. The shells came whining overhead, falling into the water with great plumes of spray. The Royal Marine Commandos [in assault craft] fanned out behind the gap and leapt ashore. The enemy put up a smoke screen. Presently this was added to by smoke from a fire in the lighthouse itself. It was hard to tell what was going on. The reports from shore were good but the men at sea were having a very rough time. They seemed to be presenting sitting targets . . . here and there we watched them being hit, pouring out smoke from their sterns . . . while the little motor boats dashed through and picked up the crews.[5]

The newspapers, whose journalists had time to sharpen their pencils, were even more dramatic. The *Daily Mirror* on 3 November described it as:

> Running unflinchingly and directly into the fire of the mighty German shore batteries, small, thin-hulled British amphibious support vessels fought a fight the like of which sailors who were at Dieppe or Normandy had never seen before. There were heavy losses. The little ships kept their guns hot until they went down or were forced to retire with holes in their sides and bleeding men on their decks.
>
> The German guns opened up. Suddenly fire belched aboard one craft, she swung around in the water, another got a direct hit, and another raced into shore with all her guns firing, and turned out again with a single officer left on her bridge and holes torn in her side. The

Headquarters ship LCH 269 was nearly blown out of the water three times. It was a fight that lasted five hours. . . . The Commandos . . . cut open the gun positions with flame throwers and grenades.

Not to be outdone, the *Daily Mail* reported that 'after inadequate preparation the little craft of the Close Support Squadron, outranged and outgunned, forced their way inshore. . . . Those craft which survived long enough to get within range shot it out with the coastal batteries and succeeded in silencing many of them'. The casualty toll of the SSEF in that report was given as 172 killed and 200 wounded, although in total 280 men of the Royal Navy lost their lives. The *Daily Mail* quoted Gen Eisenhower as saying that this operation was 'one of the most gallant of the war. It was in the true "little ship" tradition'.

Frederick Weston, with 41 Commando, was suffering in the ungainly, wallowing Buffalo which appeared to be surrendering to the lashing waves again and again. However, the worth of the vehicle was evident as it changed from fish to animal, its tracks latched on to the beach, and, with the marines ducking behind its iron bulwarks, it roared through the worst of the gunfire. Orders were given: 'Debus!' Jumping out, the men found themselves already in a village street. Ahead was a strong point located in the solid base of the lighthouse. The marines ran to orders and mustered in a house which was partly destroyed and waterlogged. Halting to take a deep breath they were astonished to find some 'old hands' already there. And brewing tea.[6]

As A Troop of the Commando came in to attack they saw a rocket ship blow up, and 'the sea boiling with explosions'. Although they drove on to 'dry land' they found the street beyond the beach mainly under water. The street was dominated by the lighthouse and apart from the post in the base the Germans were firing from the top of the lighthouse and dropping grenades as the marines appeared.

Bill Sloley, in command of P Troop, found that the enemy strong points 'were like forts, or castles several storeys high, linked by tunnels'. His impressions of the attack related to the constant loss of casualties, all good friends. 'Brind Sheridan was killed attacking one strongpost, and Peter Heydon was killed attacking another – a sniper got him. Marine

Moses went out to help him and got killed as well. . . . A lot of 48 Commando were killed when one of their Buffaloes went over a mine'.[7]

Buffaloes, Crabs, bulldozers and other 'funnies' were provided by 79th Armoured Division whose records spelled out the cost of the landing.

> Two Buffaloes loaded with ammunition were burning fiercely; in fact the beach was covered in smashed and burning vehicles and casualties were mounting. . . . Fifteen Buffaloes were put out of action in landing or on the beaches. Little difficulty was experienced with obstacles; stakes on dykes were easily snapped off and 'hedgehogs' mostly avoided. In places large stones were encountered and vehicles trying to avoid them became bogged. Many vehicle casualties were caused by mines and shelling . . . it was an unpleasant job as the seas were running high and shelling persistent.

Frederick Weston's party had little time to drink their tea before they were ordered out to attack the lighthouse. They charged along the street, firing almost wildly to keep the enemy heads down. CSM Stokell blew the door in with a PIAT bomb. The troop commander, Capt Sheridan, was first in and fell dead to the last shots. A brief moment later the enemy in the strong point were all surrendering. Weston could only ponder that 'it was one of those damn things where they were thinking of giving themselves up and then somebody decided not to'.

Weston had no chance of further reflection for they were ordered to do a circuit of the remaining sea-wall rim. This entailed a forced march and careful negotiation of a vast crater left by bombing and partial collapse of the wall. Weston had been suffering from dysentery but refused to fall out. In his unavoidably soiled condition he was the recipient of a number of curses from near neighbours 'for it was not very palatable to my mates'.

The Commandos landing at Walcheren, numbers 41, 47 and 48, were ostensibly British but with quite an infusion of other nationalities, especially South Africans. The medical support was provided by Canadian medical teams. Major John Hillsman was an American who had renounced his citizenship in order to join the Canadian Army before

Pearl Harbour. He was in the first group to land on the Walcheren sea wall and was immediately called upon for aid. Many casualties suffered from burns as their vessels or vehicles were set on fire. During that day Hillsman and his team treated over 150 casualties.

To make their task worse, next day three Buffaloes loaded down with ammunition were hit, set on fire and engulfed in a seemingly endless series of spontaneous explosions, wounding both British and Germans. Hillsman and his transfusion medic, Capt Lou Ptak, crawled on their bellies, while the exploding ammunition sprayed shrapnel over their bodies. He wrote that 'we lay on our faces in the sand, dressing wounds, stopping haemorrhages, and splinting fractures. That task completed, things became, if anything, even worse as a gale blew up while we were operating in a small totally exposed tent'. In a space of six feet by nine with a medical team of five men, when Hillsman needed to change from one side of the patient to the other he had to crawl under the operating table.[8]

Frank Himsworth and his crew, having fired at the church tower which was a hide for German snipers, settled down in their tank (which had no night sights) in the street and hoped for a little sleep. The driver complained that his feet were cold and wet, a statement which seemed a little unnecessary in the wettest of battles. Frank decided to investigate and found that the waterproofing of the tank had been damaged during the landing, the engine had become flooded, and the vehicle was out of action for the time being.

Walcheren was no place for idle hands so Frank and his crew busied themselves loading ammunition and other supplies into Buffaloes which were running through the gaps in the dyke and supplying troops around the new inland sea. One Buffalo sank into the soft sand and came into contact with a mine which exploded under its track. Frank was blown bodily into the air. As sometimes happened so close to the root of an explosion he was not wounded by the mine itself but was badly injured with broken bones by the fall. Medics strapped him up and put him aboard a Buffalo which was returning to Breskens. Frank was tied into two lifebelts as he would not be able to swim. His vicissitudes had not yet ended. As his Buffalo came into its destination in Breskens it crashed into the breakwater, spinning around several times before deciding not to sink.[9]

As so often happened, the Germans yielded one strong point after another but did not immediately break and run. For five days heroic feats were required of the attacking Marines. As they landed on or behind Walcheren sea wall, 41 Commando went left towards the village of Domburg, 48 Commando turned right towards Zoutelande, and 47 Commando followed in the steps of 48 in order to pass through and continue to Flushing, where they would link with the disembarkation in that area.

On the afternoon of 5 November Cpl Frank Nightingale of Y Troop, who had been wounded on D-Day, was still involved in subduing coastal batteries near Domburg. Battery W.18 was occupied by 200 enemy soldiers. Nightingale's citation for the award of the DCM described the action.

During the fighting in the battery, Cpl Nightingale was forward with his section officer and one other marine. They were heavily engaged by enemy m-g and rifle fire from the surrounding woods. The marine was killed and the officer [Lt Holmes] seriously wounded. Cpl Nightingale attempted to carry on the fire-fight with his bren gun but this fired only a few rounds and stopped. Cpl Nightingale seized a captured German MB 34 and continued to fire this until the enemy was forced to withdraw.

After a while the enemy counter-attacked in a determined manner but Cpl Nightingale once again drove them to ground and alone held on to this flank until the remnants of his section were able to advance and join him. Through this NCO's personal disregard for safety, and his determination to kill the enemy, the troop was able to hold on to the position.

Simultaneously with the seaborne assault on Walcheren the port of Flushing was being attacked in a similar amphibious operation. The main difference between these two elements of Operation Infatuate was that the Flushing attack was mounted across the Scheldt from the

Breskens area. As the mouth of the river was thickly mined no help could be anticipated from large warships. On the other hand the objectives of the Flushing assault were within range of the 'land mattress', the barrage of massed heavy rockets.

Off Breskens, PO William H. Cheeney was, like Basil Woolf, at the mercy of high tides and big guns in one of the frail support ships. Twenty-five of those small craft set out with the fleet of Buffaloes inside the smoke corridor across the Scheldt, which at that point had all the appearance and propensities of open sea. They had been warned that there would be no air support because of the weather. Also, because the estuary had been mined, they could not expect close aid from the battleships. The 14-inch guns of the capital ships could reach Flushing but would be shooting blind and with even more guesswork than against the Walcheren sea wall.

Cheeney's group made several runs to support the waves of infantry. As one after another of the small craft staggered under the impact of enemy fire, burst into flame and sank, Cheeney became aware that the Germans were firing intelligently. They did not waste shot and shell while the narrow bows of the craft were pointed directly at the beaches. The support craft had to turn in order to make the run back to Breskens and at that point, as they became beam on, the Germans raked the target which was several times longer than during the approach. Sixteen of the twenty-five ships were sunk.[10]

The assault on Flushing was allotted to no. 4 (Army) Commando Group, which would be followed by men of the newly arrived 52nd (Lowland) Division. The first men ashore landed on a refuse dump code-named Uncle Beach where their progress was partially hindered by defensive stakes driven into the ground. However, that shore was within range of more than 300 Allied guns from the Breskens area, as well as the land mattress of rockets. The Germans avoided losing heavy casualties on the open water front and waited for the Commandos and the 4th King's Own Scottish Borderers (KOSB) in the streets of the town.

Commando Capt E.L.K.A. Carr, known to all as Knyvet, commanded the mortar section. As his landing craft came into the beach it struck a mine and sank. The beach was under heavy crossfire, urging everyone to run for the comparative shelter of the nearest houses. Knyvet got his half-drowned men to some kind of safety and then went back through the bullets to the wrecked craft. He had the mortars set up, directed their fire and went to contact his machine-gun section colleague to coordinate action. When that colleague was wounded Knyvet commanded the two sections for twenty-four hours, during much of which they were cut off from the main body.

Major Myers, commanding Knyvet's Commando, was of the opinion that 'Knyvet's Military Cross was one of the best MCs the unit has ever won. Into the overturned craft a German m-g poured a continuous stream of bullets but Knyvet quite unconcerned continued to salvage the mortars and help pile them ashore'.[11] If it be queried how a man could survive such a hail of bullets, the answer might be in the fact that although the German Spandau m-gs fired more than twice as rapidly as Allied equivalents, this seemed to affect the accuracy to some extent. Also the Allied shell and rocket fire would cause even the most intrepid of enemy gunners to keep their heads down and fire in a general direction rather than aiming precisely.

After several runs across the water Cheeney's luck had at last evaporated. As they turned to starboard away from the beach they were hit on the port side by an armour-piercing shot which bored into their wing petrol tanks. Normally they carried 4,000 gallons of high octane petrol in eight tanks, a sure prescription for a violent explosion. However, before leaving Ostend originally they had been recommended to pump out the petrol from the exposed tanks and fill them with sea water. So the AP shot did not cause a petrol explosion. The friction of its passage through the wooden planks did set them on fire, which quickly began to rage through the entire vessel.

They started to abandon ship but the weather was very rough and they could see people from other sunk ships drowning in the heavy waves. Cheeney managed to get one engine started. At the vital moment Lt Tiplady, RN, steered his craft alongside. Tiplady's crew hooked on and rigged a fire-fighting pump from their own ship to supplement the hose on Cheeney's vessel. With both wooden craft in considerable danger and still under gunfire, the two crews managed to quench the flames. Tiplady's ship then guided them back into safer waters, an act of bravery on the part of all Tiplady's men greatly appreciated by Cheeney's pals. Several of the nine surviving craft were like their boat, battered and charred, and might well have foundered if they had been in the open sea and not within reach of the safe harbour at Breskens.

Another small craft, an LCA (auxiliary) smoke layer, had been maintaining the wavering smoke corridor across the Scheldt. The German fired blind into the smoke but with minimum effect. But at about 1600 hrs a chance shot holed the LCA and it quickly sank. At that moment it happened to be at the Breskens end of its regular beat and the entire crew was able to swim ashore. This was fortunate for the water was icy cold and some other survivors from sunk craft, endeavouring to swim to safety of a beach or another craft, had succumbed to the cold, become paralysed and drowned.

The smoke screen had served its purpose and was then closed down, allowing it to drift whither the elements might dictate.[12]

On the far shore the British had returned to the Britannia Hotel after five years' absence, but not as holiday tourists. The Commandos and the KOSBs (these latter being newly inducted into front-line warfare) now found themselves in 'a dirty, bloody fight . . . hour upon hour of crawling over rooftops, edging down narrow alleys and back gardens, even "mouse-holing", blasting holes through walls of houses', and yet in a 'macabre sort of carnival atmosphere. The more courageous civilians ventured out to see their streets liberated'.[13]

Apart from the normal hazards of street fighting the attackers faced two less usual problems. Snipers had nested in the tops of cranes and gantries at the docks. And the Britannia Hotel stood like a huge fortress high above the flood waters, with a 20-mm quick-firing gun located on its flat roof dominating the landscape. The Scots had been trained as a mountain division and still had some of their original equipment with them. This included a portable mountain gun of quite large 3.7-inch calibre. They hauled this in parts up to the top floor of a tall Dutch house, reassembled it and, having dislodged the first sniper, kept on firing until the weight of the gun caused the attic floor to collapse.

The hotel was a more costly affair as the Royal Scots Fusiliers attacked on 3 November. Two coy commanders were killed and the battalion commander, Lt-Col Melville, wounded. The intense fighting, now hand-to-hand, set the building on fire, and junior commanders led the rush into the hotel which was also the German HQ. Three lieutenants, smashing their way into the hotel's vast cellars, found that they contained a bomb-proof shelter. And in the cellar huddled several hundred enemy, all ready to surrender, and, no doubt, in the case of those who belonged to the White Bread units, their barely cured stomach complaints suffering substantial relapse at that point.

The battle had been frantic and at least one Scottish officer blessed the hard training which his lads had undergone in Scotland. Professor D.C. Simpson, then of the Highland Light Infantry, remembered thinking:

Thank goodness I really put my boys through what fire is like. We used to go up on the moors of Glamis and we used to have live firing on the moors, which was totally illegal, and we set the moors on fire by mistake. But, as a result, the Jocks all knew what gunfire was like. And were familiar with the sounds of mortars. We used to do a lot of smoke mortaring which is what set the moors on fire.[14]

The joyous citizens, knowing little of the hard facts of warfare, had been in continual danger for three days. Snipers, hidden, camouflaged and virtually invisible were firing smokeless ammunition from any high point and the Jocks were responding by spraying suspect areas with generous amounts of bullets and mortar bombs. At one house a figure appeared momentarily in an upstairs window. Bursts of fire riddled the figure before the Jocks realised it was a woman, most probably a curious civilian. Throughout the three days it was impossible to provide shelter for the wounded who had to lie out in the bitter cold, lashed by icy sea spray, while the unwieldy Buffaloes and tiny wooden craft battled with an ever more hostile storm wind, which was sending waves crashing inshore to fling the rescue vessels sideways-on against the sloping beach.[15]

The third element of Operation Infatuate required an east to west attack from the direction of Woensdrecht and the causeway. This would menace the main city of Middelburg and prevent the enemy from drawing reserves out of the area to reinforce Walcheren and Flushing. This part of the operation had to commence some days before the Walcheren landing. In fact it was almost a continuous advance from Merxem to Woensdrecht and then on to Goes.

In 1944 Walcheren was more properly an island than in modern times. It was cut off from South Beveland by the Sloe Channel, now mainly drained and narrowed into Sloehaven and Quarleshaven. In 1944 there was just the single causeway through the channel which linked the two districts. Thus the attack from the east could be both by land along the causeway and by water across another part of the channel. The Canadian infantry would continue their relentless march but the fresh units of the 52nd Division were being ferried to their reinforcement and eventual supersession.

But before this the Canadians had to fight their way across South Beveland itself. While the Germans were willing to make tactical retreats they required strong pressure, with casualties, on each resistance point before moving back to the next. Once again the Canadian 5th Brigade advanced across featureless country through tiny meaningless centres of population.

The Maisonneuves waded through flooded fields to set up a successful pincer attack on Kloetinge as the only road was covered by an enemy battery of five 40-mm guns. One 'Maisie' was killed. The battalion witnessed the unusual sight of the local people wearing traditional costume, gathering around a quickly dug grave in the local cemetery, which was still in the front line, while the padre, Hon. Capt Marchand, buried the soldier in the course of a brief but emotional religious service. The more usual procedure was to wrap the body in a blanket and leave it for later impersonal disposal.

The Black Watch carriers had driven into Goes, where orange flags were already flying everywhere. To the south the Essex Scots had forced their way through Nieudijk to the farthest western edge of Beveland. At this point the advance ran into the awesome enemy defences at the start of the Walcheren causeway. The Royal Regiment of Canada was pushed through the Essex Scots to take over the charge.

Sgt W.R. Bennett with the intelligence section of the Royals studied what confronted them: mud, rain, exposure and booby-traps in the dark, to say nothing of tank guns firing at long range straight along the causeway.

The Causeway, 1,000 yards long, 100 feet wide and perched atop a dyke 15 feet high, with swampy reed mud-flats on both sides, negating the possibility of an amphibious crossing. The Causeway carried simply a single track rail-line, the main road and a bicycle track. The fields [at either end], called polders, liberally serviced with irrigation ditches, were divided and protected by dykes about 15 feet high, some with secondary roads atop. Anyone on top of a dyke could see for miles. Many roadways were mined and booby-trapped. Days of rain had made travelling soggy. Going into this action, the Regiment was near half strength.[16]

Checking reports from his intelligence section and viewing for himself, Lt Col Lendrum might have considered this a true 'mission impossible'. At the beginning of the causeway itself the Germans had constructed a strong point with barbed wire, mines in the ground, booby-traps on wire, doors and fences. Out of concrete shelters 200 enemy soldiers wielded flak and artillery guns, well-sited m-gs and an unending supply of mortar bombs and hand grenades.

The Royals were now old soldiers and attacked in small groups of a section or platoon, at that day's strength about seven or eight men to the section and perhaps twenty to the platoon. They advanced at 0200 hr on 31 October, working along ditches and gulleys or water-worn creases in the ground, squirming through liquid mud and flood water, hiding their movements by immersing themselves almost totally. No brave, reckless wave of attackers racing as pin-point targets over the fields. As a strong point opened up Lt Maurice Berry crawled alone up to the gun slits and lobbed grenades inside. Lt Alan Gillespie dragged a flame thrower up to another strong point and silenced that. Then, as more Royals found their way forward, there was a sudden, short rush and the garrison capitulated. Berry and Gillespie both won the MC.

As the Black Watch came up to relieve the Royals, the Germans counter-attacked along the causeway but were driven off. Among the casualties of the Royals was B42737 Pte Joseph T. Perry, wounded in Normandy on 12 August, wounded again near the Seine on 30 August, and wounded for the third time now in South Beveland. Statistics can never tell the entire story.

It was time now (31 October) to cross the causeway, fan out, attack Middelburg, and distract the enemy from Westkapelle and Flushing. The Calgarys, who had some men trained for amphibious work, were ordered to cross the channel alongside the causeway while other troops probed across the causeway itself. The Canadians had expected the new Scottish division to arrive by now but they were still 'on the way'. To compound the problems, engineers surveying the channel and its apparently adequate waters found that 'there was not sufficient water even at high tide to permit such an operation . . . the ground was too saturated for movement on foot and there were too many runnels in the mud flats to permit "Weasels" to operate'.[17]

Rapidly the Calgarys were switched to an attack straight over the Causeway where the Germans themselves had formed more defences. An artillery barrage, lifting fifty yards every two minutes, saturated the narrow link and allowed the Calgarys to fight forward to the far end of the causeway. But a more distant high-velocity gun was still firing straight down the road and proved difficult to locate in the dawn light. German response was typical, officers fell in combat and the forward troops were under tremendous strain. They were inspired and emboldened by their popular young colonel, Ross Ellis, who, 'freshly shaven, neatly dressed, and apparently calm and good humoured', walked unscathed around the besieged front positions. Maj Hees, a staff officer, and Capt Newman, the artillery FOO, volunteered to take the place of evacuated officers, as A Coy was left with only one officer, Capt Wynn Lasher, who was already wounded.

As the Maisies hurried along the causeway to reinforce their comrades, the 52nd Division artillery opened up for the first time, but in the confusion the first shells fell 300 yards short, hitting both Maisies and Calgarys. At the outset the lead coy of the Maisies numbered only forty men but that included people like the inimitable Lt Charlie Forbes and his comrade-in-arms, Lt Guy de Merlis. For eight hours they held off furious German counter-attacks. When a 20-mm gun became a nuisance a signaller, Pte J.C. Carriere, volunteered to deal with it. He crawled four hundred yards along a flooded, shallow ditch, dragging a PIAT, in order to get near enough to knock out the gun. He was wounded but survived.[18]

The condition of the survivors can be understood from the description of Lt William J. Smith, who came up that day to replace Lt Stewart of the Calgarys, killed on the causeway:

It was a battered, depleted Platoon I took over. They had been in hard fighting from the time the push to clear the Scheldt estuary first started. I was addled with a legacy of nine 'ghosts', men who should have been with me but were unaccounted for. I was able to report very few facts and those I could were painful. I was accompanied by two other 'new' Lieutenants. Brown was killed, shot in the kidneys by a sniper. Doakes died of diphtheria in a hospital somewhere in the Netherlands. I was wounded on patrol in December.

On the Causeway facing the 5th Brigade were dug-in fixed-fire machine guns and Oerlikon rapid-firing 20-mm anti-aircraft cannons, the belts of which carried cartridges in a fixed order of 1 armour-piercing shell, 1 high explosive shell and 1 tracer. The troops of 5th Brigade had no advance knowledge of this lethal mix but they soon knew what they were facing. It took a high calibre of men to run the gauntlet of the withering fire in such an exposed situation. It's not surprising that the infantryman's unofficial motto was 'It ain't our business to die for our country; our job is to make the other guy die for his country!'[19]

In their odyssey from the Glamis moors to the Beveland swamps, the HLI had found themselves in the unfamiliar Buffaloes, which D.C. Simpson thought 'seemed rather safe because they were very low in the water'. They crossed a rather anonymous sheet of water and found themselves in a little orchard among three farms. There they were pinned down by their first taste of close enemy small-arms fire.

There was a machine gun with a very high rate of fire but it was very inaccurate, but it could kill anyone in a great big cone right across this field where we were pinned down. We were in an angle of the dyke, so I got up on the dyke with one of my Bren gunners. I asked him to fire so that when the German responded I could see where it was coming from. The second time I asked my gunner to fire, he didn't. I looked round and he had a hole in the centre of his forehead. I was quite shaken because our heads were really side by side.[20]

Cpl R. White was with the 52nd Division's Glasgow Highlanders and after moving up on 1 November jotted down some impressions, commencing from dawn on the next day.

'D' coy line up below embankment. Move up embankment. Meet some Canadians coming down. Pass each other in silence. [Some Canadian thought that 52nd Division had delayed and left them with the hardest tasks.] Reach causeway. See our first dead soldiers. Heavy machine-gun-tracer fire from Germans. Move slowly from shell hole to shell hole amidst an avalanche of fire from artillery firing over open sights. My folding bicycle thrown away in the confusion. Our medium machine-gun is targeted and expertly destroyed by enemy. Stalemate!

Rocket firing Typhoon fighter bombers give us some respite as we continue slow advance. At one stage our line breaks due to a panicky young lieutenant. When the rocket Typhoon went in to strafe the Company Commander suddenly shouted 'Forward "D" Company'. I immediately jumped out of the shell hole I was sharing with 2 NCOs and ran behind the O.C. It was a 2-man attack only. I remember the amused looks as I advanced passing hole after hole of sheltering infantry. 'Tired of living?' they shouted.

Still at daylight the first enemy prisoners come streaming down. The Germans machine gun their own surrendering comrades. Shouting, with their hands in the air, they present an amazing bloodstained crowd a few feet from our positions on their way to the rear.[21]

Fortunately two Royal Engineers had discovered a place in the channel well south of the causeway where it was possible to wade through the low water and over mud. Another fresh battalion, 6th Cameronians, guided by white tapes laid by the sappers, crossed in single file. The mud and sand were treacherous, but all crossed without casualties. They had thus outflanked the causeway and were on a serviceable road to Middelburg.

The guns now concentrated to shepherd the infantry into Middelburg. It was at this juncture that ten-year-old Jan Wigard heard the big BANG as the ammo ship and warehouse went up in one huge imitation of the world's worst thunderstorm. The guns were firing from three directions and there was some later competition for the distinction of which gun hit the ship. *Warspite* put in a claim although it was standing out to sea off the other end of the island. In later days Jan Wigard and other enthusiasts researched fragments from the battle and awarded the honour to the Canadian guns around Breskens.[22]

Another event impressed Wigard even more than the big bang. On 6 November, as the KOSBs were entering the town, a group of German prisoners was being herded in front of them, hands held high. Three yards away from Jan, one of the prisoners in a very tired gesture lowered his hands. He was immediately shot dead by a guard. At the time the Dutch lad was elated as he had been taught that 'the best German is a dead German'. In later years Jan was saddened by the memory of the dead man's unfortunate and unintentional lapse. 'Did he have parents? A wife and children? Was he buried in a mass anonymous grave?' After research he was able to identify the shot man as Willy Paugstad, a conscripted lawyer's clerk from East Prussia. He also found Paugstad's grave and was able to send photographs to Paugstad's brother, the only surviving relative from the war.

The epidemic of surrender was now affecting the German survivors on Walcheren, surrounded as they were. The KOSBs and Royal Scots found Middelburg largely flooded, and in many streets the civilians had taken refuge in the third or fourth storeys of their houses. It fell to a Royal Scots lieutenant to encounter the garrison commander, Lt Gen Daser. But when the general heard the rank of the only officer in the vicinity he refused to surrender until a senior British officer should approach him. The Scots subaltern went away, borrowed some extra 'pips', promoted himself to full colonel (acting, temporary, unpaid) and was delighted to find that Daser felt his dignity to be thus preserved. Middelburg garrison capitulated.[23]

Among the prisoners emerging from the old Britannia Hotel in Flushing was a dishevelled Col Reinhardt, the commander, looking anything else but commanding. He was in great distress as a Commando officer tried to interrogate him:

He was far too upset by his recent experiences to be coherent about anything. . . . During the interview he both wept and urinated freely. . . . His adjutant gave the impression of being a somnambulist, so utterly dazed was he after the bombardment. He was shaking violently and uncontrollably and when he did speak he poured out curses at the destruction wrought by water everywhere on the island. They had been mentally disoriented by the horrors endured as targets of the massed rockets [of the land mattress] which they could not identify and to which they did not know how to respond.[24]

About the same time the 8th Canadian Reconnaissance Regiment, roaming freely across South Beveland, reached its northern limit and found themselves opposite North Beveland with no enemy in evidence. Their Lt Col Alway promptly commandeered a long barge and some fishing boats tied up at the ferry station. He boarded a small force, including a group of members of the Dutch Resistance.

They first captured a German hospital ship and then dashed for Kamperland, the main town. With some insolence they demanded the surrender of the enemy commander. He was not disposed to comply. Suddenly a squadron of Typhoon rocket planes appeared and swooped over the town. The German commander frantically waved a white flag. He was not to know that the Typhoons were actually destined for Walcheren. Alway and his men took nearly four hundred prisoners with no casualties at all among themselves.[25]

The BBC's Dennis Johnston was now on his way home in the one remaining small craft from Walcheren 'with a hole in our bow as big as a window' and 'carrying the casualties of three or four other craft'. He saw a young naval lieutenant fall into a deep sleep from which he could not be awakened immediately. After fifteen hours defying the enemy guns and picking up survivors from the sea, his own ship was sunk. He was heard to say that he had 'enjoyed' Dunkirk a great deal better.[26] And on a noticeboard near the bunk was a cutting which read 'Stop purring. The War isn't won yet.'

Casualties were high, unnecessarily so. But many of those who were there, like Whitaker and Blackburn, exonerated Simonds from any blame. The artillery man considered that

A disaster equalling Dieppe might have occurred without Lt-Gen Guy Simonds's insistence on Bomber Command opening up four great gaps in the saucer-like outer rim of the island, thereby letting in the sea and rip tides and forcing friend and foe to take refuge on scanty high ground or in upper storeys, reducing German mobility and cutting his supply lines.

A major worry for the Canadians at this time was the number and condition of psychiatric cases being invalided back to British hospitals. Dr Robert Gregory of the Canadian 3rd Infantry Division noted that in October 90 per cent of these cases were men who had been in action for more than three months. He thought morale might be cracking. There was 'lack of volition to carry on. The foremost cause of this seemed to be futility. The men claimed there was nothing to which to look forward. . . . The only way one could get out of battle was death, wounds, self-inflicted wounds and going nuts'.

Many other observers had been worried about the reaction of the local Dutch people to the massive damage caused by flooding, with sea water soaking into polders laboriously reclaimed over many generations. Many advancing troops anticipated some kind of animosity from the distressed gardeners of Zeeland. They were surprised and delighted, if a little chastened, to be treated unreservedly as victorious liberators.

Marine Capt Dan Flunder noted a particularly extreme example of forgiving and forgetting. They had found a farmer and his wife dead in the ruins of the farmhouse where the troop was to spend the night. During the night they were awakened by two young sons of the dead people. The lads had waded five miles through the floods to look for their kin. Together they made the bodies presentable until they could be collected for burial. The sons waded back in the dark. Next morning the two appeared again, this time carrying a sack of bread which they had collected from neighbours in Middelburg, having noticed that the marines were hungry and short of supplies.[27]

The 'funny' vehicles of Maj Gen Stobart's specialist 79th Armoured Division had been more than ever invaluable in the unusual conditions of battle, and the division had paid a material price, in addition to four officers and fifty-nine OR casualties.

Out of 10 flails sent in, 6 had sunk. Out of 8 AVREs used, 4 sank and 2 went up on mines. Out of the 4 bulldozers used, 2 were lost. Out of 104 Buffaloes employed, 27 were immediately sunk or destroyed. At the end of Operation Infatuate, the remaining 77 Buffaloes had to be written off as mechanically unfit and not repairable, due to the extraordinarily hazardous conditions encountered.[28]

Basil Woolf had breathed a sigh of relief, having survived the day of the Walcheren assault. He was to be disillusioned. That night they were attacked out at sea by one-man submarines, scuba divers and E boats. Some of the few surviving small craft were sunk. Only the hospital ship and Basil's LCH 269 remained, although some badly damaged craft had managed to limp back to Ostend. LCH 269 set off for home with the hospital ship to starboard. The rough seas drove the ships too far inland. An enormous explosion told that the hospital ship had hit a mine. Woolf saw it break in half and sink within minutes. There were no survivors.

Eventually the LCH crept lamely into Poole harbour, the only one of the small craft to come home. Cdr Sellar was convinced that they had been deliberately sent on a suicide mission 'to keep the Germans busy'. After all that, Basil Woolf was not impressed when, as they approached Poole, the skipper chose to play over the loud hailer the only record which he had, the song 'Tiptoe through the Tulips'. There had been no Dutch spring tulips in the Garden of Zeeland, desecrated by sea water, high explosive and decaying corpses.[29]

CHAPTER NINE

More Arrows on the Map

'I was tied by the wrist with wire attached to the next sentry. All twelve
sentries were attached by wire. The sergeant held the loose ends. This
was to prevent the sentries from deserting in the night.' So admitted a
German prisoner of war.[1]

While German paratroopers, SS and other front-line *Wehrmacht* units
were fighting all the more fiercely as they were pressed back towards the
Fatherland, in some units desertion had become a major problem. This
mainly affected non-nationals who had been reasonably reliable in the
heady days of victory and, on some fronts, ample loot. Now it seemed
apparent that Germany had lost the war and there was the possibility of
reprisals as occupied countries were liberated. The non-national German
soldiers were seen as traitors in their homelands and needed to disappear,
perhaps with a convenient change of nationality, maybe merging into
local civilian populations.

As the tide of Allied incursion into the Netherlands increased, German
strategy was more and more based on skilled resistance at specific points
rather than the old system of a continuous front line. Towns became
important not only as vital traffic junctions but also as easily defended
strongholds along the routes, Breda, Tilburg, Roosendaal, Bergen-op-
Zoom, 's Hertogenbosch.

While main efforts concentrated on opening the seaway to Antwerp,
more arrows were being drawn in on the war correspondents' maps.
These aimed at protecting the right flank of the Walcheren attacks and
also closing off escape routes from that area and from the Channel ports
which still resisted.

On 20 October British I Corps (two-thirds of which was non-British) had pencilled in three new arrows. The Polish Armoured Division was to drive towards Breda on the right flank. The 4th Canadian Armoured Division was directed towards Bergen-op-Zoom on the left. The 49th (Polar Bears) Infantry Division would be in the centre heading for Roosendaal. To avoid confusion it is useful to follow each of those arrows separately, although the advances in each direction kept pace with those of their neighbours.

In the centre the 2nd Essex led off. They were somewhat dismayed when ordered to make a frontal attack on what would be undoubtedly well-prepared and hotly contested enemy positions. However, a considerable artillery and mortar barrage enabled some troops to reach their objective within quarter of an hour. Other platoons were less fortunate, as Lt Alan Vince explained:

> At the village of Stepelheide, every hedgerow was honeycombed with weapon pits. Throughout eight hours, 'C' company supported by flame throwers fought from ditch to ditch. They lost twenty-five men and had an entire troop of supporting tanks knocked out. But as darkness fell three hundred prisoners had surrendered and the four mile advance to Loenhout had been successfully achieved.[2]

The 1st Leicesters had ridden on tanks to a vital area designated as 'Stonebridge'. Inevitably the Germans counter-attacked with panzers, self-propelled guns and infantry in force. Some positions were overrun but Capt V. Rousel of the Leicesters, with artilleryman Lt D. Marriott, stood firm with anti-tanks guns and m-gs at almost point-blank range for three hours. Eventually they were forced to withdraw, but did this in good order under cover of smoke. Then six German panzers drove at speed down the main road, intent on breaking the British front. Four of the panzers were knocked out and the enemy in turn began to withdraw. Both Rousel and Marriott, as also another artilleryman, Lt H. Frost, received the Military Cross.

Well might Rex Flower of 1/4th King's Own Yorkshire Light Infantry remark that 'it was like Normandy again'. He had seen a Churchill tank blow up on one side of his slit and a lighter Honey tank brewing on the other side. The driver of the Honey escaped but the rest of the crews were still in the blazing tanks, 'what was left of the poor devils'. The Honey had been hit by a hand-held *Panzerfaust* at close range. One tank man, Denis Whybro of 1st Fife and Forfar Yeomanry, described how 'the *Panzerfaust* can create hell with a determined bloke behind it. Nothing's more lethal than a *Panzerfaust* well camouflaged a few yards away. He can put you out of action quite easy, whatever size of tank you're in'.[3]

The presence of Marriott and Frost, within a hundred yards or so of the main enemy advance, underlines the fact that artillery observers were not safely hidden away behind the 'forward defence locations'. In fact, often enough, they could be in front of most of their infantry as they directed the artillery barrages and counter-fire which were such an important part of the Allied success. A young Salford lad, Wallace Brereton, had several hair-raising experiences. Located in a conspicuous church steeple he was well aware of the vulnerability of himself and his captain.

From the highest level we were able to survey the scene from slits in a louvred aperture. Only a couple of hundred yards ahead German vehicles of all types were moving in both directions whilst even nearer, in the fields just beyond the churchyard, German infantry crouched below a hedge. They were too near us to bring our guns on to them. We were working on co-ordinates when they started to shell the church. The slender spire shook as though it were made of jelly and pieces flew off it.

I knew it would only be a matter of time . . . and I inched myself towards the ladder that poked through the floor. When the big bang came I felt a flash around my head but I was able to scramble down the ladder. I was anxious about the fate of the captain as I looked up. Then I saw his feet on the top rungs of the ladder and knew that at least he was mobile. We came out of the church leaning on each other. The captain had an injury to his leg whilst I had a deep cut over my left eye.[4]

After having their wounds dressed, Brereton and Capt Green jumped back into their carrier, code-name Roger Fox, and headed for the next conspicuous church steeple. Like Brereton, the men of the Hallamshires were now true veteran soldiers after their advance from the Normandy beaches. They were heartened to hear that they would be relieved by a newly arrived American unit from the 104th (Timber Wolf) Division. The motto of the 104th was 'Nothing in Hell can stop the Timberwolves'. During the first action the German force assembled by Chill did their very best to stop the Wolves. The Hallamshires' colonel was impressed, and then saddened.

> They eventually arrived, in vast numbers. To our surprise we found that their infantry battalions had very little transport, and the men had to carry on their backs articles which we put on our carriers. Their companies were so large that they had to dig many extra slits, but otherwise they took over our dispositions as they stood, which was very complimentary of them.
>
> I heard next day, to my horror, that they had advanced over the open plain and had lost heavily in their first taste of battle. I drove across to see them. Their CO had been wounded. Their wounded were still being attended by stretcher bearers. The enemy had reserved his fire and caught the defenceless battalion in the open with everything he had. It would have been contrary to our training to advance across 3,000 yards of open ground without the friendly cover of smoke or darkness.[5]

Hallamshire Lt Col Trevor Hart Dyke was at least able to report that after that first bitter taste of battle, the Timberwolves 'continued to be unstoppable in a number of future actions'. By 26 October the Hallams were back in front-line action enduring the worst kind of late autumn 'Chill', icy cold and perpetual rain or mists, as Gen Chill's ghost battalion continued to appear and disappear at strategic points of dispute. Capt Chris Somers, nearing Roosendaal, had to spend the night by a burning farmhouse. When he found it possible to descend into the cellar he and his colleagues were able to sleep down there, luxuriating in the 'central heating' while the shell of the building continued to smoulder above them.[6]

Such a risky attention to creature comforts can be understood when it is realised that the infantry were still advancing across mainly flat exposed countryside, in the face of unrelenting m-g fire, where the only feasible mode of advance was by wading armpit-deep in the ditches on either side of the roads. Casualties continued day by day, not always in large numbers but always with their impact of horror and sadness.

John Ellis was one of only three Hallams to receive the DCM. He was a pioneer corporal and had done sterling work in finding and defusing mines, doubtless saving many lives. Now at the point of the arrow on the map and nearing the objective, he squatted down to defuse yet another mine in the ground. He did this in his usual cool way but, as he lifted the now harmless mine, it became apparent that the enemy had laid it on top of another mine to which it was connected. The lower mine blew up and killed Ellis, while his officer, Lt Hawkins, was wounded. The mine had been located because the ration truck had run over another mine nearby and had been blown up. Breakfast porridge was scattered far and wide. One man emerged covered in porridge. For a moment it had become a great joke. Until Ellis's death.

The important town of Roosendaal now lay just ahead. About half a mile from the nearest houses a stream had been modified to form a well-constructed defensive position. Several 49th Division battalions were now 'arrowheading' in along feeder roads towards the town. Every advance route was exposed. Men of the Duke of Wellington's could only crawl forward, almost as though swimming the breast stroke, in the water of a stream. The Leicesters lost casualties on the open ground. For a while the open space was vacant except for Red Cross flags marking the search for wounded men.

No doubt with the experience of the Timberwolves in mind, Lt Col Hart Dyke protested to his brigadier about the suicidal nature of a casual advance across the 1,000 yards of ground short of the town's built defences.

In the dawn mists next morning a small patrol crept across the menacing spaces and discovered that the enemy had evacuated the defences, no doubt aware of the dangers of encirclement. The Hallams hurried forward in force, only to hear the cheers of the populace as men from 1/4th KOYLI came in first on the flank. The population was doubly delighted because the city had suffered very little battle damage. The weary, wet troops perked up as the civilians accorded them a jubilant welcome, with comfortable billets and overjoyed new friends for a day or two.

The advance, substantial in terms of Normandy progress rates, still involved danger at all levels and hard sweat for those not actually firing guns. The brigadier of 56th Brigade died of wounds. The colonel of the Gloucesters was hit by shrapnel while shaving at the kitchen sink in a billet. As to sweat, the Royal Engineers had to construct seven bridges in three weeks in order to cross considerable waterways. The 49th Division was ostensibly a Yorkshire division and no doubt had some local pride in the Bailey bridges erected by the sappers.

Their inventor was Donald Bailey, a Yorkshireman born in Rotherham (Hallams country). His quick-fit bridges came in sections, the heaviest of which could be man-handled by six men and carried in ordinary three-ton lorries. Two panels, each 10 ft by 5 ft, were joined by girders to form a 'bay'. Any number of bays could be bolted together to achieve the necessary span over canal, anti-tank ditch or river. The structure was mounted on rollers on the near bank. It was then rolled out across the obstacle. Weights on the landward side held it horizontal. Finally wooden sleepers formed a floor across which tanks could travel. For longer bridges floating supports would be added. An original bridge is still in use near Rotherham.[7]

Mines continued to be a main obstacle to fast advances. George Learad of the Hallams had worked out his own way of dealing with mines, even though the system might have horrified technical experts. George simply cleared enough dirt around the mine to be able to clip a hook on to a lifting handle. He then retreated and pulled a long chain attached to the hook. The mine either exploded or obediently slid to the side of the road where it could be dealt with later by trained engineers.

While he was dealing with the mines his concentration was so intense that he had no sense of bullets zipping over his prone body. After one episode his officer, Lt Nicholson, said, 'Didn't you hear the bullets?' to which he replied, 'They must have been bad shots.' Such concentration was offset by moments of near farce. Assisted by a Sherman tank of the Canadian Sherbrooke Fusiliers, leading men of the Hallams rushed into a farmhouse to find that the enemy had evacuated the place with such speed that they had left a pan of chips cooking on the stove. The chips were quickly 'liberated'.[8]

Such moments were rare. Pte Eric Rolls of the 11th Royal Scots was distressed to see the body of a ten-year-old girl lying beside the road as the unit advanced. In contrast Rolls and his mate were billeted with a Dutch family who had a very attractive daughter 'most charming and pretty'. The two soldiers vied for the daughter's favours . . . until the local civil authorities arrived to take the girl away on a charge of collaborating with the Germans.[9]

Another of the Hallams, Arnold Whiteley, remembered some of the contrasting horrors of battle:

> We had a nasty time. There were trees all round and we had no clear vision but we took about thirty prisoners. They were put in a barn when a shell hit a tree and burst and all the Germans prisoners inside and the one English lad guarding them were killed. A German Panther tank came round a house and we'd an anti-tank gun at this side. We'd put it there because we thought it were faulty. But they must have put it right because as this German came round they got him.

What actually happened with the Panther, a more powerful tank than the ordinary British Sherman, was that the 6-pounder anti-tank gun had hit the tank's rear three times, halting it but not destroying it. The German crew then tried to reverse the long gun to the rear. However, the gun barrel struck a tree and jammed there. More shot from the smaller gun eventually set the Panther on fire and the crew bailed out with their clothing aflame.[10]

Small events, rather than mass slaughter, often evoked the greatest pity and sadness in the hardened fighting men. Hallam Les Sewell had been asleep in a Bren gun pit when a loud bang awoke him. A figure a few yards away was in the act of throwing a bomb. Les fired a burst which killed the man, a German sergeant. He then found a wounded corporal and carried him back to the aid post, after which he found his overcoat saturated in blood. His disgust was forgotten when his own sergeant met him with more bad news.

> He said, 'That first bomb you heard was this patrol chucking a bomb into the hole where these two lads were'. They were L/Cpl Johnny Green and Pte Joe Clayton and both were killed. Next day the mail came up and there was a parcel for Johnny Green. It was a cake which his wife had baked and sent to Johnny. His wife had just had their baby.

The arrow on the map relating to the Polish Armoured Division pointed towards the ancient fortified city of Breda. The Poles already had bitter experience of another ancient fortified city, Falaise in Normandy. At the closure of the notorious Falaise pocket the Poles on Mount Ormel had experienced some of the most ferocious fighting of any war. Many of them had been in action or in transit since 1939. A British soldier fighting alongside them was not surprised to see how tired some of the Poles looked.

Denis Whybro, Fife and Forfar tank NCO, commented, not unkindly:

> They put a Polish brigade with us. I mean, that was a pantomime. . . . the poor devils had been in action since D-Day I should think and they must have been shattered. 'Cos they was going along sweeping mines and there was mines all over the place and one bloke was sweeping with this detector, and the bloke behind him spotted he'd missed a mine, walked right past it, waving the detector over it, like asleep as they walked. When his mate pointed out the mine he missed he took his detector earphones off and threw them on the ground in disgust.[11]

The Poles were now faced by men of 711, 719 and 346 German Infantry Divisions, all in reduced numbers but reinforced from 51 Flieger Regt and 11/6 Parachute Regt. The Polish units had been largely on the defensive from 6 to 20 October and were desperate for reinforcements. Their infantry had been reduced to 50 per cent of normal strength and their tank crews to the two-thirds needed to crew tanks (that is even eliminating a co-driver). All armies were similarly afflicted at this time.

In Britain only 43 cadets of the current session had passed out of the Sandhurst armoured course as against 171 authorised places. Among other ranks a report stated that 'demands still cannot be met in tank crews.[12] In the Polar Bear Division the former anti-aircraft platoons were now acting as normal infantry units, this being made possible by the dearth of *Luftwaffe* activity.

Twenty-year-old Cpl Cliff Brown, now a veteran among veterans, had bitter experience of the reinforcement problem. In reserve behind the line, he was awakened by loud shouting of '*Hände Hoch*!' He thought it might be a practical joking rookie with no understanding of the danger in perpetrating such a jape. Then bursts of *Schmeisser* fire and grenades indicated that a German patrol had infiltrated their lines. Cliff yelled, 'No rifle fire', for his men were surrounded by friends as well as enemies. Hurriedly he handed out hand grenades, shouting 'throw them that way'.

As the noise abated with the enemy patrol slipping away into the darkness, Cliff became aware that he had heard very few explosions from the grenades thrown by his men. Quick enquiry revealed that the new reinforcements had not realised that it was necessary to pull the pin out of the grenade before throwing it. They had no infantry training at all. There followed two incidents of black comedy. L/Cpl McInnis had been seriously wounded by a German grenade. Cliff Brown carried him back to the aid post. McInnis was bleeding profusely. Cliff arrived at the post covered, face and uniform, in blood. The MO insisted that the unwounded Cliff looked worse than McInnis and should be treated first. McInnis was not amused.

As Cliff's coy started man-to-man training on infantry weapons, one veteran to one reinforcement, it was decided to set up a night tripwire with a flare attached in front of their slits. In the dark small hours the flare burst into flame and there was loud squealing. The nervous Lincs jumped for their guns, ready for another German patrol, only to confront two stray piglets which had been caught in the tripwire. History records laughter but not the fate of the piglets.[13]

The Poles were able to obtain a few recruits from liberated French and Belgian volunteers with military training. There was also an inflow of Polish prisoners of war who had been conscripted into the German Army and were anxious for revenge. Cliff Ellwood was with the 4th Lincolns advancing towards Breda. He had just returned to the battalion after recovering from septic bites from the infamous mosquitoes in the marshes around Caen. He saw Polish conscripts in German uniform deserting and asking if and where they could join the Polish Army.[14] Walter Shea, a Royal Artillery anti-tank gunner, reported a similar experience as the Germans troops were pulling out fast, trying to extricate themselves from the merging arrows on the maps.

Reinforced by the Canadian 2nd Armoured Brigade the Poles had been directed to make a holding attack towards Oosterhout, the purpose being to draw German attention away from other attacks on either flank. As sometimes happened, the holding attack was more successful than the other attempts. Unexpectedly the Poles broke through to Gilze and Haansburg. Now given the responsibility as the point formation, they set up a fast two-pronged attack on Breda. Their weariness transformed into fresh enthusiasm, over two days they made a rapid advance, entering Breda without the need of prolonged air or artillery destruction.

Their general, Stanislaw Maczek, called it an 'epoch of carnival'. The streets were thronged with delirious crowds. In shop windows notices appeared with inscriptions in the almost unknown Polish language, 'Thanks to the Poles!'. The enthusiasm reached its climax as Maczek himself arrived at the town hall and officially installed the former mayor who, during the German occupation, had been obliged to remain in hiding. The local people were extremely relieved because Breda was a fortress city surrounded by a canal and could have been expected to offer stern resistance, with catastrophic results for the inhabitants. This had happened during vital sieges in 1577, 1581, 1590, 1625, 1637, 1793, and 1813, so why not in 1944?

The restored mayor, van Stolbe, had read his history and noted that a Polish prince had once visited Breda to study military tactics. During the civic reception held to honour the liberating Polish troops the mayor remarked, 'In the seventeenth century during a siege your Crown Prince

Ladislas had studied the art of siege work in this city and how to vanquish the resistance of a city. Perhaps we can think that his acquired experience had not been forgotten for, three hundred years later, it enabled the Polish armoured division to liberate our town in one attack'.[15] Fanciful words no doubt, but justifiable in the euphoria of liberation. And a satisfying tribute for the Poles after their five-year odyssey.

Walter Shea, the anti-tank gunner supporting the Poles, was a member of a self-propelled gun crew. Their vehicle had a tank chassis and a gun mounted within armour but not in a turret with a 360° traverse system. The limited traverse did not detract from the efficiency of the S-P when well situated and camouflaged. However, Shea's vehicle, even with its tracks, could not operate on the terrain which varied between total waterlogging and deep yielding mud. So Shea and his crew 'had to leave our tanks in hides and fight as infantry. We lost a number of soldiers ambushed there'.

Along the next arrow on the map, the Canadian 4th Armoured Division also found that for most of the route the tanks were unable to give much more than distant fire support to the infantry as they squelched forward. The conditions became ever more hazardous. Cliff Ellwood of the British 'Lincs', mentioned earlier, had been bitten by the mosquitoes near Caen. The commander of the Canadian 'Lincs' (the Lincoln and Welland regiment), Lt Col Cromb, had also been bitten and had been suffering from a bad attack of malaria. Now, with the Lincs headed towards Bergen-op-Zoom, Cromb had returned to his command, just as his replacement, Maj Young, succumbed to another painful and distressing battlefield hazard, dysentery.

In front of the Canadian 'Lincs' and their companion battalion on 19 October the enemy had withdrawn into an ideal defence location, Camp de Brasschaet, on the heath named Maria ter Heide. The camp had been a training area and rifle range of the peacetime Belgian Army, while the Germans had added an aircraft runway and hangars. Its flank was guarded by a railway embankment. There was a dense wood in which was a large château. Permanent obstacles like barbed-wire entanglements, tank traps, rifle butts, mines and booby-traps were in profusion waiting for the enemy. Lt Col Cromb held his O group at the top of a water tower giving an excellent view of the terrain. The view did not prompt optimism.

The infantry attacked with grenades and repelled counter-attacks with bayonets. B and C Coys captured and held the hangars against the odds. The situation was considerably confused when A Coy went too far along the railway and insisted on the radio that it was at the correct objective. An ominous gap had opened up. Cromb assessed the situation and directed A to its correct destination. Atoning for sins, A Coy's Maj Lambert performed what was described as a 'bizarre manoeuvre'. With his men in extended line along the railway, he spaced out a squadron of tanks which came up the tracks to give him support. The battalion history recorded the 'bizarre' sequel:

Maj Lambert ordered his men to 'right turn', which meant that they were facing across the fields in a single long line. Waving a peaked cap which had come through both world wars, he led his company across the open fields, shouting 'Peanuts, popcorn and programmes' at the top of his lungs. The enemy were so startled that they gave themselves up in droves. This enabled 'B' coy to move . . . some 2,000 yards to its objective, just as darkness set in.

Advancing on the flank the Algonquin Regiment remembered the attack for 'the 150 prisoners taken in this operation [who] provided the last of the great windfalls of local money, to the delight of all, except the prisoners'. The Algonquins reasoned that the exceptional sums of local money found on the prisoners were probably looted from civilians. Speaking of excess, the battalion also found more mines around the château of Brasschaet than they had seen anywhere on the continent. They then set out in single file through the minefield to continue in a night advance.

On 24 October the Lincoln and Welland men continued the attack in great hopes as they were now supported by a troop of Sherman tanks, two troops of Crocodile flame-throwers as well as artillery and mortars. After about 500 yds the tracked vehicles once again became bogged down and the foot men had to continue alone. Fierce counter-attacks resulted in one soldier achieving some kind of record for brief service. Lt W.E. Edwards had just been commissioned at an officer's training centre in Britain. He had arrived in the depleted battalion as a much appreciated reinforcement. At 1300 hr he was given command of a platoon. By 1600 hr the platoon had been surrounded and he was taken prisoner.

The day had been more propitious, although most painful for Lt C.H. Chirnside. Having spearheaded C Coy attacks to a point where they were well ahead and being subjected to constant counter-attacks, and though badly wounded, he walked back on his own and found his way to battalion HQ in order to ensure that Lt Col Cromb was fully acquainted with the situation. He was awarded both Dutch and Belgian gallantry orders, the battalion now being in battle astride of the old national border. At the end of the day the redoubtable Maj Swayze of D Coy and his runner decide to set up HQ overnight in a barn. Opening the door they found more than fifty enemy soldiers, who promptly surrendered at the threat of Swayze's pistol.

The village of Esschen straddled the Belgian–Dutch border and was taken by surprise as a result of the night march. The Canadians were now only about seven miles from Bergen-op-Zoom but the men of the Hermann Göring Regiment, sent forward by Chill, were determined to fight for every bend in the road. As one account has it, 'the picture that emerges over the next five days details a series of intense isolated battles for the small villages of Wouwsche Plantage and Centrum. . . . The progress was slow: the woods, verges and sandy tracks were heavily mined. With nowhere to go, the armour became easy targets for the German artillery set ahead on the road bends'.[16]

Cliff Brown was once again 'attacking under very heavy artillery, mortar, rifle and machine gun fire. We tried digging a trench but it filled with water immediately so we kept moving forward'. Then occurred one of those freak incidents which battle could produce:

We reached a barn where a cow had been tied up outside. One soldier was standing on the other side of the cow when a shell hit close by. Both the soldier and the cow took the full impact of the shell and were killed while I was covered with mud and blood, and lost my hearing for a short while.

We had to clear the barn as we knew there were Germans inside firing at our advance. My men flung the door open and I attempted to spray the interior with my Sten gun. It failed to fire. However the Germans in the barn immediately gave up. The Sten gun was an unpredictable weapon. Not my first such experience. But it was a very effective weapon 99% of the time. [The Sten was a simple, somewhat crude sub-m-g, mass produced in hundreds of small workshops and not always of standard quality.]

On 26 October the German FM von Rundstedt decided to withdraw the 15th Army 'to the general line Bergen-op-Zoom–Roosendaal–Breda–Dongen–west of s' Hertogenbosch' in order to preserve some kind of cohesion and avoid further isolation of units. That same day Col von der Heydte called in Mayor Lijnkamp of Bergen and ordered him to evacuate the city immediately to enable a continuing German defence. Lijnkamp refused. There were fierce arguments and consultation took place on the German side. Finally von der Heydte agreed not to continue defending the city. He insisted on conditions such as a curfew, banning of civilian gatherings and the surrender of any German weapons or uniforms held by civilians.

In the uneasy interim as the German troops moved back, demolition squads went to work, blowing up radio towers, the telephone exchange, church towers, dock installations and railway lines. Many citizens died during continuing artillery duels. Some civilians moved into deep shelters. Others tried to contact the Allied troops with news of the changing situation.[17]

Forming a pincer movement on the outskirts of Bergen, Cromb of the Lincs and Lt Col Wotherspoon of the South Albertas discussed the reports being filtered through by the local Resistance. Eventually Wotherspoon turned and said to Cromb words which have become legend to both Canadians and Dutch: 'Hell, Bill, let's take the damned place.'[18] Their immediate advance coincided nicely with the withdrawal of the last of von der Heydte's troops. At the same moment an underground Dutch newspaper was being printed in a basement hiding place with the equally evocative headlines, 'De Tommies zijn hier'.

Another large town at the point of another arrow on the map, Tilburg had been liberated at the same time. But it was not all a fairy story of sweet liberation enchantment. Victory could be inebriating. Wine flowed in civilian toasts. But sometimes it flowed illicitly. A Canadian review of those days cited one incident.

> The men took in movies, meals and dances. They also drank from a distillery liberated during the fighting. Harry Lumsden remembered being ordered to secure the building: 'You couldn't stop anybody. They were coming in the doors, the windows, everywhere, throwing cases out. I said, "OK. One case per man only" . . . I don't think anybody there was sober'. On 30 October the Dutch Military authorities [forbade] civilians to give liquor to soldiers. Others were not happy because the Canadians had taken over a dormitory that the Dutch had established as an emergency hospital. . . . So too did the Canadian soldier take advantage of the shortage of Dutch men to court Dutch women. . . . Still the grumblings were relatively minor.[19]

For some of the Canadians there was little opportunity for such shenanigans. Factories in the industrial outskirts of Bergen were still occupied by the enemy. For three days the Canadian Argylls and the Lincs fought from one factory building to another, Capt Lambert winning the Military Cross before the area was cleared of all enemy. In the confusing huddle of buildings, men of C Coy of the Lincs were badly hit by friendly fire from their own artillery.

There was still no prolonged relief from the battles. By 2 November the troops were moving again towards Steenbergen with the final objective of reaching the great river barrier of the Maas and denying all road exits to the remaining German troops on the west.

The supply of reinforcements had again failed to make up for the continual drift away of casualties. In sober words, the Lincoln and Welland history relates that 'realizing how much each man counted', Pte G.K. Taylor of D Company refused to be evacuated, although badly wounded at the beginning of the battle; instead, he continued to fight with his Bren gun until by morning he could no longer move his legs. He was then ordered to the rear by his company commander, and was later decorated with the Military Medal.

Similar motives inspired Charlie Kipp to insist on staying in the front line of action. Charlie had landed in Normandy as Cpl Kipp in the Lincoln and Welland regiment. Within three weeks he was leading a platoon, due to a shortage of officers. He was a sole survivor of his section during the carnage around Tilly-la-Campagne. Promoted to lance-sergeant, he continued to command a platoon for two months. On 22 October he collapsed from exhaustion and hypertension. For four days he was carried, unconscious or partly conscious, in 'one of the most dangerous places I could have been, the back seat of my Coy commander's jeep'.

On 26 October the MO, Capt A.W. McKenzie, diagnosed a heart problem and recommended repatriation to Canada. Charlie refused to go. As volunteers the Canadian soldiers had some say in their own destiny. He continued to take part in the Lincs battles. In January 1945 he was wounded for the ninth time. When the war ended he was still there, acting sergeant-major of his company.[20] However, on 25 October that other apparently indestructible Normandy survivor, Cpl Cliff Brown, was shot through the chest and right shoulder at Wouwsche Plantage. This time there was urgent need for the MO to save Cliff's life. There was no question of Cliff refusing the inevitable evacuation to England on a stretcher.

There is a note of legitimate pride in the historian's record that 'On 5th November, ten days ahead of the time planned, the Division [4th Canadian Armoured] had reached the Lower Maas. The Carrier Platoon patrolled as far as Boompjes van Drogendijk, a hamlet within sight of the estuary of the Schelde . . . in Dinteloord . . . it also met elements of the 49th British Infantry Division'. The arrowheads were converging.

The significance of that entry is that the Germans now had no access to a viable bridge crossing of the great river, the 51st Highland Division having secured the bridge at Geertruidenburg to the east a few days earlier. All resistance on Walcheren had ceased by 9 November, but the first cargo ship, after awaiting mine-clearing operations, did not sail into the river towards Antwerp until 28 November. The Belgian Resistance had recommended clearing the Antwerp entrance on 4 September when it was quite feasible.

The Dutch people in the liberated cities were initially delirious with happiness as they were liberated. Very soon the happiness was tinged with worry and desperation as news leaked through about the conditions in the remainder of the Netherlands which would still have to wait more than four terrible months for liberation. Teresia in Breda, who would later marry tank driver Brian Carpenter, remembered the 'hunger winter' which afflicted those areas:

We heard that people there had to resort to chopping up their doors and even their floorboards in an effort to keep warm during what was one of the worst winters in living memory. For many there were no rations and their food consisted of tulip and crocus bulbs. When eventually food parcels were parachuted down, people had to eat sparingly to avoid stomach upsets having been deprived of proper nourishment for so long. Many older people did not survive this severe spell.[21]

The first train to run from liberated Roosendaal across to Flushing was in the charge of driver Koppernol. He sensed the unique nature of the occasion and as he drove he found words to describe his delight in crossing the liberated land. But very soon the delight was marred by the realisation of the suffering and sacrifice which had secured the ultimate prize of freedom. He later wrote down some of those impressions in his poem 'Along Track 46'.[22]

> Sun was shining,
> gulls back in the sky,
> countryside full of colours,
> pastures fresh and green,
> and Man was finding back his brightness.
> But then . . . ! A wooden cross

roughly thrust into the ground;
a steel helmet . . . a panzerfaust . . .
a little mound,
and a rifle . . . BROKEN!

It was if something broke
inside my soul,
over there
in the land of the Zeelanders.

CHAPTER TEN

Massing towards the Maas

A month had passed since the Arnhem failure of September 1944. That protruding thumb on the map was still virtually unprotected on its left outline. It was essential for the Allies to consolidate along the River Maas.

Commencing as the Meuse in French-speaking territory to the south, the great river had been flowing consistently northwards, changing its name as it came into the land of the Dutch. Then, just short of Nijmegen, it veered to the left, as though to take advantage of the great bridge which had been built for it at Grave. On veering leftwards it seemed to yield to the attraction of the sunset and moved at an angle of ninety degrees westwards, widening into the Netherlands Diep and entering the sea.

This vast corner of land within the great bend of the Maas, once liberated, would give the Allies left flank protection. By reaching the Maas around Den Bosch ('s Hertogenbosch) and marching along the south bank of the river, the Allies might also trap the German forces still active around Walcheren and down the Channel coast.

But on 22 October Will Lagarde in his bakery at Oss was still worried about the German raids into the food warehouses. Maria van Breugel, busy making miniature clogs as souvenirs for Allied soldiers, was still scared of the random bullets and nearby explosions around St Oedenrode. Two hundred yards away a newly arrived tank regiment had formed its laager outside a farm. At night prowler guards were posted around the laager. Guards were ordered to patrol in pairs, back to back. They were told that infantrymen, sleeping in the ditch beside the main road to Arnhem, had been killed by a German patrol the previous night.[1]

The tank regiment at St Oedenrode with the 51st Highland Division was part of the vast mass of Allied reinforcement which was now rolling from the last positions of the Normandy campaign into the new locations for the Lower Maas campaign. Welshmen of the 53rd Division were moving alongside the Scots, while the Desert Rats, the 7th Armoured, had also been called forward. They would again face the problem of attacking empty spaces, dealing with poor-quality German units of Lt Gen Poppe's 59th Infantry Division, and then, from time to time, running into some of the enemy's best and most tenacious men, like paratroopers of the Bloch Battalion, fired by the knowledge that this was virtually part of the front line of the Fatherland itself.

The new arrivals from Normandy knew what war was all about. No heroic illusions remained. Bill Moseley (of the Northants Yeomanry), waiting in his tank on the farm at St Oedenrode, reflected on recent experiences:

Some of us were detailed to help the 'Jocks' to collect and bury the dead. Although the sight of a dead body was not new to us, this was the first time we had to actually handle one – the 'Jocks' laughed at our squeamishness – since to them this was all part of the day's work. Their fighting was man to man, whereas ours was impersonal in that we seldom fired at an individual man and saw him die, but at an object, tank, vehicle, gun, building.

The bodies were treated with respect which soldiers have for one another, friend or foe; each was searched for Pay Book, identity tags and personal belongings (which were sent back to the family eventually). As we laid one German in the temporary grave which we had dug, a 'Jock' remarked 'There ye go, Fritz. Nae mair soldiering for ye. Aie, ye was some paur maither's son like me, ye paur bastard.'

Such recollections of hands-on encounters with death, usually preceded by ghastly wounding and disfigurement, inevitably gave the soldier reasons for apprehension as he waited for the next D-Day and H-Hour sometimes just a few yards along the road. Bill Moseley recorded the feeling of waiting for the 'IDB':

'Imminent Deadly Breach', a phrase encapsulating for the tank man, thoughts of impending action, causing physical pain as the stomach muscles tighten involuntarily. Shakespeare said it all with 'Once more unto the breach, dear friends, once more!' Everyone had his own method of dealing with the anxieties and apprehensions of an impending action – for those of us so far unscathed 'how long our luck would last? Not for ever!' Mostly we would laugh and joke while preparing for the next Big Push. It was now obvious that the war wasn't going to be over by Christmas 1944.[2]

IDB for Operation Colin, clearing the Lower Maas, was indeed imminent for the Scots and their associated tank men. As the Highlanders assembled, some of their units were still in the fields bordering that main Arnhem road. The second anniversary of El Alamein was on 22 October, and the 51st Highland Division had been conspicuous there. It augured well for Operation Colin.

Maj Gen Rennie launched his men into the thick woods at Eerde which was the junction between two German units. In the dark hours of 22/23 October, 5/7th Gordons burst through into Wijbosch. Then 5th Black Watch with 4RTR advanced at dawn under a smoke screen aiming towards a stocking factory at Schijndel. The morning's silver mist and artillery's black smoke caused the troops some delay in identifying landmarks as they pushed forward. When they eventually reached the stocking factory, well on time, they were astonished to find their CO, Lt Col Bradford, already there waiting for them, he having rushed overland in his jeep, steering on a compass bearing.

To their left the 5th Camerons ran into solid German defences and needed to shed the requisite amount of blood to force their way into the western outskirts of Schijndel. The Seaforths (2nd and 5th) found holes in the German defences. Some of them walked along the railway line (known to local residents as 'the German Line', as eventually it headed into Germany). Their objective was the railway bridge over the substantial River Dommel. They became the first victims of a frustrating hazard which would be repeated throughout Operation Colin. The moment the first Highlander came within spitting distance of the bridge, the Germans blew it up.[3]

Sherman tanks of Bill Moseley's regiment took up the charge beyond Schijndel. An enemy trap, based on a huge tree felled across the main road, was outflanked and destroyed. The old church tower at St Michielsgestel gave the Germans good observation so that they could direct their guns on to the approaching tanks. One of the Shermans was knocked out and another damaged, but the remainder bombarded the tower, drove off the anti-tank guns and roared through the village towards their objective: another bridge over the Dommel.

Sgt Jack 'Randy' Ginns, head out of the turret, in the first tank ordered gunner Harry Graham to douse the bridge with m-g fire. They were so near, twenty yards, but so far. A huge flash warned Ginns, who dived into the turret, slamming the hatches tight behind him. A moment later the tank was hit by a raging whirlwind of fire, blast and debris. More than a ton of bridge remnants, concrete, wood, metal, tarmac, shredded into tiny shards, crashed down on top of the tank. Another bridge blown.

Randy swore later that he thought he heard sounds of German laughter from beyond the far bank of the Dommel. But the German soldier who, seeing that the electrical trigger was not working, jumped under the bridge and set off the explosives manually, blowing up the bridge and himself at the same time was silent.

It would again mean a wait for engineers to come up and build a Bailey bridge over the Dommel in the dark. While they waited Capt Charlie Robertson and his men of 7th Black Watch found a rowing boat without oars. Using rifle butts as oars they crossed the river during the night, 'the khaki shapes hunched close to the water's surface like primeval water beasts'.[4]

Meanwhile the leading Yeomanry Sherman had progressed carefully to the objective at the end of St Michielsgestel's main street. As one of the crew remembered:

Every corner and bend is yet another dying time. Every lurch forward into another stretch of open street is to savour all the imagined agonies of wounding . . . ripping of flesh, mangling of bone, shredding of muscles, laceration of nerves. . . . The village seems a hundred miles long and the day lasts a hundred years.[5]

The reality was to be a little less horrific on this occasion. The lead tank had motored alone to the far end of the long straight street, as was the custom, with the second tank and supporting infantry waiting under cover at the previous bend to assess the danger. The Sherman then fell prey to another frequent Dutch hazard. Halted at the roadside, its weight caused the verge to collapse, toppling the tank, with thirty tons of gravity impetus speeding it down, into a huge ditch. The squadron ARV (armoured recovery vehicle) was soon on the spot while the forlorn crew prepared to defend the objective armed with a couple of pistols and a Sten gun. By the time the second tank was alongside, the ARV was pulling the fallen tank back on to the road. The only casualty was a corporal with injuries severe enough to merit evacuation back to Blighty.[6]

The East Riding Yeomanry also had a story about ditches around St Michielsgestel. Their B Sqn was commanded efficiently by Maj Salman, a Belgian officer whose permanent rank was only that of captain. Among reinforcements there arrived a British cavalry major of greater seniority. He was to take over the sqn. First, though, the colonel sent him off on a recce. Passing through St Michielsgestel the cavalry man disappeared and was reported missing. He had driven through the German outposts, tried to reverse his scout car, and, like the earlier tank, crashed into one of the huge ditches. He was captured but later escaped. Having been wounded he was evacuated after his one ditched mission. And Belgian Maj Salman continued his happy relationship with B.[7]

Allied staff officers appeared to be particularly influenced by anniversaries of great battles: Colin commencing on the anniversary of Alamein, Totalize (in August 1944) on the anniversary of Amiens 1918, and so on. One anniversary which seemed to go unnoticed occurred as the Highlanders battled into nearby Boxtel. Just 150 years before, in

1794, another British soldier entered Boxtel. His name was Tommy Atkins. British (and sometimes Canadian) soldiers have generally been known as 'Tommies' or 'Tommy Atkins' ever since. The Germans invented the term 'Tommy Cooker' for the Sherman tank when it burst into flames. Some authorities are of the opinion that 'Tommy Atkins' was a random, fictitious name invented by the War Office. Perhaps they had never heard of Tommy of Boxtel. Now Boxtel was captured again by the Tommies.

One extraordinary event at Boxtel launched a myth which persisted for many years. As the Seaforths liberated the town they were met by another group of strange soldiers, some 106 Allied men whose presence was not expected. They were American and British airborne soldiers whose troop-carrying planes had crashed or landed in the wrong place. They had gathered together and hidden in the woods around Boxtel for a month. Seeing the airborne men, many civilians thought that they had been liberated by an airborne drop, and, in the 'fog of war', the myth was perpetuated.[8]

As the Highlanders pushed forward from St Michielsgestel they were delayed by the enemy blowing yet more bridges over the meandering Dommel and its tributaries. Their engineers worked full-time, enabling tanks and infantry to advance on the next major objective, the town of Vught. It is possible that none of the advancing troops had ever heard of Vught. But for the Dutch population it was already a name of terror to compare with Belsen, Buchenwald and Auschwitz.

Here was one of the two major concentration camps in the Netherlands, housing a mix of Jews and non-Jewish resistance leaders. From here the 'German line' constantly rattled under the wheels of cattle trucks conveying Dutch civilians (some 14,000 of them) to the mechanised extermination camps in Germany. Many did not have to go so far because there was a 'Shooting Place' in the camp itself.

The Germans had tried to evacuate and clean up the camp before the Allies arrived. This was in vain. As Lt Col Derek Lang and his Camerons walked in on 27 October there was no hiding the appalling reality of the place: stinking barrack huts with pathetic shreds of clothing lying around, barbed-wire barriers, hastily buried corpses, blood-stained sod at the

Fusilierplaats, a few surviving evaders and many more local citizens to tell the story, and the unmistakable aura of such places where no birds will wing or sing among the dense trees.[9] At that time many British soldiers were unaware of the vast extent of the Nazi extermination operation carried out by Himmler's special squads. The example of Camp Vught was a forceful incentive to fight and liberate the remainder of the Netherlands.

The Camerons may have walked into Camp Vught without interference but there had been nightmares to endure en route. Bill Moseley was alongside in his tank:

Our objective was to cut and block the main Vught–Tilburg road, preventing the enemy's retreat from Tilburg, which was being attacked by the Polish Armoured division. The road ran through a thickly forested area. The Sqn deployed, entering the forest via several grassy tracks with the Cameron Highlanders riding on the tanks; suddenly all hell broke loose as mortar bombs rained down on us and Spandau fire sent the 'Jocks' diving for the ground to take cover behind the tanks. We kept up a hail of m-g fire to give them cover as we 'jinked' off the track into the undergrowth, trying to pinpoint, in the gathering darkness and gloom of the forest, where the fire was coming from.

Eventually a Cameron officer, using the infantry telephone fixed to the back of the tank, was able to direct our fire and we let rip with HE shells hoping to hit something, though many of our shots ricocheted off trees, exploding prematurely, adding to the general confusion, especially for the PBI Jocks.

I couldn't see a blind thing through the periscope sight and had to rely on [Maj] 'Dickie' Courage to spot the enemy flash as their guns fired. 'Right a little bit . . . stop! Up a little bit . . . stop! Fire! Right a bit more . . . Fire!' After some considerable time things quietened down. The Camerons then reported that they had wormed their way on their bellies under our fire, right up to the Jerry positions, silencing them with hand grenades and securing the road.[10]

The mission of the 53rd (Welsh) Division could not have been more different to that of the Camerons in the forest. The Welsh were being asked to set up possibly the biggest attack of a city, with intense house-to-house fighting, yet required of a British unit. In Normandy a number of large towns had capitulated before major street-fighting could take place, Bayeux, Caen, Rouen, Le Havre. Now Den Bosch, capital of North Brabant, stood in the Allies' way. Its full name was 's Hertogenbosch (The Duke's Wood). It was surrounded by wide waterways like outsize moats, with good-quality German troops prepared to defend it.

But first the Welshmen had to advance from the area of Will Lagarde's disputed bakeries and warehouses near Oss, coordinating the advance with the 51st Division. Like the Highlanders they encountered a mixed reception. Sometimes luck, often bad luck, intervened. One coy commander of 4th Royal Welch Fusiliers (RWF) had assembled all his officers for an O group. A random shell descended and wiped them all out.

Like the Highlanders the Welch were frustrated by the blowing up of essential bridges in this waterway-riven land. The Germans were astute even in this mechanical operation. 1/5th Welch had successfully rushed a platoon across a bridge before it could be blown. The Germans then blew the bridge by remote control, leaving the platoon of about thirty men stranded and doomed, facing three self-propelled 103-mm guns and an overwhelming force of counter-attacking infantry. A Coy of 6th RWF had also succeeded in penetrating the German defences, only to be surrounded and viciously counter-attacked, only for 7th RWF with tanks of 5th Dragoon Guards to drive off the counter-attackers, and for the gallant but badly wounded commander of A Coy, Capt R.G. March, to die as he was being evacuated.[11]

Lt Col G.F. Dickson of 7th RWF was informed that all the bridges over the canal in front of him had been blown but that the lock gates were still standing. Early in the morning he arranged for tanks and flame-throwers to be assembled on the near side of the canal and to commence covering fire. His A Coy then performed the virtual tightrope circus act of rushing across the tops of the lock gates and seizing the German positions on the far side. While they held firm on the far bank, 555th Field Coy, REs came up and erected a Class 40 bridge (capable of bearing the weight of a tank) over the canal.

Capt Travers Cosgrove was one of the engineers responsible for the apparently interminable task of replacing bridges. Setting out from the area of Oss, through half-grown forest, he had in his command half-track Sgt Les Bourne, his batman, a driver and two wireless operators. They quickly found that sand among the trees was a greater obstacle than mines. It was virtually impossible to steer the vehicle intelligently. No matter which way the driver steered the vehicle and which way the front wheels were pointed the half-track continued to slide right ahead. 'Fortunately that was the way the track led.'

Driving towards Rosmalen they came on a deserted hamlet which was thoroughly mined. 'First I had to ask the OC, who had just reached us, to be careful with his feet; he was standing on a "Box" mine' (designed to react to the weight of a vehicle). Having put the OC right they then managed to reverse on to another mine. 'Four letter words flew!' A small fire was started which set off some phosphorous flares. Les Bourne selflessly grabbed the flaming flares and threw them away. There was then a brief delay while the MO checked that Les could continue with burned hands.

Suddenly they came on a tree-lined main road to Den Bosch which 'looked green, quiet and open in the morning light', but, the big 'but', was it mined? A Dutchman materialised and pointed to a fine white horse lying badly wounded by a mine. The Dutchman pleaded 'Can you shoot it, and then we can have something to eat'. Cosgrove shot the suffering animal. More civilians then appeared, armed with knives to help in the carving. Sometimes the events outside of the immediate battle zone seemed to lodge more firmly in the long-term memory than those in the hectic fury of the front positions.[12]

All this had to happen before the 53rd Division could approach the outskirts of Den Bosch and the nearby large village of Rosmalen. Capt J. McCann was the MO with 2nd Monmouths and was used to blood and pain. But the sights he saw in Rosmalen still appalled him. As Rosmalen was stormed more than 200 German prisoners were captured – at a price.

The price we paid was six killed and forty-four wounded. It was at this engagement that our Capt Dmitri Garitzin, a real Russian Prince known to us as 'The Cossack', was fatally wounded. He died in my arms. All of us knew him as a friendly and very brave man. On entering Rosmalen we met a very sorry sight, many dead and wounded soldiers and civilians. We dressed the wounds of those who had been caught in the crossfire from the artillery from both sides.

The sight of Germans who had been flamed by flame-throwers was sickening. All the hair and skin had been burned to a crisp. Two burned Germans came to us in a terrible state and all we could do was to give them morphine and send them on their way.[13]

Tpr Joseph Ellis, of 141 RAC, driving one of the flame-throwing Churchill tanks, remembered that 'the only way you can get into 's Hertogenbosch is over a bridge; water all around, like a river running round it'. Ellis was to come to grief in that water:

Two o'clock in the morning we were ordered 'forward to that wood over there!'. We had to climb up a great embankment and over a railway line. Then they said 'put your foot down. Head straight for that wood'. So I put my foot down on the accelerator and all of a sudden 'Poom!' We were down in the water. Three bombs had fallen into one flooded crater. It was all marshland. The tracks would not bite. We had to sit on the turret until another tank came back to take us off. They could not move our tank. My mate had the BBC over there fifty years later to try to find the tank. It's still in the hole.[14]

Many of the armoured vehicles were relatively clumsy and difficult to drive in narrow streets. John Downs was in an M10 self-propelled armoured vehicle mounting a large anti-tank gun of 340 anti-tank battery. He was not impressed by the way in which his battery was switched from one sector to another: with the Guards at Nijmegen bridge, with the American 'Screaming Eagles' (101st Airborne) back down the Arnhem road, then with the Welsh Division heading towards Den Bosch.

Downs and the battery had one moment of amusement when they captured all the mail of a retreating German division. Then they were used in indirect shoots which was not their forte. Finally they were driving into Den Bosch, with roof slates crashing down on top of them and problems of working the huge protruding gun around sharp bends. However, they had the satisfaction of taking seventeen prisoners and knocking out one of the enemy's prized Tiger tanks, hitherto regarded as the king of the battlefield. To compound his dissatisfaction with arrangements, John had no military maps but was issued with an old Michelin guide. He was at first unable to find 's Hertogenbosch, for the French version logically read 'Bois de Duc'.[15]

In those twisting streets, among tall, narrow houses or sprawling factories, enemy snipers came into their own. Norman Gaunt Marshall was also a driver in 51st Anti-Tank Regt. Feeling exposed as he sat with his head out of the driver's hatch in order to see the route more clearly, he reflected:

We hated snipers worst. They could be anywhere, behind any bush or tree, or in a window or doorway. Favorite places were in church steeples or factory towers. There were two kinds of snipers: the 'amateur' left behind by his comrades as they retreated, and the professional purposely placed. The amateur would bang away as long as he could and shoot as many as possible, trying to get out of a tight corner. He very quickly gave his position away and would soon be blasted to hell.

With the professional he would take one shot and a man would drop, usually with a bullet in his chest. Then he would lie still for several minutes, before another crack. Another one down. We still had no idea where he was. The good sniper would get six or seven victims and then disappear. But his presence was still with us. We didn't know that he'd gone. All our movements were running, doubled-up, making ourselves as small targets as possible. These acts of self-preservation stayed with us for several hours.[16]

Marshall was not a naturally martial man. He had been brought up in an atmosphere of music and song. His father had been the conductor of the world-famous Black Dyke Mills band. But he quickly learned the facts of battle life. When out of his tank, even with snipers around, 'it was surprising how little cover was necessary for a feeling of security. In towns or villages, for example, a five inch kerbstone in the street at the end of the footpath could feel as good as a two foot deep foxhole during a mortar attack. But the front line man was not averse to admitting his close acquaintance with fear in such situations':

Oh, yes, we knew what fear was. It seemed to fade away in action but it was always there in the background. Having seen dozens of dead soldiers and, worse, obscenely wounded men with arms or legs held in position only by their battledress. After having seen tanks and half-tracks when they explode while still full of men, as the uninjured scrambled out of the inferno; and heard the screams of the wounded as they tried desperately to escape the red hot blazing shell. Oh, yes, we knew what fear was. We knew that one minute the village seemed as quiet as a churchyard, flowers blooming in the garden, birds fluttering in the trees. What we didn't know was whether there was a Tiger tank just around the corner.

That fear was no doubt felt by many of the Welsh units having to rush bridge after bridge and then find ways of crossing bullet-swept water as bridges were blown in front or behind them. The East Lancs and 7RWF had fought their way towards the strategic railway station. By the time they reached it the station was burning fiercely. During the night they continued to clear the enemy out of surrounding buildings working by the light of the burning station. Tersely the division history relates that 'the German garrison had resisted fiercely. Every street, and every house had to be cleared. The system of defence had been devised with the usual German skill and the demolitions carried out with the customary thoroughness'.

The action around the law courts was typical. The East Riding Yeomanry had been moved from their usual supporting role with 51st HD as it was thought that their Shermans would be more suitable tanks for street actions than the thinner-skinned Cromwells which normally accompanied the Welsh units. The ERY's B Sqn linked with 1st East

Lancs came under fire from an imposing yellow building which turned out to be the law courts. The 'Intrepid Belge', Major Salman, ostensibly commanding the tanks, spent most of his time out of the tank, his pistol drawn, leading infantry groups into buildings, yelling out in German orders for the enemy to surrender. He brought up two Shermans commanded by Lt Jon Davies to douse the law courts with high explosive shells and then led the infantry in clearing the building floor by floor.

As twenty prisoners were led out of the law courts, Davies's tanks pressed on to the next bridge. There they came face to face with an enemy anti-tank gun which promptly fired and set Davies's tank on fire. All the crew bailed out except for the driver. Realising that the man was still in the blazing tank, Jon Davies ran back, climbed up the front of the Sherman and pulled the driver free. As the officer carried his driver back to safety the other tank drove off the enemy gun. Meanwhile C Sqn's Sgt Townsend in his Sherman encountered a new problem. Civilians were looking out of top-floor windows watching the battle while Germans on lower floors were lobbing grenades at the tanks. The Shermans could not elevate their guns sufficiently at point-blank range, to engage the higher windows. The tanks had to close down their turret flaps and continue a fierce fire in order to cover the infantry following up and entering the houses.

Sgt Morrell's tank was trapped by the collapse of a building. An enemy anti-tank gun around the corner commenced shooting down the wall of the building to try to get a bead on the tank. Other tanks came quickly to the rescue. Norman Gaunt Marshall's fear about snipers was fully realised in the case of Lt C.W. Laing, who, commanding his tank with his head in the open as most commanders did, was shot through the head by a sniper and killed.[17]

Capt McCann was now encountering problems in dealing with the number of wounded, British, German and local civilians:

One of our Bren gun carriers ran over a large mine which blew up the carrier, resulting in the deaths of the driver, his mate and ten other soldiers. This new type of mine was covered by a piece of wood so that it made it difficult for mine detectors to locate. Several other woundings resulted. I personally carried wounded men out of the mined area because we had lost so many stretcher bearers wounded.

We set up our RAP in an old dynamite factory. Four of our stretcher bearers were killed and another four were taken prisoner. I had to round up some RAMC stretcher bearers who normally worked farther back at surgical units, to come right up the line to evacuate casualties. This was the only time I saw RAMC stretcher bearers in the front line [British stretcher-bearers were recruited from among the fighting personnel].

It was a doubly horrific experience for the civilians caught up in the firing without the necessary training for evasion and taking adequate cover. Above all the children suffered as they witnessed sights for which nothing could have prepared them. One little girl remembered all too well:

> Then came the day when an Allied tank across the street got hit right in the muzzle. Its barrel split open like a flower and we heard the soldiers screaming inside, but they couldn't get out. The whole tank was burning and the curtains on the bank across the street caught fire. The next thing we knew the house next door and our roof were ablaze. Our parents got us out in a hurry. We ran along several streets until we came to an army tank that was shooting at the German soldiers. We ran on through the streets. We eventually ended up in a public washroom where the smell was overpowering.[18]

Joseph Ellis, who had been sunk in the flooded bomb crater, was now driving another flame-throwing tank and was in action again as the three-day battle began to wane:

> There was a lot of bridges blown up. There was some factories in the town. The infantry couldn't get across this bridge. There was a factory there on the other side. It must have been full of Germans with m-gs and they were giving our infantry hell. So all we did, from one side of

the river to the other, we flamed and set the factory on fire. As soon as that happened, well, they more or less packed it in. That was about the end.

It had been a grinding, grisly progress through the streets in the face of the skilled, resolute soldiers of the German 712th Division. There had been little light relief. There had been some laughter when soldiers were awaiting the arrival of an assault bridge on a Churchill chassis, a huge contraption, which would quickly bridge the canal. As the mechanical colossus swung through the streets it was seen to be 'festooned with all the tram wires from the whole city'. Soldiers cheered when they saw comrades emerging from a German HQ building bearing a huge red and black Nazi battle flag, requiring about four men to wave it triumphantly. On the other hand the men were depressed when they learned that local civilians had to supplement their scarce rations with meat from dead German horses.

After four days in the streets of the city and its environs the capture of Den Bosch sealed off all direct land escape routes towards the main body of enemy forces for all German troops to the west. Only two major bridges over the Maas, the Moerdijk and the Keisersveer bridge near Geertruidenberg, remained available. Great credit was due to the able commander of the Welsh Division, perhaps the most underrated and least lauded senior commander of the campaign, Maj Gen R.K. Ross, DSO, MC.

Corps commander N.M. Ritchie stated, 'I must tell you how tremendously impressed I have been with the fighting qualities of the 53rd (W) Division. . . . I do not think any formation could have shown greater enterprise and resourcefulness throughout these operations.' A similar tribute came from the commander of the German garrison, Maj Riehl, who was captured. He stated 'that he had been ordered to hold the town at all costs; but he was greatly surprised by the speed of the 53rd Division's advance, and impressed by the resolute manner in which the infantry crossed the River Dommel and the prompt manner in which the Sappers bridged the river for the passage of the anti-tank guns'.[19]

Across the waterways from Den Bosch the Highlanders with 33rd Armoured Brigade were pushing on from Vught. Recce Sgt Kenny Jack, MM, had been the first soldier to enter the ruins of Caen from the north. He had climbed over the debris and craters left by the huge RAF bombing raid because the tanks were unable to penetrate the chaos, and he had walked alone into the centre of the city. Now outside Vught he and colleague Cpl Clague had already towed away one of the trees which the Germans seemed to love to fell across the route of the advancing armies.

Kenny now ordered his driver, Tpr Ovens, to speed up in their Honey light tank as 1st Northamptonshire Yeomanry probed along various roads and tracks. Another felled tree blocked the way. Unlike the previous undefended one, this one bristled with muzzle flashes. Kenny had Ovens reverse around the bend. Then, releasing and dragging the big .5 m-g from the turret top, they crawled through a field and found themselves in a farmyard. And quite quickly they had reached a spot behind the tree barricade, with a full view of the section of enemy soldiers crouching behind the obstacle.

An old cartwheel lying in the farmyard gave Kenny an idea. Finding some old rope they lashed the m-g to the cart wheel, and as the wheel lay horizontally on its hub the m-g had acquired a traversing wheel which span easily. Kenny and Ovens quietly dragged the whole contrivance out into the open behind the enemy who were still watching their front. From fifty yards they opened fire, swinging the gun so that the large 0.5 bullets doused the barricade, setting it on fire. Some Germans fell but most thrust their hands high in the air, yelling 'Kamerad!' through the echoes of the gun.[20]

Another 1NY driver, Johnny Byrne, was very unhappy about his own encounter with enemy prisoners nearby. As the Highlanders reached their objective and consolidated, Johnny, from his tank, watched two Germans climb out of a ditch, waving white rags. Several others began to follow them. The battle had been won. Unexpectedly an m-g started firing from an oblique angle. The surrendering Germans were caught in the open like petrified hunted animals. One rogue gun acted as a trigger for more firing. Infantry, tanks, artillery joined in the renewed slaughter. An hour passed before the noise died down. At last Johnny could climb from his cramped seat and stretch his legs:

> He counted up to forty bodies strewn like the proverbial rag-dolls across the tiny battlepatch, not large enough to be termed a battlefield. And, central to it all, three – only three – Germans sat on the ground, unkempt in their baggy uniforms, and all three weeping the grief of bereavement, betrayal and dereliction. Johnny turned to a Black Watch lieutenant standing nearby. Troopers did not normally address strange infantry officers unless invited. Honest Geordie Johnny snarled, 'The man who pulled the trigger of the bloody gun when they were surrendering ought to be shot himself.'
>
> 'Itchy fingers', replied the officer soothingly. 'It happens in war'. 'I'd chop the bloody fingers off so that they wouldn't itch any more,' and Johnny turned away to his tank, forgetting even to salute an officer of another unit. The Scot shrugged his shoulders and called to a corporal to move the prisoners along.[21]

By 28 October the Desert Rats were advancing on the key village of Loon-op-Zand and were unfortunate enough to hit one of the tough areas of German defence. The village was at a crossroads and near to an area of sand dunes which would make the advance physically difficult. It was essential to capture the village in order to reach the Geertruidenberg crossing. The Germans had left an infantry battalion and five 75-mm anti-tank guns well dug in there. It was a potential killing ground for the tanks. The attack petered out but inflicted serious casualties on the defenders.

Commanding 4CLY in the Desert Rats was Lt Col Gray Skelton, who had commanded the squadron which eliminated the elite Wittmann Tiger troop in Normandy. Lt C.J. Lawson, who later took holy orders, commented that Skelton, like many heroes, 'was a quiet shy person, one of the few officers whom I recall coming to communion services on the rare occasions when they were possible'. He recalled a moment of typical harsh comedy and tragedy in the command Sherman tank:

We approached a hump-backed bridge over a canal. As we crossed there was an unpleasant 'WHOOSH!'. We realized we were on fire. We reversed but the tank slipped into the ditch. For safety, as we were in full view of the enemy, Gray ordered smoke to be laid, and then 'Bail out!'. I was at the side of the big gun with a small escape hatch over my head. As I grabbed the maps I also picked up two bottles of whiskey and stuffed them into my jerkin. With that load I was too fat for the small hatch. A moment of panic as I ducked under the gun to reach the turret hatch.

At this moment an air-burst shell exploded directly overhead. When I had bailed out I found poor Gray collapsed in the ditch. I left other crew members to care for him but later I heard that he had died. I ran to the other tanks of HQ where our 'B' sqdn commander took over the regiment. Mounting another tank, confusion reigned. All of a sudden as we moved to more secure ground there was a terrific jolt and instantly the turret was filled with blue flames pouring through the engine bulkhead.

We went through the hatches like wet soap, the drivers escaping through their hatches as well. It appeared that we had been shot clean through, for a lump of armour was missing on the home side too. The tanks we had at that time were Shermans powered by Wright cyclone 5-cylinder radial aero-engines burning high octane fuel. I discovered why the Germans called them 'Tommy Cookers'. We were very fortunate having lost no more than the hair on the backs of our hands and our eyebrows. I had also been hit by a splinter in the knee.[22]

As the race to close German escape routes became more and more pressing, much responsibility devolved upon the recce troops. Frank Gutteridge was a lieutenant commanding the recce troop of 1RTR as they accelerated past Loon-op-Zand. He found the going very heavy. Roads were perched up between deep dykes and any attempt to leave the road usually ended in ditching. It was rumoured that ditching had become a court-martial offence.

The Honey light tanks and Daimler scout cars were deemed less expensive, if lost, than the bigger Cromwells. So as these light vehicles were sent along the exposed roads, it meant, as Frank quickly observed, that 'to avoid almost immediate death at the outset, some ingenuity had to be used to have some chance of survival'. They were in open farmland now, with little cover:

I sent my troop sergeant over to the left as we approached the next village of Oosterhout. I had picked up a brave Dutch Resistance man who insisted on sitting on the front of the tank to guide us. My sergeant started things off by destroying a dug-in 20 mm cannon, setting fire to the ammunition. This caused a dense cloud of white smoke to drift across our front, causing, I was told, some hesitation behind us. We drove on through the smoke and had a short altercation with a German infantryman who tried to shoot us and the Dutchman, but then ran away behind a farmhouse when we machine-gunned him.

Coming out of the smoke I noticed that in front of a large barn an earthwork had been thrown up. I had the gunner fire HE at it. This set the barn on fire and made an even greater cloud of smoke across the front. It turned out subsequently to be a gun emplacement. Why we were not fired on I do not know, as three other tanks involved in the attack were knocked out by the anti-tank gun.

When we entered the village I dropped off the Dutchman and worked over to the left in a field covered with bathroom and lavatory items. There was some sniping, as I heard bullets whizz past my ear but the fighting soon stopped. Fortunately I did not open fire at troops moving on the far side of the Wilhelmina canal as they turned out to be from the Polish Armoured Division! The inhabitants of Oosterhout were most welcoming to us. The village had suffered relatively little damage.[23]

Other civilians in a nearby village were not as lucky. At Kaatsheuvel on the direct route to the Maas crossings the Germans had decided to take root, boosted by three of the huge 105-mm guns. It took an artillery barrage of more than 8,000 shells to open a way through for 5/7th Gordons and 4th Royal Tanks (the former 144 RAC). In the process twenty-eight civilians were killed. The German force on the main road could not avoid being outflanked by a flood of attackers including 7th Argylls, 7th Black Watch and Shermans of 1st Northamptonshire Yeomanry.

Tpr Les 'Spud' Taylor of 1NY saw one of the neighbouring Shermans brewed up by a *Panzerfaust*. The operator was pulled out by the other crew members but died on the road – 'he was so terribly mutilated'. He was buried by the wayside. A white cross was placed over his grave. For some days Les had to travel up and down that road and 'that spot with its white cross gave me the creeps every time we did so'. It was no compensation to Les to hear that in the regiment's battle fifty of the enemy were killed, three anti-tank guns knocked out and over 700 prisoners taken.[24]

Stan Whitehouse, of the Black Watch, with his mate 'Popeye' had an encounter with 'Goliath', one of the immense physical supermen which the German Army seemed to be able to produce from time to time. Stan and Popeye had advanced into a ditch where they could hear German voices on all sides. The enemy were firing *Panzerfaust* bombs designed to knock out tanks. As another one skimmed Stan's hole he became almost hysterical, yelling 'Come on, you Hitler bastards, come on!' Then he saw this 'huge German rising from the opposite ditch and pointing a *Panzerfaust* at us':

I froze as he climbed out and crossed the road towards us, snarling and uttering guttural sounds. I was convinced that this was my last moment on earth. In sheer, futile desperation I picked up a grenade and threw it at him without bothering to pull the pin. The grenade hit his body and bounced away. Screaming deliriously now . . . he emitted a ferocious bellow and lifting the bazooka high, slammed it down on our heads. I recall groaning 'Oh, Mum' and then blacked out.

It looked like the ideal moment to write 'to be continued in our next edition'. How could one survive a moment like that? In fact Stan quickly revived, to find comrades wrestling with the German in the ditch. Then there was a distinct 'pop' which seemed no louder than a cork exiting a bottle. Popeye had recovered his rifle and shot the German at a range of inches. Goliath survived and was eventually marched off towards a doctor and the prison camp. Stan confessed later, 'I had a sneaking admiration for my adversary. He was tough and he had tried to kill me – the bastard, but inexplicably I wished him well'.[25]

Many survivors cherished unusual sights along the way. Pte J.D. Ingham was a company runner with 5/7th Gordon Highlanders. He was sent back to fetch the intelligence officer to interrogate some prisoners. Hit by a shell he lost most of his right leg. He was then seen hopping on one leg for more than 200 yards to complete his mission before being caught by stretcher-bearers and loaded on top of a jeep.[26] Rex Jackson, sitting in the co-driver's seat of his tank just a few yards back from the point of the attack, was astonished to see 'a beefy, red-faced padre', walking along, overtaking the tank, waving cheerfully to all and sundry, as though he was doing some sick visiting in his home parish on a quiet Sunday afternoon.

Perhaps the padre was going to conduct a temporary burial. But it might have been his calm, detached manner, and similar examples from other commanders, which inspired Rex himself to gain a Military Medal on the sand dunes. 1NY had been sent into the dune country outside Loon-op-Zand, and found progress difficult in the soft terrain, while the enemy held the advantage of clear vision at long range. Rex's tank was knocked out. Cpl Percy Sumner's tank alongside was also hit, a shot exploding on the turret and filling Percy's face with minute steel fragments. The injuries were not enough to cause Percy's evacuation but fifty-seven years later his optician would remove one of the fragments from Percy's eye.[27]

In the meantime Rex Jackson had bailed out, but for the moment was not too sure of where he was. As his mind and vision cleared he realized that he was headed towards the enemy lines. He quickly turned and, walking towards safety, saw that his tank was on fire. But it was not totally brewing up in the 'Tommy Cooker' tradition, although the flames in the turret might reach the ammunition and the petrol tanks very quickly. Unsure still about the fate of his comrades, Rex climbed back into the smoking tank, found the fire extinguisher, doused the turret fire, put the tank into reverse gear and drove it back into cover.[28]

Spud Taylor was already 'fazed' by passing that white cross by the roadside. Now he saw his commander, Mike, digging a hole. Spud asked what he was doing. 'I'm digging a hole to bury you in, Spud'. The fact that 1NY sedulously buried all its rubbish even on the worst strewn battlefield and that Mike was simply getting rid of food tins, did not help to settle Spud's mind. Something evil was about to happen.

They moved off down the road. Spud was in the co-driver's seat with a good clear view of the road ahead:

What happened next was like some horrible dream. I saw the armour piercing shot coming towards me! It had a red tracer and it seemed to take hours as if in slow motion. It hit our tank with an almighty clang. 'Old Faithful' shuddered in her tracks and filled with smoke, and once again we smelt that awful acrid odour. The Sherman on the right immediately knocked out the anti-tank gun. We all seemed OK so we did not bail out. The AP shot had left a perfect imprint of itself, grooved out of the side metal, behind which was a rack of 75-mm shells and my head. Mike's earlier crude joke had come within an inch of becoming fact.

Mike was now busy with the binoculars. We passed a lone bungalow which was on fire and an armoured car of 7th Armoured which was still burning. Mike gave me orders to shoot up the woods with the co-driver's Browning. I must have done well because Mike said, 'Very good shooting, Spud'. At that moment there came absolute confusion in the turret which began to rotate at full speed, anti-clockwise. And at every revolution of the turret Mike's face, on a level with my eyes, passed by, covered with blood. He had been shot through the head. He had fallen on top of gunner Titch, jamming Titch's hand on the traverse control.

We were ordered down the road where the Blood Wagon would meet us. It was a hell of a job getting Mike out of the turret. He kept slipping through his great coat. Why he wore the thing I do not know. It took the combined effort of all of us to get him to the ground. He was later laid to rest temporarily in the grounds of a hospital. I felt sorry for the tragic parents of Mike for this was the loss of the last of their three sons in the war.[29]

The little village of Raamsdonk now became the last critical point of German resistance because beyond Raamsdonk the bridge over the Maas at Keizersveer would be in full view of British artillery observers and also within range of the tank guns. The remaining German defenders were deployed in the streets and outskirts, supported by six half-tracks and at least four large self-propelled guns. The Northamptonshire Yeomanry were ordered to seal the gap, taking with them infantrymen of the Black Watch in armoured Kangaroo carriers, ten men to each vehicle. There was little the tanks could do but line up and charge towards St Lambert's church and the Kuijsters' white farmhouse, the final objective of the campaign. This meant that the spearhead could only be one tank wide in the narrow streets.

The resistance would last for two days, but in vain. L/Cpl Reboles, like many young lads, had suddenly been elevated to command of a tank but only to an unpaid rank because the regiment's establishment of senior NCOs was already full, though many of them were away in hospital. He led the way into Raamsdonk. Lt Wall followed him. The two tanks were seen to turn a bend and then the village became an inferno of fire and smoke. Roland England bailing out was blown into a ditch. He was rescued by Germans and an enemy surgeon would skilfully remove shrapnel from his brain. Other tank men perished.

Behind them young farm lad Piet de Bont came up from his cellar where the family sheltered, to check on the cows. He saw German soldiers setting up an anti-tank gun in the farmyard. Across the field the tank of Stan Hilton appeared and at long range, before the astonished gaze of Piet de Bont, Hilton's first shot crashed into the German gun and blew it to pieces. Burning Shermans and enemy half-tracks now blocked that route into the village.

Next morning more tanks repeated the rush along another street. Four tanks burst into the village centre. German S-Ps retaliated at tank's length range. Road edges collapsed and tanks became ditched but continued firing. The German tanks blazed. One Black Watch officer seeing an unburnt S-P in front of his Kangaroo, ordered his driver to charge the S-P and disable it bodily. Crew of one tank bailed out. Driver Wally Tarrant was hit on the head by a hand grenade which did not explode. He threw it back. Cpl Ginns and L/Cpl McKenzie took shelter in a nearby cottage which they would share for the night with scared Germans upstairs.

Troop leader Lt Bobby McColl descended from his tank to confer with the infantry commander and sort out the chaos. A last enemy m-g poured bullets into him. The ditched 1NY tanks dominated the entire street with continuing fire. McColl's driver, Don Foxley, ran into the church seeking cover. He found himself sharing the pews with German wounded and the Kuijsters family.[30]

As the German effort in the village waned, Black Watch Lt Col Cathcart filtered infantry around the main battle, over the low ridge and into view of the coveted bridge. Meanwhile, Maj Lindsay of 1st Gordons, motoring along another route alone in his jeep, was so intent on getting a sight of the River Maas that he drove down to the bank, saw thirty Germans rowing across, and then was greeted by a hail of Spandau fire, causing him to reverse and speed away. At the Keizersveer bridge the word was '*Alles Ausgehen*' ('Everybody go back!') as German engineers hurried a few survivors over the bridge, prior to blowing it before the tanks could power down.[31]

The aftermath found triumph sullied by continuing tragedy. An MC, a DCM, an MM and several Mentions in Despatches were awarded for the Raamsdonk battle. The Kuijsters family's little boy, with other lads let out to play in the new joyous flush of liberation, picked up a discarded phosphorous bomb. It exploded and he was burned to death.

Some soldiers were still counting their lucky stars, like Bill Bellamy's 8th Hussars tank troop. In Loop-op-Zand an enemy 75-mm anti-tank gun had fired at close range. He heard a whooshing noise. The shot 'went diagonally left to right . . . missing us by inches, then struck the ground in front of Bill Pritchard's tank, passed straight under it, emerged at the rear and ricocheted over Alan Howard's turret before disappearing noisily into rear areas'. There were no lucky stars for the enemy gunners.[32]

Frank Gutteridge, sent back to base to collect two new officers, was castigated by the base commandant for not wearing a uniform belt. He was accused of being scruffy and disgracefully badly turned out. When he replied that he had only just come out of the line, the colonel threatened him with arrest and court-martial.

Sgt Danson of 1NY, obtaining one of the first leave passes to the flesh pots of Antwerp, went to the cinema, which was hit by a German V2 rocket. 'Danny' Danson and an untold number of others, civilians and soldiers, were killed as the building collapsed.

CHAPTER ELEVEN

Guns towards the Fatherland

As troops moved to clear the enemy around the right-hand base of the 'thumb', conditions provided a kind of penal servitude. Simonds had needed to sink Walcheren but to the troops in the notorious Peel marshes it seemed as though the earth was sinking spontaneously. Weather again dominated all other considerations.

Fortunately for tank crews, like Ian Hammerton's in XXII Dragoons, new one-piece, padded, relatively insulated suits arrived to replace the thin denim overalls, 'initially one per crew, so we gave one to the driver of each tank. No one, except a tank man, knows how wet and cold you get in a tank, especially when the vehicle is moving through rain. The engine creates a tremendous draught as it sucks air through the open cupola. . . . It also, of course, sucks in rain, dust or mud.'[1]

Another tank gunner found that 'the ground was sodden, swamped, awash from incessant rains. A vast sump of mud across the entire region of the regiment's ordained plan of advance'. It was 'cold . . . damp . . . dark . . . deadly'.[2] The Grenadier Guards reported the area being 'as desolate as an enormous Irish peat-bog in the depths of winter . . . rains came lashing down and within a few hours the surrounding area had been transformed into a sea of mud . . . a terrible concoction of Nature'.[3] Capt Pat Dyas of 4CLY remembered being 'permanently frozen' around Weert, 'damp, dirty, miserable all day long, and the nights indescribable'.[4]

While the airborne troops had been landing around Arnhem and the Guards' tanks were racing up that main Arnhem road, the 11th Armoured Division, with its charging bull emblem, was advancing to the south and east of the main road, providing a parallel protection on the right flank of the exposed advance. From 20 September their tanks were working around the outskirts of the key town of Helmond, seeking to outflank it rather than become committed to costly street fighting. By 25 September a unit from true bull country, 1st Herefords, had cleared the town of the enemy. This resulted in the Germans retreating into the fastness of the almost trackless Peel marshes, like Hereward the Wake in English history. But it seemed that Allied forces were now moving with irresistible impetus.

As yet the Allied columns were thin on the ground. Suddenly, on 27 September, elite troops of 9th SS Panzers and 15th Panzergrenadiers smashed into a gap near Meijel and advanced 6 miles in two days into the still narrow 'thumb'. The whole corridor could still be precarious. More Allied reinforcements were brought up. The Charging Bull men found themselves next to a newly arrived 7th Armoured Division. But this was not the familiar formation of Desert Rats. It was an American unit with the same numeral and similar élan. During the week 1 to 6 October the Americans pounded away at German positions near Overloon with little success.

The Americans, like the British, had been informed that they were facing hastily assembled remnants of the armies shattered in Normandy. They were astonished by the quality of those remnants, so quickly assembled by the astute Gen Student. The very experienced Charging Bull HQ stated of Student's parachutists that they were 'the staunchest soldiers . . . capable of sustaining their desperate role. Like the SS they were picked troops, but their reputation rested less upon propaganda than that of their rivals. Nowhere did they admit the superiority of the SS. . . . Magnificent infantry.'[5]

The British comment noted that the paratroopers were merely the nucleus of the widely varying enemy troops, Germans, young and old, fit and decrepit, as well as foreign conscripts. The German high command was not at all confident about the quality and determination of the whole force. Morale was understandably low among so many men who had seen their units disintegrate and had needed to find means of retreating for hundreds of miles. The authorities acted quickly to stiffen the resolve of the troops.

Hitler was still pinning his hopes on differences arising between the Allies. 'The time will come when the tension between the Allies will become so great that the break will occur. All coalitions in history have disintegrated sooner or later'.[6] The age of universal military service was extended to include those between fifteen and eighteen years of age, and those between fifty and sixty. During September and October some 500,000 men were found from these groups and from combing through reserved occupation and non-combatant units. Strangely the Nazis were averse to mobilizing women and only 182,000 women were employed in war-related work, as compared to some 2,250,000 women from the smaller population of Britain.[7]

Fierce, deterrent orders of the day were made known to the German troops. FM Model's 14 October dictum was given as 'The Commandment of the hour: None of us gives up a square foot of German soil while still alive'. He continued that 'every bunker, every block of houses in a German town, every German village must become a fortress which shatters the enemy'. He made the point that, although fighting continued on Dutch soil, 'on widely separated fronts we must defend . . . the sacred soil of the Fatherland with tenacity and doggedness'.[8] Some of the extreme punishments, both of deserting soldiers and of their families, invoked to reinforce such orders have already been referred to.

Some German soldiers took little account of such propaganda. SS tank commander Gerhardt Stiller was one of those who escaped through hedgerows and ditches from the horrors of the Falaise pocket. Although seriously wounded and wearied from five years of war, he was already back on duty. He saw comrades fighting on even though all was lost, 'their houses destroyed by air attacks, often the young wives, their families, their friends dead . . . most of us had become automatons, most of the soldiers brutalized, dulled, unable to think. But holding their position. All men of my company were standing to the banner and there were no desertions. . . . Prussian tradition!'[9]

On the British side there was great suspicion of propaganda in any form. Montgomery has been credited with boosting the morale of his men, more by personal encounters than by his brazen and misleading public declarations. Glyn Sherrington of the Fife and Forfar Yeomanry remembers Monty halting his jeep as some of the Yeomen were relaxing on a village green. They all stood up to salute but the field marshall, in his best voice of command, yelled 'Sit down!' In a more friendly tone he asked, 'Have you seen the *Daily Mirror* today?' (an impossible mailing feat for ordinary soldiers). He then commanded his driver to hand around copies of the newspaper. 'When do you think this war will end?' he queried. One of the troopers varied considerably from Monty's estimate. The commander then bet the trooper half-a-crown on the outcome. Months later the trooper realized that he had lost the bet.[10]

Most British servicemen had received some kind of religious education in Sunday schools or day school. It was logical that, in the face of the many horrifying manifestations of death visible on the battlefield, men should think more seriously about eternal affairs. Lt Peter White found that 'for any faith in continuity at all, one had to search for something outside of human structure and organisation on which to rely'. Therefore at church parades or impromptu religious gatherings in the fields, 'we were all much more thoughtful than usual and sincere in prayer'.[11] During the advance through the Peel marshes nine soldiers of 1st Northamptonshire Yeomanry were allowed time off to be confirmed by the Bishop of Dover, who was visiting front-line regiments.[12]

Canadian Russ Clarke had a truly enlightening religious experience. A voluntary church parade was being held in a school, the only substantial building available. Even the school had holes in the roof. The service took place in dim light. Hymns and a sermon proceeded solemnly. Then, as Russ and others went forward to take communion, the sun suddenly shone for the first time for days. It pierced like a searchlight down through a hole in the roof, raying directly on the kneeling men and reflecting off the rain-soaked floor. It was like a sacred vision. Another soldier turned to Russ as they knelt and said, 'I think we'll make it'. (Russ confesses, 'I am not a deeply religious soul', but the moment was sublime, unique, inextinguishable.)[13]

Morale boosting among front-line troops more often resulted from extempore humour, often in grim situations. As crews of the Northamptonshire Yeomanry listened anxiously for news on their wireless earphones, the ever-cheerful Recce Sergeant Kenny Jack, who had made contact with the Dutch Resistance, called HQ. 'Hullo, Sugar 6. I have made contact with the Chief of the Underground.' HQ immediately replied, 'Good! Take a ticket to Victoria on the Circle line.'[14] Capt Ian Hammerton, during a moment's break in battle turmoil, looked for his bottle of whisky to share with the frozen, soaking-wet men of his troop. He found the level in the bottle suspiciously low. So he challenged his driver, Basil Frost, who looked him straight in the eyes and stated emphatically, 'Evaporated, sir!'[15]

One engineer unit long cherished the recollection of a sarcastic, foul-mouthed, unpopular sergeant-major who was superintending the building of a pontoon bridge. Stepping off a pontoon to get into a small boat he misjudged his distance and landed on the bows of the boat, which tipped over and launched him feet first on to the water. After one or two frantic running steps he sank into the canal. One of the sappers instantly proclaimed, 'He might think he's Godalmighty, but he can't walk on water'.[16]

Bill Moseley, of 1NY, and some mates had found a large, fairly clean pigsty near Helden. The single indolent sow seemed amenable to their sharing residence with her. Next morning the black beret of one of Bill's mates was missing. Eventually they discovered that the pig had eaten the beret, but had left the badge. Amid raucous laughter the Yeomen, scions of a humble peacetime part-time regiment, vowed, 'if it had been an 11th Hussars or 17/21st Lancers badge the bloody pig would have eaten that as well'.[17]

As indirectly with the pig, morale could be boosted by contact with animals. Echelon driver C.J. Teague arrived in a front-line village:

The village was being bombarded by the enemy. A very frightened dog was in a yard, tied up and unable to move as Moaning Minnie mortar bombs with their siren noises fell into the area of the house and exploded. Risking both the bombs and the wide-eyed, snarling, frothing German Shepherd, two or three of us went into the yard. We offered the dog some corned beef. We gingerly loosened him and then led him off into the shelter of a ditch. That dog became our constant companion, sitting in the cab of our lorry and guarding it from all comers, friend or foe.[18]

Men of the King's Own Scottish Borderers noticed a peculiar fact about goats. A few goats had survived in a farm which was under constant bombardment. The men noticed that, long before any sound had reached human ears, the goats were diving for cover. Soon a batch of Moaning Minnies arrived, normally six of them. After the explosions the goats emerged from cover again. With their acute hearing they had learned to associate the remote 'pop' of the mortars being fired with the eventual 'CRASH', flame and shrapnel of their landing. The KOSBs thereafter took their cue, diving for cover with the goats as long as the unit stayed in the farmyard.[19]

Sgt Jack Pentelow, accustomed to riding in a noisy tank, learned a similar lesson when shepherding some veteran German infantrymen back as prisoners. Without warning the men dived into a ditch. Jack was still standing wondering when the first batch of bombs fell around them. So, for the rest of the walk back, when the enemy dived, Jack, partially deafened by riding in tanks, dived too.[20]

For most of the fighting soldiers, most of the time, there was a monotonous absence of enthusiasm and exhilaration. Then in brief moments there occurred opportunities for heroism or deadly quirks of fatal circumstance. Sgt G.H. Eardley with 4th King's Shropshire Light Infantry found the way forward near Overloon blocked by three m-g posts occupied by the skilled and resolute paratroopers. The KSLI attack had stalled. Armed with only an unreliable Sten gun and a few grenades, surprising friend and foe alike, Eardley charged forward alone, destroying the posts one by one and driving off the enemy. He was awarded the Victoria Cross.

George Harold Eardley volunteered for the army in 1940, already twenty-seven years of age, and married and with three children. Eventually he was posted to 4KSLI. He joined them in Normandy on 31 July 1944 as a private. Incredibly he won the Military Medal on the next day, 1 August, crawling unobserved through deep mud alone to attack an m-g post. By 15 October, his VC day, he was an acting sergeant and, at thirty-two years of age, a really 'old' soldier.

Surprisingly he was of slight stature – no bully boy at 5ft 6in and weighing only 9 stone. His father said of him, 'He was never a daring lad but he was good at sport', particularly cricket. Harold (to his family) Eardley continued in the army until 1950, achieving sergeant-major's rank, and then became a Rolls-Royce electrical engineer. Having prodigiously escaped wounding in the war, he found civilian life not so kind. In 1964 his car was hit by a train at Nantwich, Cheshire. His second wife was killed and he lost a foot in the accident. He died in 1991.[21]

The two commanding officers of 3RTR and 3rd Monmouthshires were thinking of nothing more alarming than a conference with Brigadier Harvey as they joined him at a roadside rendezvous which seemed safe enough. Just then an attack from another direction flushed out two German half-tracks which sped towards the O group, firing furiously. The brigadier and his brigade major were both wounded, the latter seriously. Lt Col Silvertop and Lt Col Orr were killed instantly. They were highly esteemed veterans who had survived all the horrors and extreme dangers with the lead tanks of the catastrophic Operation Goodwood in Normandy.[22]

The wild marshes and woods of the Peel in the Zwarte Plak (Black Acres) around Helden were ideal places for hiding from the enemy. Evaders were mainly Jews, known Resistance workers and escaping Allied air crews travelling the 'Pilot Line' of Dutch, Belgian and French hosts. Here the Resistance became very bold. Because of food rationing they raided food offices to obtain food coupons for persons in hiding. They held up registration offices to find blank passports and other official papers. They also deleted Jewish names from municipal rolls so that the Germans would not search for those persons. One famous massed raid took place successfully in July 1944 on the Helden-Panningen registration office.[23]

The Germans retaliated with raids on churches and businesses and organised forced collections of war goods, such as bicycles, radios, food, church bells and heavy transport. On 8 October, with the Allies approaching, the Gestapo arranged a manhunt in Helden, Sevenum, Heythuysen and Helenaven. On Sunday they surrounded the Sevenum church during the crowded mass, taking away every male between sixteen and sixty-five years of age. These churchgoers in their Sunday best were marched away, soon to become slaves in fine rags as they dug trenches and tank obstacles along the Maas.[24]

Meanwhile the main Allied offensive in the area had been postponed for two days because of the incessant rain. Then on 12 October the soldiers were astonished to look up into radiant blue skies with brilliant sunshine. It was time for the battle of Overloon, which has become memorable, not only for the details of the fighting but also because local people decided to leave part of the battlefield as it was as a memorial. This led to the establishment there of a Dutch National Museum of Remembrance.

The battle has been described, and is still talked about in the museum itself, as 'the only tank battle' which took place in the Netherlands during the war. Perhaps 'only major tank battle' is more correct. There were a number of occasions when tanks fought tanks in lesser numbers in the Netherlands.[25] One Dutch authority has commented that:

There was also something reminiscent of the trench warfare of September 1916 . . . [when] the very first tanks used in battle trundled forward on the Somme front, dispersed among the infantry, but hampered by the pot-holed, shell-cratered ground, unable to carry out any independent task. . . . The battle for Overloon is more an echo from the past rather than an example of modern, mechanized war of movement, which had been characteristic of the fighting during the preceding months.[26]

The terrain again conditioned the style of battle. Douglas Waller, an NCO with 1st Rifle Brigade, remembered 'there was a big forest. We got quite involved in a big battle there. It was a ghostly sort of place. You didn't really see anything, just fleeting glimpses in a forest. And you were always firing at shadows'.[27] Capt Arthur Rous, the adjutant of 1st South Lancs, was happy that there was now some effective cooperation with the tanks, but not so happy about other aspects of his responsibilities:

I felt that it was not until we got into the Netherlands that we really knew how to cooperate with tanks. It was in the Netherlands that we were first able to go behind the tank and speak to commanders through a phone attached to the tank. After the American division had tried at Overloon, our 8th Brigade attacked. It was a particularly unpleasant battle because of minefields. The weather was deteriorating again. There was no shelter of any kind and the ground was unsuitable for tanks and vehicles. We had great difficulty in actually feeding our men. We had one coy which did not get a meal all day until 2 a.m. – the only occasion in the war where we had a coy which didn't get a hot meal during a battle.[28]

The tanks available were from the 6th Guards Tank Brigade and consisted of 4th Grenadier and 4th Coldstream Guards. An independent tank brigade differed from an independent armoured brigade, being equipped with the much slower (than Shermans) but more heavily armour-plated Churchills. These were intended mainly to attack stationary strong points. Their 75-mm guns were not efficient against better German tank guns. They were to support the 2nd East Yorks of 3rd Division, who were directed to a 'dog-shaped' wood outside Overloon. 1st Suffolks would move to the right of the Yorkshiremen. They were encouraged by a barrage laid down by four artillery regiments. The American fighter bombers roared in overhead to blast enemy positions.

Unfortunately many of those positions were in built-up areas from which the Germans had tried to evacuate civilians. Not all civilians had left their homes, while in the Santa Anna 'asylum' (psychiatric hospital) near Venray refugees had congregated. On 30 September an air bomb had killed sixteen patients. On 5 October another bomb hit a ward where the extreme cases of 'lunacy' were treated.

Now, on 12 October, Sister Marie-Godelieve of the Sisters of Mercy had 1,500 patients crowded into the cellars, with more refugees coming to seek shelter. The hospital was at the epicentre of the bombardment but fortunately the cellars were deep and the walls strongly constructed.[29] However, the psychiatric effect of the noise, vibrations and dust clouds on critically ill patients was beyond estimation.

In a nearby maternity ward where women were in labour the impact was more physical. As Mrs Jannsen was giving birth her neighbour in the next bed was hit by shrapnel and severely wounded in both legs. When the wounded woman was separated from her baby and taken away to be operated on, Mrs Jannsen found herself compelled to breast-feed both babies as the battle raged on. Many other civilians, hiding for safety in the woods, found that the battle tended to centre on the trees. Numbers were killed or wounded.[30]

The barrage assisted the advancing troops but stiff German resistance still caused problems. A Coy of the Suffolks had walked as far as a burned-out windmill when they were hit by well-concealed snipers. Seven men were killed, including the coy commander, and a sergeant had to take charge. The East Yorks, moving through the dog-shaped wood, saw tanks of the Coldstream Guards blowing up on mines which had been sown profusely. The East Yorks D Coy also encountered mines and their leading men, including the coy commander and all their officers and senior NCOs, became casualties. A corporal took over the remnants of the company.

Their CO, Lt Col Dickson, was blown over by a Moaning Minnie bomb. He was able to continue directing his men and the remaining tanks into Overloon, clearing the village, but later he was found to be badly harmed physically by the blast. Overloon was free, but at a considerable price.

As the battle continued the tanks of the Grenadiers rendered valued service in rescuing wounded infantry from areas sown with *Schü* mines, potentially fatal to walking men but with insufficient power to harm a tank. Spr G. Duncan in a Churchill of 617th Assault Sqn experienced both types of mines:

We hit a mine more powerful than the previous one which we had hit but had not disabled the tank. This one blew the bottom of the tank in, injuring all of us in different parts. The driver and front gunner both had broken ribs and cracked skulls. We in the turret all had leg injuries. The officer in our tank climbed out and was immediately killed by a sniper. So we stayed put until the medics came up a while later. [Churchills did not 'brew up' as rapidly as Shermans.][31]

As the advance rolled forward, men of the Royal Engineers had the formidable task of probing into unknown territory to check for minefields. The flail tanks could open narrow paths but it was necessary to clear wider stretches of country as infantry and supply services moved up. Lt P.H. Dixon was one of those who ventured out on recce in this way:

> There were a number of empty mine boxes lying around, so it was obvious that some had been sown along the way. It would take a long time with mine detectors to find and clear the mines. I therefore requested that the brigadier should loan me a tank. He gave me a light Honey tank driven by a tank sergeant. We drove along looking for patches of disturbed earth. Then there were three successive explosions. These blew me right out of the tank but also blew my helmet and glasses off sending them up higher than my head. Landing outside on the ground, when I tried to get up I found my leg had been broken by the blast and I was carried off wounded. But at least the location of the mines had been discovered![32]

Ian Hammerton and his Dragoons in their flailing 'Crabs' were now experts in dealing with mines. In Normandy the battlefields had largely been clear of civilians. Now there were 'streams of refugees, adults and children, lugging their bundles of possessions along the farm tracks'. And, of course, along the tracks the anti-personnel mines were strewn in most profusion. 'How could we warn them of the deadly dangers? It was impossible of course.' The Dragoons were under great pressure with their own military duties. They could only look on appalled as distant civilians were blown up on mines.

Even the Dragoons themselves were not supermen when out of their vehicles. Ian's crew had offered some passing infantrymen tea, which was easily brewed on or even inside a tank. The footmen joked, 'That's better tea than we get. Why do the tankies have better tea than us?' Wireless operator Bob Burdett jumped off the tank to show the infantrymen the tin of 'compo' tea issued to tank crews. He landed on the path where hundreds of feet had already trodden. But he landed right on an undiscovered mine and one of his feet was blown off. Hammerton was saddened but reassured by the fact that Bob could be immediately carried to an aid post a few yards away, treated, put on a medical jeep and rushed off to Base Hospital near Weert. Within hours Bob was on a plane returning to England.[33]

The 51st Highland Division had been switched from the north-west section of the River Maas down to the edge of the Peel marshes at Nederweert. The Shermans of the Northamptonshire and East Riding Yeomanries and 144 RAC had come with them. Where good roads existed it was possible, against crumbling enemy defences, to make a 4-mile advance in a day. The infantrymen were able to ride in the Kangaroo carriers, which reduced casualties considerably.

The Germans could not destroy 144 RAC but the War Office could. In the arcane manner of military HQ, the men of 144 were simply told that they would henceforth be known as 4th Royal Tank Regiment (4RTR), thus resurrecting a battalion which had been wiped out by Rommel years before in the Western Desert. Nobody explained why.

Bill Moseley with 1NY was more concerned about trying to keep dry in the persistent rain and mist. He was also fascinated by the fact that the signal lights on canal lock gates were still working in spite of the total blackout everywhere else. Capt Rathbone was preparing to go forward to explore ways over the canal ahead, when he was met by a staff officer who informed him that a captain had no right to be so far forward. 'Send a sergeant!' he was told. So Sgt Huitson was sent to recce.

Huitson's troop leader, Lt Edward Vaughan Green, then led his tanks over lock gates to the other side of the water barrier. Vaughan Green was a peacetime schoolmaster and a poet of some note. In the evening he was called to an O group in the local school. By some freak of war, one single salvo of six *Nebelwerfer* bombs was launched at random and landed around Vaughan Green in the school yard. Ken Lyke and Shorty Coleman from his crew rushed to the place but could do little to help. Capt Rathbone, who had been a master at the same Brackley school as Vaughan, emerged from the school and quickly confirmed that the voice of a poet of considerable potential had been stilled for ever.[34]

Capt Ian Hammerton had already avoided enough fatal dangers for one lifetime. As the advance continued from Weert to Helden-Panningen he experienced perhaps his luckiest escape of the war. His tank went roaring up a Panningen street with the impetus of 30 tons of armoured steel, propelled by an engine capable of exceeding a 30-mph limit. Hammerton turned round in the turret for a moment to check that his other vehicles were following in good order. At that point he was struck a tremendous blow on the head. His helmet was knocked into the street and his wireless headset roughly ripped off. He had collided at speed with a taut signal cable strung across the street.

If the cable had caught him across neck or throat he could have been decapitated instantly. It was an accident quite familiar to tank commanders. His billet that night was inside a brick kiln. But the fires were out and it was unbearably cold and draughty.[35]

The lottery of war casualties never ceased. Cpl David Bucke had served the maximum time in the Middle East under the 'Python' scheme, became due for long home leave, and was then sent to 1NY as a reinforcement. Coming to the regiment at this time he was given command of Vaughan Green's tank. 'You'll find us a helpful lot', said Shorty Coleman as they shook hands. They mounted the tank.

Less than ten minutes along the road Shorty saw a 'black, sharp missile' rushing at immense speed across the fields towards them. It slammed into the tank, which 'brewed like a blast furnace'. 'Bale out!' was Bucke's single order. And then in the ditch, Bucke grumbled, 'Bugger that! Six bloody months to get here. One sodding day in command. Ten flaming minutes of battle. Would you credit it?'[36]

Ken Ward had driven his tank out of Helden, leaving behind the emerging civilians with their cheers, wine, flowers and kisses. Ahead was what appeared to be an uninhabited wilderness in a sea of brown paste. His tank began to tip and sway as though about to sink into bottomless depths. 'Halt!' Another Sherman was burrowing its snout in the deep mess, like a pig at a trough. The squadron recovery tank was trying to pull the Sherman out, but the weight of the combined tanks was drawing the recovery vehicle down into the mud. Dragoon tanks on the flank, with their flails beating the earth as though trying to dig a trench, were also sinking helplessly. Once again an attack had stalled as the weather gods dictated.

The German Army was being squeezed out of that part of the Netherlands, but as the enemy soldiers reluctantly retreated it was often the civilians who suffered worst.

Ger Schinck would one day become Burgomaster of St Michielsgestel. During the Limburg fighting he was a six-month-old baby. His family owned a large house and had been forced to billet sixty enemy soldiers. As the Allies approached, the civilians were told to pack up and leave, within a quarter of an hour. Ger's mother hurriedly prepared the family, three brothers, one sister and the grandmother. They took what food they could lay their hands on after the retreating enemy had looted the home.

They did not know that they would be required to walk 15 kilometres in icy weather with snow underfoot. They did not know that the walk would take two days until they arrived at a railway station. They did not know that their transport would be in closed cattle-trucks with no heating and no food supplies. They did not know if they were going to extermination camps or slave labour.

In the trucks the older and weaker people lay on straw, while the fitter people stood crammed together. Many suffered frostbite as the train wound its way first into Germany and then back into the north of the Netherlands. They lost count of time but finally agreed that about ten days had passed while the train traversed some 200 miles of bleak winter country. Some people, nobody counted the number, died from cold and lack of food and water.

At last the train stopped and they were ordered out. They found themselves in a remote, frost-stricken rural region somewhere near Groningen. Local people, themselves on short rations, did their best to give the refugees shelter and some support. It was almost as bad as riding in the cattle trucks. The winter of 1944–5 was one of the worst in living memory in the Netherlands. Old people and babies died. When the war ended Ger's uncle drove in his truck to the north to find the refugees from their tiny village. Eighteen of them had died, all either babies or people over eighty. Miraculously Ger, not yet one year old, survived to tell the story.[37]

On 23 November 'Spud' Taylor's tank was halted in some anonymous waste land, as had so often happened all the way from the Normandy beaches. Their guns pointed whither they had been ordered, apparently with no urgent purpose. Suddenly a cheerful voice broke into the wireless silence:

> 'Hullo, all stations Yoke. Stand fast. Your guns are now pointing over the frontier into Germany itself. Range anything from 2,000 yards. Fire at random in your own time, ten rounds 75 each. That's Hitler's country in front. Good shooting! Yoke, off.'

Les thought of civilians killed and bombed out of their homes back in Blighty, mates hurriedly shovelled into unsanctified holes along the long road from Normandy, other comrades burned or mutilated and lying in British hospitals, stories of that concentration camp back in Vught. With more purpose than ever before, he began to load the big gun.[38]

CHAPTER TWELVE

Reflections on the Water

This book has not been concerned with the central events of 'the bridge too far' at Arnhem. However, the Arnhem 'failure' impinged on many events dealt with here, so a brief reference to the overall picture is relevant.

As with Operation Goodwood in Normandy, those who fought at the Market Garden bridges have resented the use of the word 'failure'. In both cases a considerable advance was made and some of the rapidly decreasing enemy strength was 'written down'. Failure relates only to the fact that action did not measure up to Montgomery's apparent intentions. In this area of misunderstanding perhaps Montgomery himself was the worst enemy.

Historians have noted that 'the wartime benefits if "Market Garden" had succeeded were potentially enormous', and that if ground forces of the western Allies had ended the war nearer Berlin, post-war politics would have been different. Poland might never have been a vassal of the USSR for more than forty years.[1]

While not unanimous, some historians and biographers have come to the conclusion that Market Garden 'failed, was always likely to fail and showed a serious error of judgement on Montgomery's part. The idea . . . was simple and potentially effective; but it ignored the realities of the situation'.[2]

Part of the problem was Montgomery's own personality. He was seen as 'so obsessed with the driving need to be right, and to persuade everyone that he was so, that he managed to persuade himself', this being a 'grotesque flaw in a rigid, frigid personality'.[3]

It is instructive to study an enemy point of view on the failure of Montgomery's expectations. An opinion authorised by the German C-in-C, West, considered that:

The main error on the part of the enemy was that 1 English [sic] Airborne Division was not set down all at once but in the course of 3 days, and that 1 to 2 further airborne divisions were not brought up into the area west of Arnhem.

11 SS PZ Corps which was resting and refitting was an unpleasant surprise for him. Here his intelligence service, in spite of the very best liaison through agents, failed. The enemy had armoured cars and heavy a/tk guns . . . [but] in the fighting for the bridges the enemy sits tight in houses situated close by. The time required between landing from the air and moving to the attack was comparatively long – 2 to 3 hours. Thereby chance of success through surprise at Arnhem was missed.[4]

Blame has, of course, been apportioned lower down in the chain of command. Gen 'Boy' Browning disregarded aerial evidence of the German SS Panzers lurking around Arnhem. His decision to ignore this, and to consign to sick leave Maj Urquhart, who vehemently and correctly argued against launching the attack, 'led to the catastrophic loss of the British 1st Airborne Division on the ill-fated operation'.[5] But Montgomery could have said 'No!'.

Looking at the larger picture, it might be relevant to comment on two issues which are less frequently mentioned. The first is the apparent assumption that, if the Arnhem bridge had been captured, by some miracle the German Army would have cut and run and that none of their troops, in the manner of KG Chill, would have obstructed the progress of the Allied Army in Walcheren, Noord Brabant or Limburg.

Given an advance beyond the Arnhem bridge, the even more extended 'thumb' might have become still more precarious. Montgomery would be looking out into the 'open plains' of Germany with some available divisions weary and at perhaps less than 50 per cent of their D-Day efficiency. Other essential divisions, like 49th and 51st, would still have been tied down hundreds of miles back as their transport had been taken away to offset the failure to open up Antwerp. Also German reaction to further advance would have been quite different to their headlong flight through France and Belgium. Several versions of the Goodwood catastrophe might have been waiting for the Allied tanks on the open plains beyond Arnhem.

A second factor which affected the entire campaign was the failure to give due consideration to the stark problem which stares out from every map of the Low Countries: water. There was a serious lack of appropriate or sufficient equipment to tackle the extent of water problems. There was also a lack of training in a realistic battle doctrine for the troops at ground level.

On the question of equipment, the unfortunate Dorsets, sent in as a last attempt to relieve the survivors of the Arnhem bridge fighting, were issued with frail kapok boats which could be sunk by a few m-g bullets, and were expected to cross water dominated by m-gs firing 1,200 rounds a minute. The Canadians suffered similarly around Breskens and elsewhere.

It must also have been obvious that the Germans would blow bridges as they retreated. The normal doctrine was to wait until nightfall and then send the REs up to put a temporary bridge across the water. In the specific instance of St Michielsgestel, Randy Ginns and other tanks of the Northamptonshire Yeomanry and infantry of 7th Black Watch stood on the near bank of the Dommel amid the ruins of the bridge and totally dominated the far bank. Had there been a tank-bearing Bailey bridge in echelon immediately behind 2 Troop of 1NY the advance could have continued almost without pause. Instead some twelve hours had to be wasted.[6]

It was not only the wide ship canals and rivers which caused water problems. Lt Bill Bellamy's 3 Troop encountered two less spacious but equally fraught hazards. Bursting through a massive hedge they found themselves in the midst of a strong enemy position with heavy anti-tank guns. They had to reverse their Cromwells at full speed. Their direct route back was barred by a 21 ft wide drainage dyke, not by any means in the top category of Dutch waterways. Their only method of crossing was to rev up engines, hit full speed, charge the ditch and jump over it like steeple-chasers or trick motor-cyclists. One driver forgot to declutch, so as to land on free running tracks, and his tank virtually stood on its nose.

In the same area, near St Oedenrode, as Bill was watching a fire fight, his driver Chamberlain, hatch closed down, was unable to see through his periscope that a narrow ditch lay ahead. Bill's tank stood on its nose down in the gully, leaving driver and co-driver 'up to their arses in freezing cold water'. The troop leader had to mount another tank while the sodden drivers helplessly waited for the rescue vehicle to pull them out.[7]

Montgomery is usually regarded as an outstanding trainer of troops but many of the situations of Normandy and the Netherlands were not contemplated in that training. The infantry officer of one of Montgomery's 'own' elite veteran divisions remarked that only at Overloon were they acquiring basic skills in working with tanks.

It would be difficult to calculate a butcher's bill related to the events in this book which were made necessary or whose problems were exacerbated by the Arnhem failure. In relation only to the failure to open the Antwerp seaway, a Canadian authority has calculated that clearing the Scheldt cost the Canadian Army 12,873 casualties. Of these 6,367 were Canadian soldiers, the others being mainly British, Polish and Belgian.[8] The entire amphibious vehicle strength of two battalions of Buffaloes had to be used up on Walcheren.

Lack of a strategy, or desire, to cross the Lower Maas and liberate more towns in the Netherlands resulted in intolerable suffering for the civilians who were thus deliberately omitted from the first flood of liberation. In this respect Montgomery's share of responsibility is less than that of those who made wider policy decisions.

Amidst all the statistics the main impact of relative failure or impeded success on the individual soldier was very personal. Statistics into the thousands meant little. It was the tiny, focused tragedy which tore at heartstrings and fed the ever-nagging fear:

the body of a ten-year-old Dutch girl, unknown;
the white cross beside the road;
the staring eyes of the dead tank commander rotating endlessly in the turret;
the sailors drowning in the waves while one's own boat was sinking;

the German prisoner who was too tired to keep his hands raised in surrender;
the nineteen-year-old replacement gunner who came up, died within minutes and was taken away, and whose name we never knew until we saw it in the Roll of Honour or on his gravestone.[9]

And often, added to the memories of the face, the voice, the form, the habits of the lost comrade there was the sense of human quality, future riches of friendship, inestimable personal value, lost for ever. Such was the loss of a quiet schoolmaster turned tank troop leader who found a way across lock gates over the water near Weert, went to an O group in a school, was hit by a single random salvo in the schoolyard and was buried in Nederweert cemetery.

Crew members Ken Lyke and Shorty Coleman had brought the dead Vaughan Green's kit to Michael Rathbone, Vaughan's fellow schoolmaster and friend. The captain had sorted through the kit and found, among other handwritten papers, Vaughan's last unfinished poem, dated just fourteen days before and ending, as far as it would ever be completed by the poet, in broken-limbed rhythm, thus:

> We now have a newer duty
> and a harder burden of thanks
> to pay to those dead without shriving,
> caught in the water-logged holes
> they had dug for themselves in the ground,
> or trapped in their burning tanks,
> younger, more tortured souls,
> who, of their little wealth of days,
> since they only had life, must give it.
> Oh long we shall look in vain
> for the young heads,
> the dark and the fair ones,
> gone now their careless ways . . .

(E.V.G. 1.11.44).[10]

Glossary

AP	armour-piercing (shot)
AVRE	armoured vehicle adapted for engineering use
bn	battalion
brigade	normally three battalions
Cdr	commander
CO	commanding officer
coy	company
Cpl	corporal
CSM	command sergeant major
DCM	Distinguished Conduct Medal (other ranks)
Division	(usually three brigades, nine battalions)
DSC	Distinguished Service Cross (naval officers)
DSO	Distinguished Service Order (military, air officers)
Firefly	Sherman tank with the heavier 17-pounder gun
F/Lt	flight lieutenant
FM	field marshal
Flg Off	flying officer
FOO	forward observation officer (artillery)
HE	high-explosive (shell)
HQ	headquarters
Honey	British name for American Stuart light tank
IWM	Imperial War Museum
KG	*Kampfgruppe*, German battle group (any mix of troops)
laager/leaguer	armoured assembly area/camp
LCA	landing craft
LCF	landing craft flak
LCG	landing craft gun
LCH	command (HQ) landing craft

LCI	landing craft infantry
LCS	landing craft support
LCT	landing craft tank
L/Cpl	lance-corporal
MC	Military Cross (normally army officers)
m-g	machine-gun
MM	Military Medal (army other ranks)
NCO	non-commissioned officer (e.g. sergeant, corporal)
Nebelwerfer	German mortar, the 'Moaning Minnies'
OC	officer commanding
O group	any group gathered to issue and receive orders
OP	observation post (usually artillery or similar)
ORs	other ranks (non-officers)
Panzer	German armour, mainly tanks and S-Ps
Panzerfaust	'armoured fist', hand-held bomb projector
PIAT	projector, infantry, anti-tank weapon
PO	petty officer (navy)
P/O	pilot officer (RAF)
Pte	private (lowest military rank)
QM	quartermaster
RA	Royal Artillery
RAC	Royal Armoured Corps (cavalry, yeomanry, RTR and numbered RAC battalions)
RAMC	Royal Army Medical Corps
RAP	regimental aid post
RASC	Royal Army Service Corps
RE	Royal Engineers
regiment	in the British Army, a battalion of cavalry or yeomanry tanks, or a complete organization like the RTR; in the German and other armies a regiment is a battle formation equivalent to the British brigade
Rfn	Rifleman
RTR	Royal Tank Regiment (several battalions)
SM	sergeant major
SP	self-propelled gun – heavy gun on tank tracks
Spandau	the fast-firing German m-g
Spr	sapper
sqdn	squadron (in the army, a company of tanks)

SS	*Schutzstaffel*, originally Hitler's bodyguard; in 1944 the SS provided front-line army units but partially under separate command of Himmler
SWWEC	Second World War Experience Centre, Horsforth, Leeds
Tpr	trooper
VC	Victoria Cross – the highest award for valour
Wehrmacht	normal Germany army units, as distinct from Himmler's SS
WO	warrant officer
1NY	(e.g.) 1st Northamptonshire Yeomanry, a regiment (battalion) of the overall Northamptonshire Yeomanry Regiment (complete organization of two battalions at least)

Notes and References

Unit war diaries or histories are not noted unless the quotation is of special significance. Because of the various methods of communication used, personal information direct to the author is noted only by the individual's name and the year. See Bibliography for publication details.

CHAPTER 1. BEGGARY AND BRAVERY

1. Local information from Karel Govaerts, Merxplas historian, 2002.
2. D. Scott, *Polar Bears from Sheffield*, and Don Scott, 2002.
3. John R. Dean, 2002.
4. Roy Simon (died 2002) per Don Scott, 2002.
5. D. Scott, *Polar Bears*, and Victoria Cross citation.
6. Royal Leicestershire Regiment history.
7. Contemporary information from Karel Govaerts, 2002.
8. Walter Shea, Imperial War Museum (IWM), taped recording.
9. John Brown and Fred Tattersall, Thorne, 2002.

CHAPTER 2. MAD TUESDAY AND BLACK FRIDAY

1. Mad Tuesday information from W.D. Whitaker and S. Whitaker, *The Battle of the Scheldt*, and other accounts.
2. W. Close, *A View from the Turret*, and 2002.
3. L. Taylor, *Tommy Cooker*.
4. W. Moseley, '*From Arromanches to the Elbe*', and 2002.
5. Tessa Carpenter, 2002.
6. Dr Ger Schinck, 2002.
7. G. Hayes, 'Where are our Liberators?', in *Canadian Military History*.

8. W.Th. Lagarde, 2002–3.
9. G. Hayes, 'Where are our Liberators?'
10. K. Tout, *Tanks, Advance!*
11. K. Tout, *The Bloody Battle for Tilly.*
12. Black Watch history and T. Copp, *The Brigade.*

CHAPTER 3. ARNHEM – THE SORE THUMB

1. Harold Lander, Second World War Experience Centre (SWWEC) archive.
2. Mileages from current maps.
3. 29 September 1944, 1 Corps Report.
4. L.F. Ellis, *Victory in the West.*
5. A. Chalfont, *Montgomery of Alamein.*
6. *Ibid.*
7. C. Wilmot, *The Struggle for Europe.*
8. 17 September, 'Personal Message to be Read to All Troops', per P. Odgers, SWWEC.
9. Author refrains from quoting average battle-worn trooper's response to 'the Lord's doing'.
10. This review based largely on Public Record Office (PRO) summary.
11. S.W. Mitcham, *Hitler's Field Marshals.*
12. Andrew Horne, 2002.
13. Lander, SWWEC archive.
14. G.G. Simonds, 'General Simonds Speaks', in *Canadian Military History.*
15. Mitcham, *Hitler's Field Marshals.*
16. H.F. Stanley, Report 19/20 September 1944, PRO.
17. M. Reynolds, *Sons of the Reich.*
18. P. Delaforce, *The Fighting Wessex Wyverns.*
19. Reg Spittles, 2002–3.
20. A. Carder, SWWEC tape.
21. Lander, SWWEC archive.
22. C.N. Barclay, *The History of 53rd (Welsh) Division.*
23. E.A. Smith, *Recce Troop Memories* (private circulation).
24. W. Moseley, *From Arromanches to the Elbe.*
25. L. Taylor, *Tommy Cooker.*
26. T. Saunders, *Hell's Highway.*
27. Reynolds, *Sons of the Reich.*
28. Spittles, 2002–3.

29. W. Rawling, 'Medical Practice in an Armoured Division', in *Canadian Military History*, vol. 6, no. 1, 1997.
30. Maria's diary per Louis Kleijne, trans. Tessa Carpenter.
31. W.Th. Lagarde, 2002–3.
32. XXX Corps history.
33. W. Brereton, *A Salford Boy Goes to War*.
34. A. Borthwick, *Battalion*.
35. Ibid.
36. M. Shulman, *Defeat in the West*.

CHAPTER 4. ANTWERP: THE GENERALS FORGOT

1. W.D. Whitaker and S. Whitaker, *The Battle of the Scheldt*.
2. W. Close, *A View from the Turret*.
3. I.C. Hammerton, *Achtung! Minen!*
4. W.D. Whitaker, own experience, 1999.
5. *Ibid.*
6. Close, *View*.
7. P. Roberts, *From the Desert to the Baltic*.
8. T. Copp, *The Brigade*.
9. W.R. Bennett, *Vignettes*.
10. W.R. Bennett, own observations, 2001 – the author agrees.
11. Also Tpr Joe Ekins, destroyer of the elite Wittmann troop in Normandy, unique feat, no decoration; see K. Tout, *A Fine Night for Tanks*.
12. Based on a member of the patrol in Copp, *Brigade*.
13. G. Blackburn, *The Guns of Victory*, and 1999.
14. A Blackburn action recorded by someone else; D.J. Goodspeed, *Battle Royal*.
15. Blackburn, *Guns*.
16. *Ibid.*, and Bennett, *Vignettes*.
17. Bennett, *Vignettes*.
18. *Ibid.*
19. Capt Bill Bellamy, MC, *Schoolboy's War*, and 2003.

CHAPTER 5. A POCKET OF SMALL CHANGE

1. W.D. Whitaker and S. Whitaker, *The Battle of the Scheldt*.
2. Bellfield quoted by Lt Gen Horrocks in Whitaker and Whitaker, *Battle*.
3. *Ibid.*

4. M. Shulman, *Defeat in the West*.

5. C. Wilmot, *The Struggle for Europe*.

6. Shulman, *Defeat*.

7. John A. Marin, taped, SWWEC.

8. K. Tout, *The Bloody Battle for Tilly* and *A Fine Night for Tanks*.

9. Charles Martin per Roy Whitsed, 2002, and with Whitsed, *Battle Diary*.

10. Polish Archives, Polish Institute, London.

11. G.L. Cassidy, *Warpath*.

12. Hammerton, *Achtung!*

13. Cliff Brown, 2003.

14. PRO.

15. J.C. Bond, 'The Fog of War', in *Canadian Military History*.

16. S.A.G. Mein, *Up the Johns!*

17. Gollnick and Nordstrom personal accounts per George Cooper, 1999–2002.

18. F. Court, 1999.

19. Hammerton, *Achtung!*

20. R. Gray, in *Canadian Legion Magazine*, 1999.

21. Cameron, taped, per G. Cooper.

22. Canadian Scottish history, *Ready for the Fray* (private circulation).

23. Tout, *Bloody Battle*.

24. Whitaker and Whitaker, *Battle*.

25. Marin, SWWEC.

26. K. McKee, taped, SWWEC.

27. Clennett and Franks in Whitaker and Whitaker, *Battle*.

28. Reg Dixon, 1999 and 2002.

29. G. Cooper, 2002.

30. D. Crockett per G. Cooper, 2002.

31. Marin, SWWEC.

32. All details and history in M. Reagan, *Two Visits to Ijzendijke*, and 2002.

33. Higgs per C. Russell Clarke, CD, 2002–3.

CHAPTER 6. CHILL GHOST OF AUTUMN

1. The main chapter outline follows Whitaker, who was there (Whitaker and Whitaker, *Battle of the Scheldt*).

2. T. Copp, *The Brigade*.

3. This kind of report often denied by German sources but author saw similar at Le Havre; see Tout, *Tanks, Advance!*

4. P.H. Dixon, taped, IWM.
5. M. Shulman, *Defeat in the West*.
6. *Ibid.*
7. W.R. Bennett, *Vignettes*.
8. G. Blackburn, *Guns of Victory*, and 1999–2002.
9. Bennett, *Vignettes*, and 2002.
10. Copp, *Brigade* (For Forbes in Normandy *see* Tout, *The Bloody Battle for Tilly*)
11. Blackburn, *Guns*.
12. Dated 16 October 1944, just as Montgomery was switching priorities.
13. Whitaker's own plan plus massive postwar research. Unfortunately Denis Whitaker died during consultation on the present book.
14. Copp, *Brigade*.
15. Blackburn, *Guns*.
16. *Ibid.*
17. Whitaker and Whitaker, *Battle*.
18. Marin, taped, SWWEC.
19. James, 2002.
20. Canadian who wished to remain anonymous, 2002.
21. Quoted in Whitaker and Whitaker, *Battle*.
22. Blackburn, *Guns*.
23. Bennett, *Vignettes*, and several sources quote.
24. Again several sources quote.

CHAPTER 7. A DUTCH KRAKATOA

1. Jan Wigard, 2002–3.
2. W.D. Whitaker and S. Whitaker, *The Battle of the Scheldt*.
3. M. Shulman, *Defeat in the West*.
4. The author quoting himself (lecture).
5. K. Tout, *A Fine Night for Tanks*.
6. G.G. Simonds, 'General Simonds Speaks', in *Canadian Military History*.
7. Whitaker and Whitaker, *Battle*.
8. J.C. Bond, 'The Fog of War', in *Canadian Military History*.
9. RAF details here onwards follow Paul M. Crucq's monumental work, '*We never blamed the Crews*', and Crucq, 2002.
10. Interviews by Paul Crucq.
11. *Ibid.*
12. Wigard, 2002–3.

13. Cheeney, taped, IWM.
14. Woolf, 2002 (he was Mentioned in Despatches in Normandy).
15. Weston, taped, IWM.
16. Himsworth, 2002.

Chapter 8. Wet! Wetter!! Wettest!!!

1. G. Blackburn, *The Guns of Victory*.
2. Basil Woolf, 2002.
3. C. Wilmot, *The Struggle for Europe*.
4. W.D. Whitaker and S. Whitaker, *The Battle of the Scheldt*.
5. Transcript per Basil Woolf.
6. F. Weston, tape, IWM.
7. R. Neillands, *By Sea and Land*.
8. J. Hillsman, *Eleven Men and a Scalpel*.
9. F. Himsworth, 2002–3.
10. W.H. Cheeney, taped, IWM.
11. Carr per Mrs Phyllida Carr, SWWEC.
12. J.C. Bond, 'The Fog of War'.
13. Whitaker and Whitaker, *Battle*.
14. D.C. Simpson, taped, IWM.
15. P. White, *With the Jocks*.
16. W.R. Bennett, *Vignettes*.
17. T. Copp, *The Brigade*.
18. *Ibid*.
19. Lt W.J. Smith per James Paul/http://www.combinedops.com.
20. Simpson, IWM.
21. R. White, memoirs, SWWEC.
22. Jan Wigard, 2002–3.
23. Wilmot, *Struggle*.
24. 4 Commando report, WO 218/66, PRO.
25. Whitaker and Whitaker, *Battle*.
26. Transcript per Basil Woolf.
27. Neillands, *By Sea*.
28. 79th Armoured Division. history.
29. Dutch enterprise, drainage skills and hard labour enabled significant restoration of quality cultivation within three years.

Chapter 9. More Arrows on the Map

1. M. Shulman, *Defeat in the West.*
2. *Et seq.*, respective regimental histories and diaries.
3. D. Whybro, taped, IWM.
4. W. Brereton, *Salford Boy Goes to War.*
5. T. Hart Dyke (DSO, Hallams CO), *Normandy to Arnhem.*
6. D. Scott, *Polar Bears from Sheffield.*
7. *Ibid.*
8. *Ibid.*
9. P. Delaforce, *The Polar Bears.*
10. Scott, *Polar Bears.*
11. Whybro, IWM.
12. Royal Armoured Corps liaison letter no. 19, 13 November 1944.
13. Cliff Brown, 1999–2003.
14. C. Elwood, also W. Shea, taped, IWM.
15. S. Maczek, *Avec mes Blindées.*
16. G. Hayes, 'Where are our Liberators?', in *Canadian Military History.*
17. *Ibid.*
18. Quoted almost identically by several sources.
19. Hayes, 'Where are our Liberators?'.
20. C. Kipp, 1999, comments just before his death.
21. Tessa Carpenter, 2002.
22. Translated and made available by W.Th. Lagarde, 2002.

Chapter 10. Massing towards the Maas

1. K. Tout, *Tanks, Advance!*
2. W. Moseley, *From Arromanches to the Elbe*, and 2002.
3. Local Dutch study: Jack Didden, *Operation Colin.*
4. K. Tout, *To Hell with Tanks.*
5. Tout, *Tanks, Advance!*.
6. This incident only of interest in that it ended the author's war!
7. P. Mace, *Forrard: The Story of the East Riding Yeomanry.*
8. Didden, *Operation Colin.*
9. As when the then Lt Gen Sir D. Lang walked the camp with the author in 1994 (fiftieth anniversary of liberation).
10. Moseley, *From Arromanches.*

11. History of the 53rd (W) Division.
12. T. Cosgrove, 2003.
13. J. McCann, memoir, SWWEC.
14. J. Ellis, taped, IWM.
15. J.P. Downs, 2002–3.
16. N.G. Marshall, memoir, SWWEC.
17. Mace, *Forrard*.
18. M.H. McKee in *Canadian Legion Magazine*, January/February 2002.
19. History of the 53rd (W) Division.
20. Tout, *To Hell*, and K. Jack, 2001.
21. Tout, *To Hell*.
22. Revd Preb. C.J. Lawson, memoir, SWWEC.
23. F. Gutteridge, 2003.
24. L. Taylor, *Tommy Cooker*.
25. S. Whitehouse, *Fear is the Foe*.
26. J.D. Ingham, memoir, SWWEC.
27. P. Sumner, 2001.
28. Tout, *To Hell*, and R. Jackson, 2002.
29. L. Taylor, *Tommy Cooker*.
30. Tout, *To Hell*.
31. Didden, *Operation Colin*.
32. W. Bellamy, *Schoolboy's War*.

Chapter 11. Guns towards the Fatherland

1. Hammerton, *Achtung!*
2. K. Tout, *To Hell with Tanks*.
3. Nigel Nicholson, Grenadier Guards report.
4. Pat Dyas, 1999.
5. 11th Armoured Division, *Taurus Pursuant*.
6. Fuehrer Conference, 31 August 1944, Bundesarchiv.
7. W. Shirer, *The Rise and Fall of the Third Reich*.
8. M. Shulman, *Defeat in the West*.
9. G. Stiller, 2002.
10. G. Sherrington, 2002.
11. P. White, *With the Jocks*.
12. 1NY War Diary, 21 November 1944.
13. C. Russell Clarke, CD, 2002–3.

14. Tout, *To Hell*.
15. Hammerton, *Achtung!*
16. Maj Tim Ellis, DSO, per Russell Clarke, 2003.
17. W. Moseley, 2002.
18. C.J. Teague, taped, IWM.
19. White, *With the Jocks*.
20. Tout, *To Hell*. Many tank crew have suffered 'one ear deafness' for sixty years but not sufficient injury to qualify for compensation.
21. Roy Eardley, 2003. A bronze statue of Sgt Eardley, VC, MM, has now been cast and was expected to be erected in Congleton during 2003.
22. 11th Armoured Division, *Taurus Pursuant*.
23. Dr Ger Schinck, 2002.
24. Local information, various sources, 2002.
25. Tank battles: e.g. the author's regiment fought in more than one such 'tank skirmish' in the Netherlands and Belgium (Ardennes).
26. A. Korthals Altes, *Overloon: the Forgotten Battle*.
27. D. Waller, taped, IWM.
28. A. Rous, taped, IWM.
29. Korthals Altes, *Overloon*, and local reports, 2002.
30. Overloon Museum.
31. G. Duncan, taped, SWWEC.
32. P.H. Dixon, taped, SWWEC.
33. Hammerton, *Achtung!*
34. Tout, *To Hell*.
35. Hammerton, *Achtung!*
36. Tout, *To Hell*.
37. Schinck, 2002.
38. L. Taylor, *Tommy Cooker*.

CHAPTER 12. REFLECTIONS ON THE WATER

1. M. Middlebrook, *Arnhem 1944*.
2. A. Chalfont, *Montgomery of Alamein*.
3. J.L. Granatstein, review of N. Gelb, 'Ike and Monty, Generals at War', in *Canadian Military History*, vol. 4, no. 1, 1995.
4. Report 1 October 1944, addressed to Wehrkreis VI, HP 2133, PRO.
5. J. Hughes-Wilson, *Military Intelligence Blunders*.
6. Author's own comments.

7. W. Bellamy, (MC, December 1944), *Schoolboy's War*, and 2003.

8. G. Blackburn, *The Guns of Victory*.

9. So 1NY's Tpr Dilwyn Price, killed in action at Waspik and buried in a local churchyard, was the inspiration for Marius Heideveld and friends setting up the organization VOGW (Waalwijk) to beautify war graves and teach schoolchildren the realities of war. Similar work is done by Louis Kleijne in St Oedenrode, Lt Kol Brouwers at Nederweert and many others around Second World War battlefields.

10. E. Vaughan Green in G. Jelley, *Rhymes of Northamptonshire Yeomen*.

Bibliography

SOURCES AND FURTHER READING

Unit histories are included only where they have some wider application in the general story.

11th Armoured Division, *Taurus Pursuant* (1945)
79th Armoured Division, *The Story of the 79th* (1945)
Alanbrooke, Lord, *War Diaries 1939–45* (Weidenfeld & Nicolson, 2001)
Baldewyns, A., *Les Batteries de Walcheren* (Rossel, 1974)
Barclay, C.N., *The History of the 53rd (Welsh) Division in the Second World War* (William Clowes and Sons, 1956)
Bellamy, W., *Schoolboy's War* (private/ SWWEC)
Bennett, W.R., *Vignettes* (Royal Regiment of Canada Association, 1944–5)
Blackburn, G.G., *The Guns of Victory*, (McClelland & Stewart, 1996)
Bond, J.C., 'The Fog of War', *Canadian Military History*, vol. 8, no. 1, 1999
Borthwick, A., *Battalion* (Baton Wicks, 1994)
Brereton, W., *Salford Boy Goes to War* (Neil Richardson, 1992)
Cassidy, G., *Warpath* (Ryerston Press, 1948)
Chalfont, A., *Montgomery of Alamein* (Weidenfeld & Nicolson, 1976)
Close, W., *A View from the Turret* (Dell & Bredon, 2001)
Copp, T., *The Brigade* (Fortress Publications, 1996)
Crucq, P.M., *'We Never Blamed the Crews'* (ADZ, Vlissingen, 2000)
——, *Aiming Point Walcheren* (ADZ, Vlissingen, 2000)
De Guingand, E., *Operation Victory* (Hodder & Stoughton, 1950)
Delaforce, P., *The Fighting Wessex Wyverns* (Sutton, 1994)
——, *The Polar Bears* (Sutton, 1995)
Dendermonde, M., *228 Seconds of Silence: an Arnhem Story* (Uitgeverij de Prom, 1994)

Didden, J., *Operation Colin* (Zwaardvisch, 1994)

Dugdale, J., *Panzer Divisions, Panzer Grenadier Divisions, Panzer Brigades of the Army and the Waffen SS in the West* (Galago Publishing, 2000)

Eisenhower, D.D., *Crusade in Europe* (Doubleday, 1998)

——, *D-Day to VE Day, 1944–5* (The Stationery Office, 2000)

Ellis, J., *One Day in a Very Long War* (25 October 1944) (Random House, 1998)

Ellis, L.F., *Victory in the West*, vol. 2 (HMSO, 1962)

Fey, W., *Armour Battles of the Waffen-SS, 1943–45* (J.J. Fedorowicz, 1990)

Forbes, C., *Fantassin: pour mon pays, la gloire et . . . des prunes* (Sillery, 1994)

Furbringer, H., *9 SS-Panzer Division* (Munin Verlag, 1987)

Gelb, N., *Ike and Monty: Generals at War* (William Morrow, 1994)

Gilchrist, D., *The Commandos: D-Day and After* (Robert Hale, 1982)

Goodspeed, D.J., *Battle Royal* (Royal Regt of Canada Association, 1962)

Hammerton, I.C., *Achtung! Minen!* (Book Guild, 1991 and 2000)

Hart Dyke, T., *Normandy to Arnhem* (Greenup & Thompson, 1966)

Hayes, G., 'Where are our Liberators?', *Canadian Military History*, vol. 4, no. 1, 1995

Hillsman, J.B., *Eleven Men and a Scalpel* (Columbia Press, 1948)

Horrocks, Sir B., *A Full Life* (Collins, 1960)

——, *Corps Commander* (Sidgwick & Jackson, 1977)

Hughes-Wilson, J., *Military Intelligence Blunders* (Robinson, 1999)

Jelley, G., *Rhymes of Northamptonshire Yeomen* (NY Association, 1988)

Keegan, J., *Churchill's Generals* (Weidenfeld & Nicolson, 1991)

Korthals Altes, A., and in't Veld, N.K., *Slag in de Schaduw*, trans G.G. van Dam as *Overloon, the Unknown Battle* (Sarpedon, 1994)

Lewin, R., *Montgomery as Military Commander* (Batsford, 1971)

MacDonald, C.B., 'The Decision to Launch Operation Market-Garden, 1944', in Greenfield, K.R. (ed.), *Command Decisions* (Methuen & Co., 1960)

Mace, P., *Forrard: the Story of the East Riding Yeomanry* (Pen & Sword, 2001)

Maczek, S., *Avec Mes Blindées* (Presses de la Cité, 1967)

Martin, C.C., with Whitsed, R., *Battle Diary* (Dundurn, 1994)

Masse, W.B., *The Netherlands at War* (Abelard Schuman, 1977)

Mein, S.A.G., *Up the Johns!* (Turner-Warwick, 1992)

Middlebrook, M., *Arnhem 1944* (Penguin, 1995)

Mitcham, S.W., Jr., *Hitler's Field Marshals* (Heinemann, 1988)

Moseley, W., *'From Arromanches to the Elbe'* (SWWEC archive)

Moulton, J.L., *Battle for Antwerp* (Sam Allan, 1978)

Neillands, R., *By Sea and Land* (Cassell, 2000)

Powell, G., *The Devil's Birthday: The Bridges to Arnhem 1944* (Buchan & Enright, 1984)

Ramsey, W.G., (ed.), 'After the Battle: Walcheren', *After the Battle*, 36, 1982

——, "'s Hertogenbosch, Then and Now', *After the Battle*, 64, 1989

——, 'Highlanders in the Low Countries', *After the Battle*, 120, 2003

Reagan, M., *Two Visits to Ijzendijke* (self-published, 2000)

Reynolds, M., *Sons of the Reich, II SS Pz Corps* (Spellmount, 2002)

Roberts, G.P.B., *From the Desert to the Baltic* (Kimber, 1987)

Rogers, R.L., *The Lincoln & Welland Regiment* (Regt Association, 1954)

Rosse, Earl of, and Hill, E.R., *The Story of the Guards Armoured Division* (Geoffrey Bles, 1956)

Ryan, C., *A Bridge Too Far* (Hamish Hamilton, 1974)

Saunders, T., *Hell's Highway* (Leo Cooper, 2001)

Scott, D., *Polar Bears from Sheffield* (Tiger & Rose Publications, 2001)

Shirer, W.L., *The Rise and Fall of the Third Reich* (Secker & Warburg, 1959)

Shulman, M., *Defeat in the West* (Secker & Warburg, 1947)

Smith, E.A., *Recce Troop Memories* (self-published, Grenadier Guards, 1997)

Simonds, G.G., 'General Simonds Speaks', *Canadian Military History*, vol. 8, no. 2, 1999

Sosabowski, S., *Freely I Served* (William Kimber, 1956)

Stacey, C.P., *The Victory Campaign, Official History of the Canadian Army in the Second World War*, vol. 3 (Queen's Printer at Ottawa, 1960)

Taylor, L., *Tommy Cooker* (SWWEC archive)

Tout, K., *Tanks, Advance!* (Robert Hale, 1989)

——, *To Hell with Tanks* (Robert Hale, 1992)

——, *A Fine Night for Tanks* (Sutton, 1998, 2002)

——, *The Bloody Battle for Tilly* (Sutton, 2000, 2002)

——, *Roads to Falaise* (Sutton, 2002)

van Gent, L., *October 1944, Den Bosch Liberated* (Atr. Heinen, 1989)

van Lith, H.A., *Liberation of Walcheren* (G.W. den Boer, 1970)

Whitaker, W.D., and Whitaker, S., *Tug of War* (Beaufort Books, 1984)

—— and as *The Battle of the Scheldt* (Souvenir Press, 1985)

White, P., *With the Jocks* (Sutton, 2001)

Whitehouse, S., with Bennett, G.B., *Fear is the Foe* (Robert Hale, 1995)

Wilmot, C., *The Struggle for Europe* (Wordsworth Editions, 1997)

Index

British Army Regiments and Battalions are listed in order of precedence.